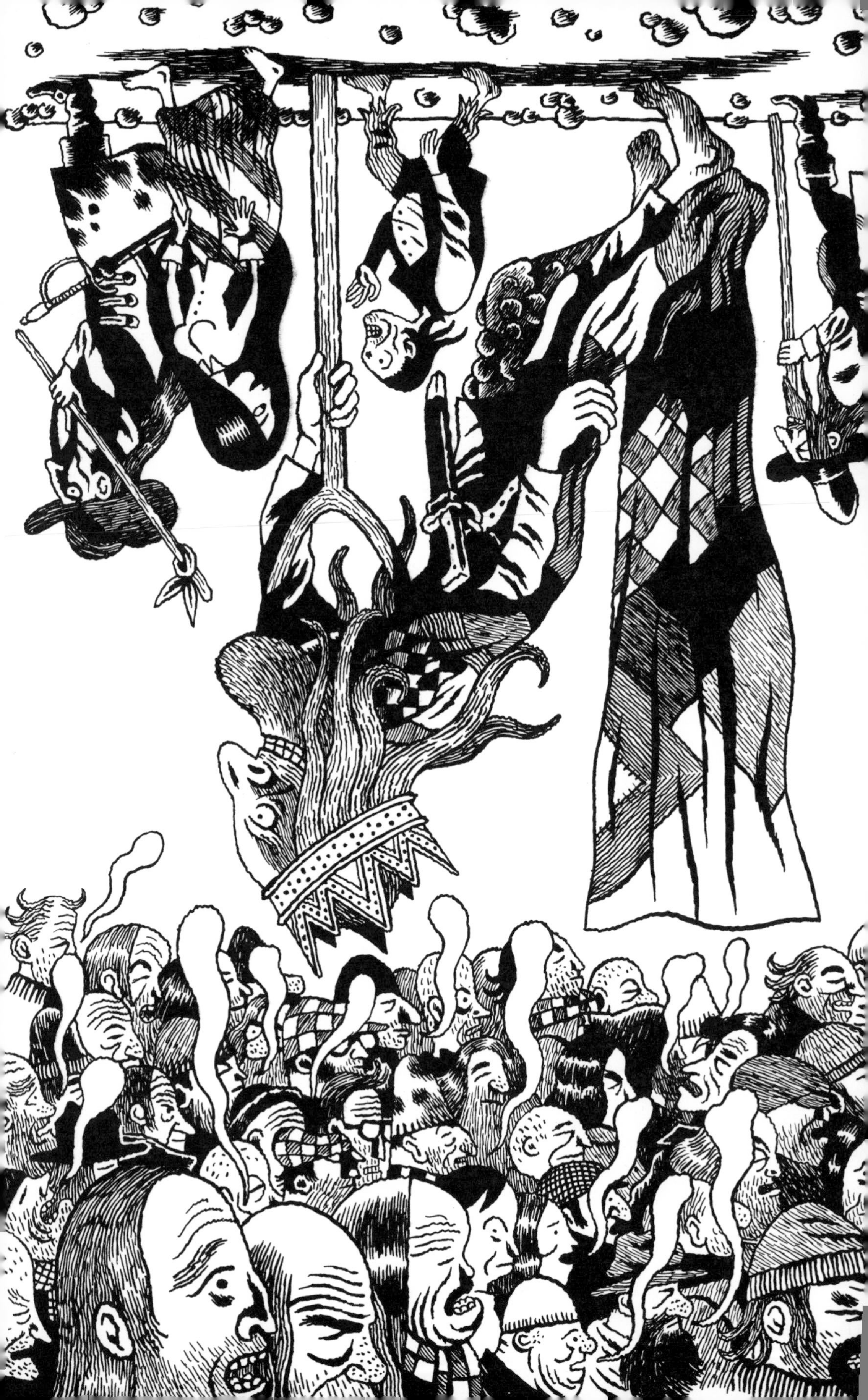

David B.

INCIDENTS in the NIGHT

Book Two

Translated by
Brian & Sarah Evenson

Uncivilized Books, Publisher

Other Books by David B.

Incidents in the Night Book One

Epileptic

The Armed Garden

Nocturnal Conspiracies

Black Paths

Babel

Originally published as *Les Incidents De La Nuit Tome 2* by L'Assо<iatiоn

Cet ouvrage publié dans le cadre du programme d'aide à la publication bénéficie du soutien du Ministère des Affaires Étrangères et du Service Culturel de l'Ambassade de France représenté aux États-Unis.

This work, published as part of a program of aid for publication, received support from the French Ministry of Foreign Affairs and the Cultural Service of the French Embassy in the United States.

Design by Tom Kaczynski
Typography by Tom Kaczynski
Production assist by Madeline McGrane and Rachel Topka

Uncivilized Books
P.O. Box 6434
Minneapolis, MN 55406
USA
uncivilizedbooks.com

First American Edition, April 2015

10 9 8 7 6 5 4 3 2 1

ISBN 978-0-9889014-8-3

DISTRIBUTED TO THE TRADE BY:

Consortium Book Sales & Distribution, LLC.
34 Thirteenth Avenue NE,
Suite 101 Minneapolis,
MN 55413-1007
Orders: (800) 283-3572

Printed in the Singapore

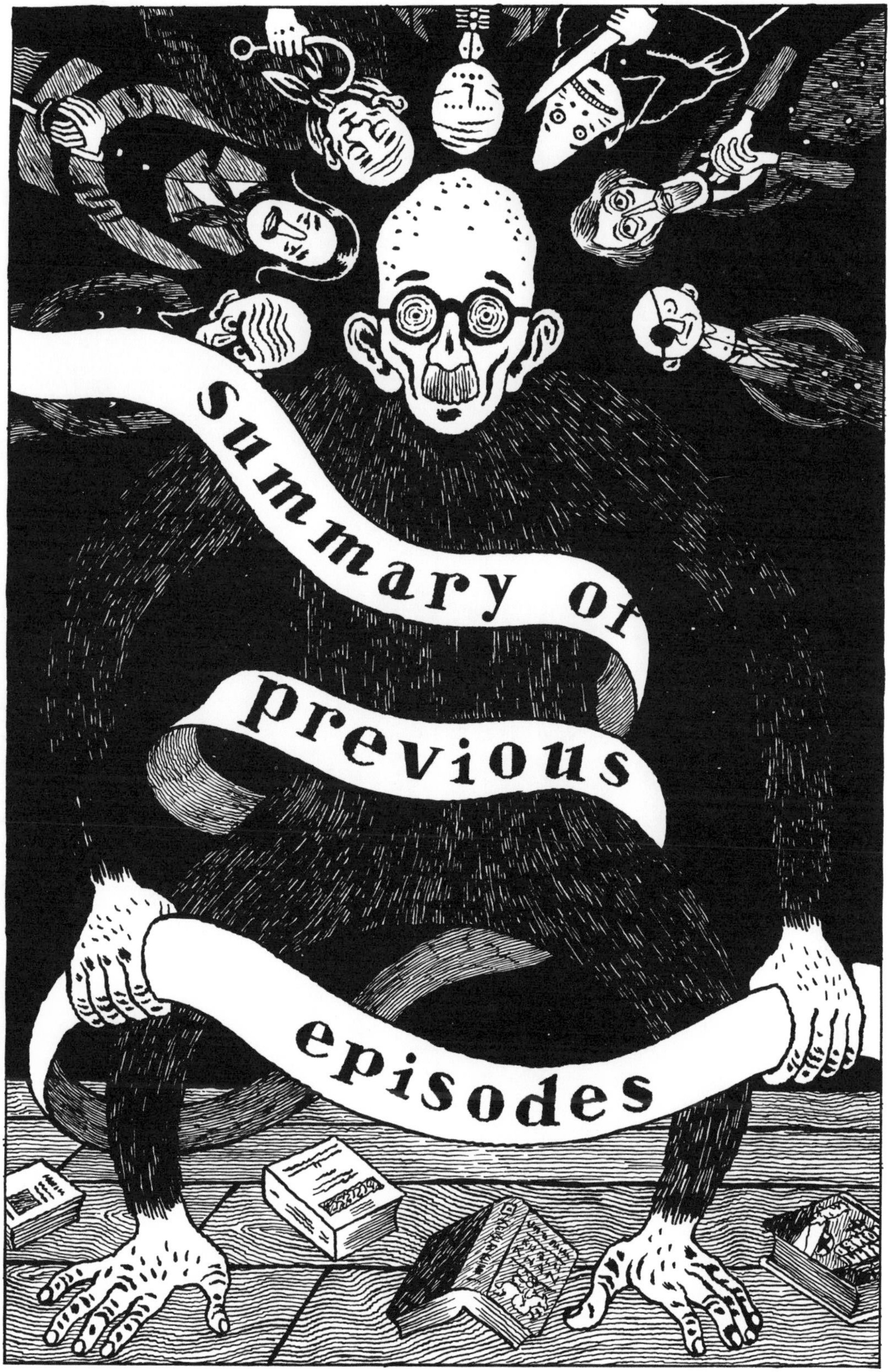
Summary of previous episodes

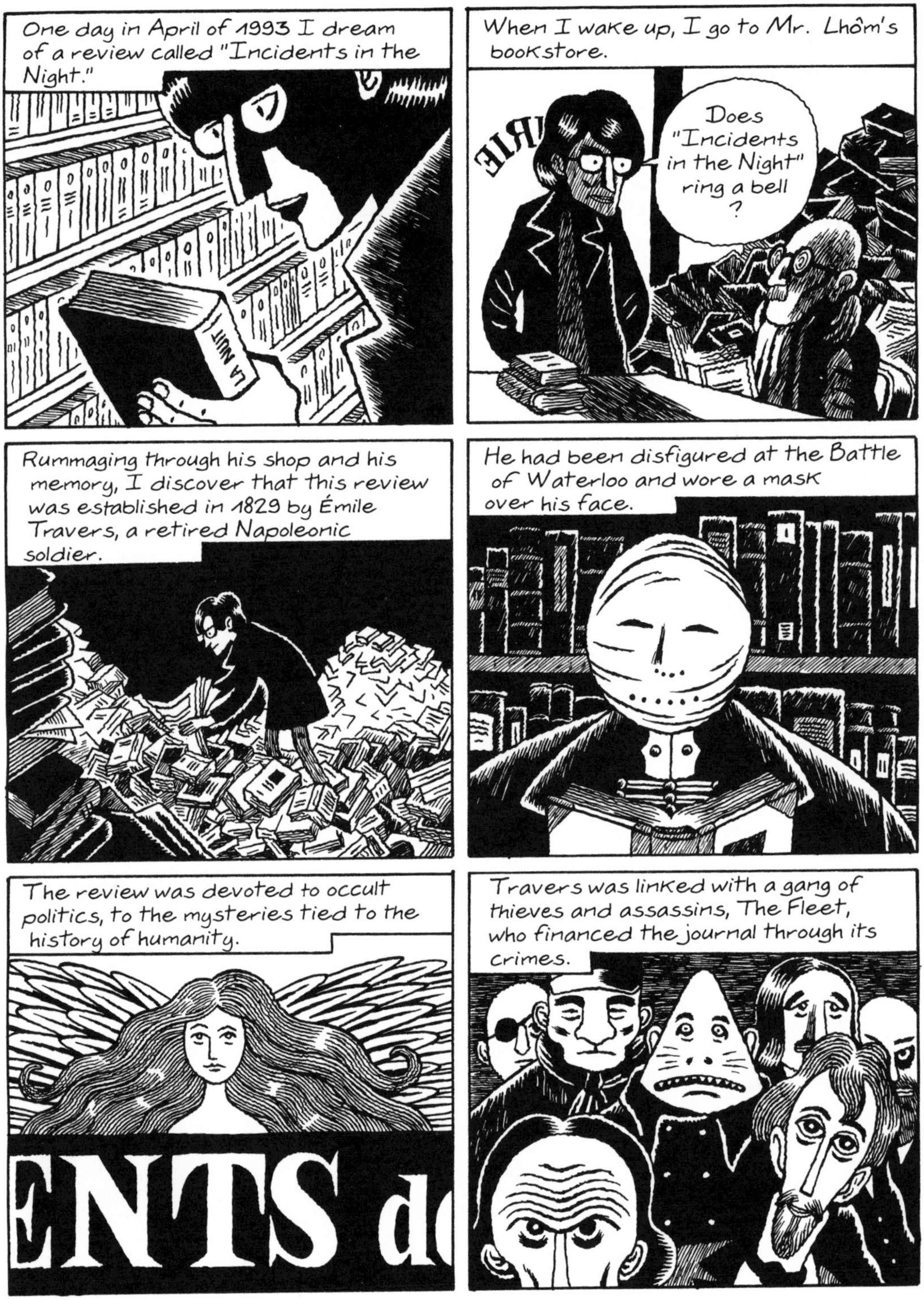

One day in April of 1993 I dream of a review called "Incidents in the Night."
LA NUIT
When I wake up, I go to Mr. Lhôm's bookstore.
RIE
Does "Incidents in the Night" ring a bell ?
Rummaging through his shop and his memory, I discover that this review was established in 1829 by Émile Travers, a retired Napoleonic soldier.
He had been disfigured at the Battle of Waterloo and wore a mask over his face.
The review was devoted to occult politics, to the mysteries tied to the history of humanity.
ENTS d
Travers was linked with a gang of thieves and assassins, The Fleet, who financed the journal through its crimes.

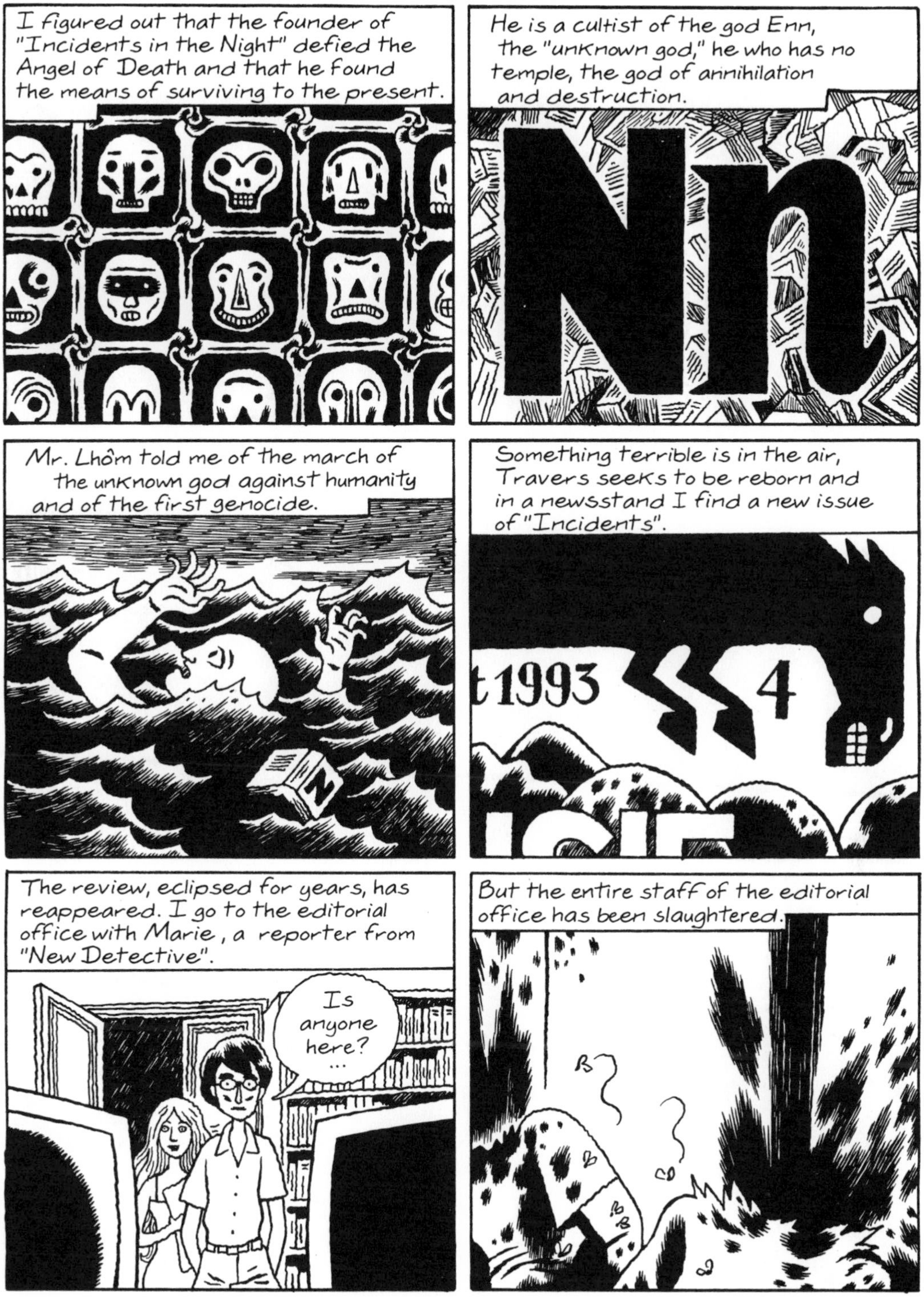
I figured out that the founder of "Incidents in the Night" defied the Angel of Death and that he found the means of surviving to the present.
He is a cultist of the god Enn, the "unknown god," he who has no temple, the god of annihilation and destruction.
Nn
Mr. Lhôm told me of the march of the unknown god against humanity and of the first genocide.
N
Something terrible is in the air, Travers seeks to be reborn and in a newsstand I find a new issue of "Incidents".
t1993
4
The review, eclipsed for years, has reappeared. I go to the editorial office with Marie, a reporter from "New Detective".
Is anyone here? ...
But the entire staff of the editorial office has been slaughtered.

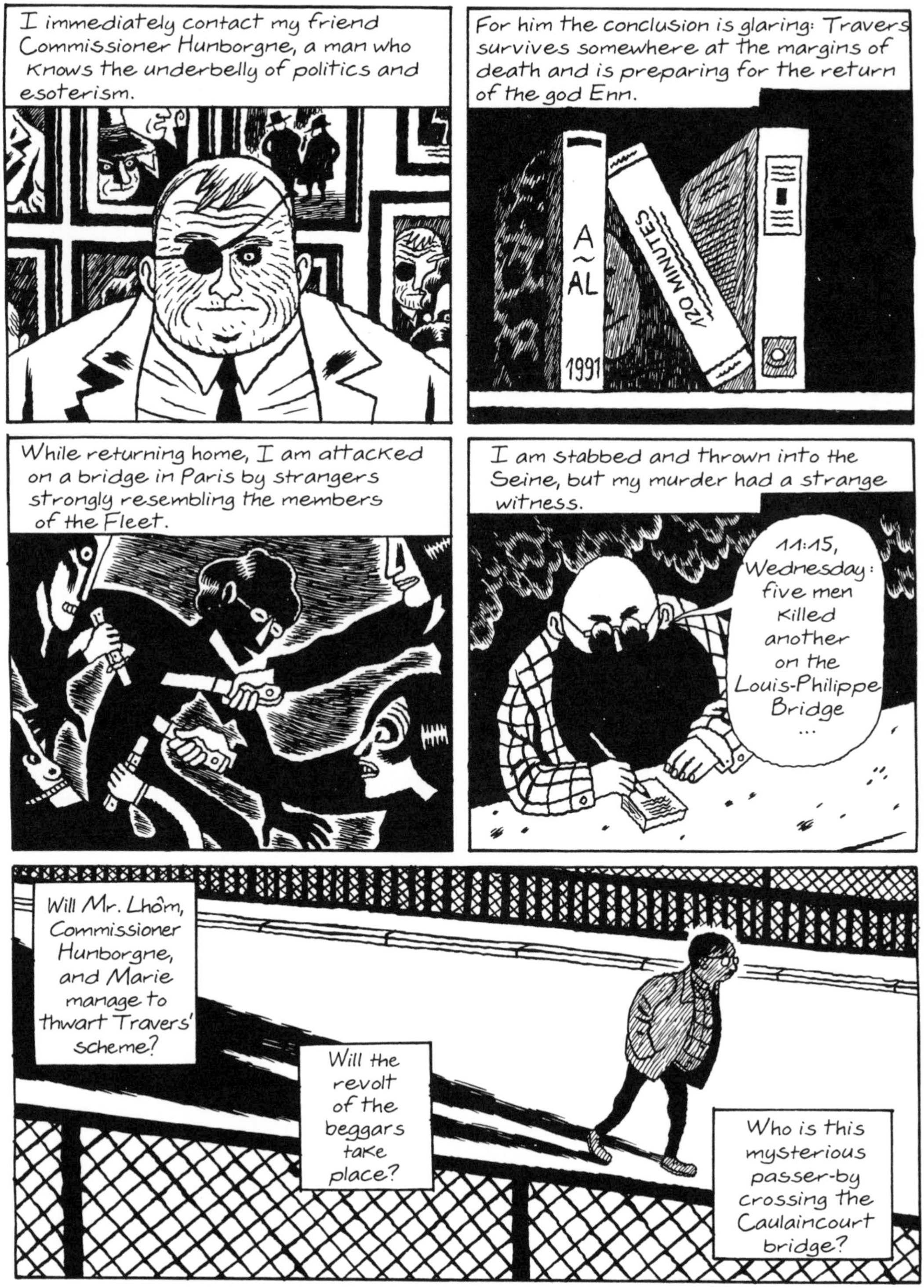
I immediately contact my friend Commissioner Hunborgne, a man who knows the underbelly of politics and esoterism.
For him the conclusion is glaring: Travers survives somewhere at the margins of death and is preparing for the return of the god Enn.
A ~ AL
1991
120 MINUTES
While returning home, I am attacked on a bridge in Paris by strangers strongly resembling the members of the Fleet.
I am stabbed and thrown into the Seine, but my murder had a strange witness.
11:15, Wednesday: five men killed another on the Louis-Philippe Bridge ...
Will Mr. Lhôm, Commissioner Hunborgne, and Marie manage to thwart Travers' scheme?
Will the revolt of the beggars take place?
Who is this mysterious passer-by crossing the Caulaincourt bridge?

Incidents in the night

2

David B.

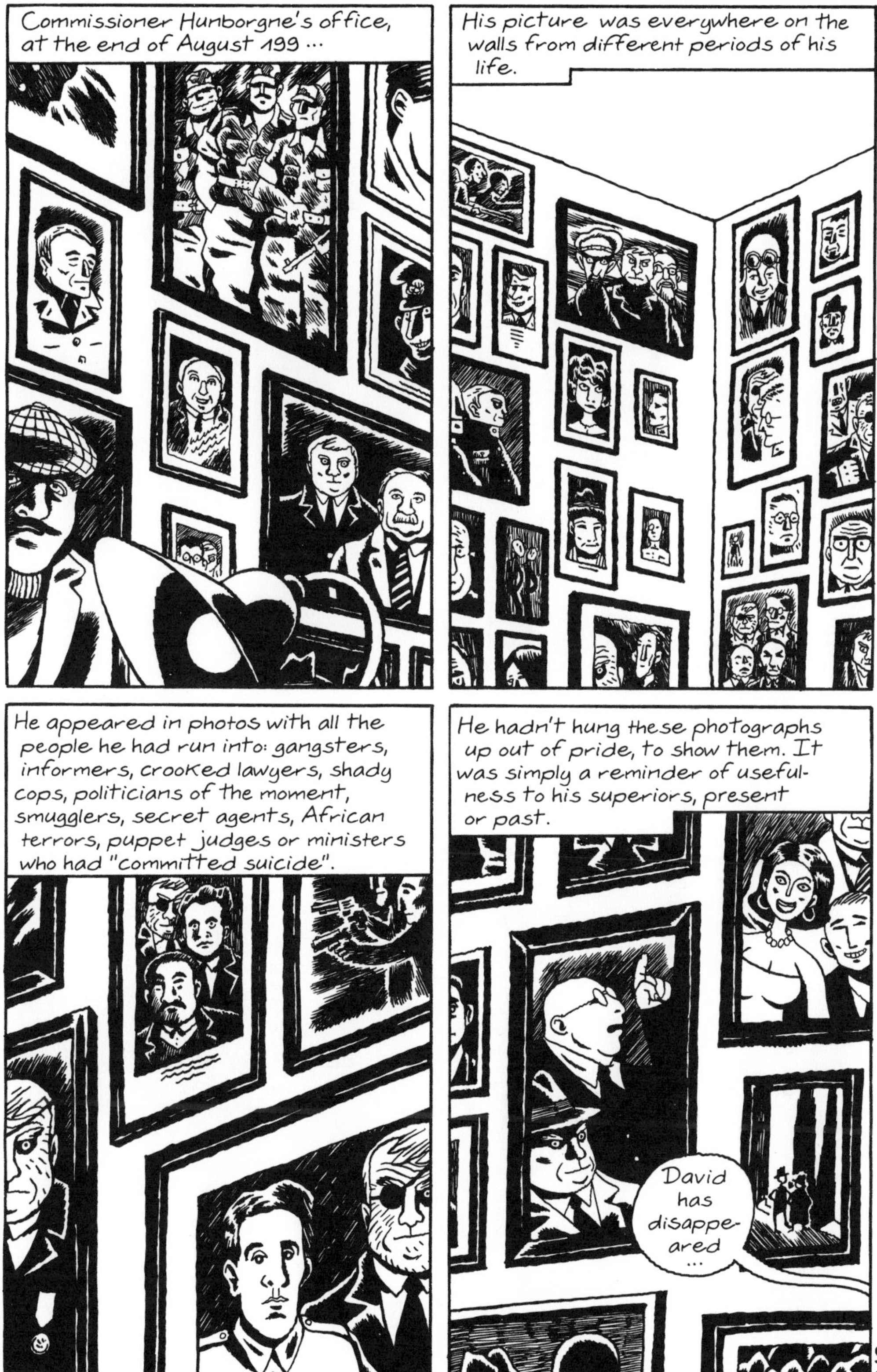

Commissioner Hunborgne's office, at the end of August 199 ...
His picture was everywhere on the walls from different periods of his life.
He appeared in photos with all the people he had run into: gangsters, informers, crooked lawyers, shady cops, politicians of the moment, smugglers, secret agents, African terrors, puppet judges or ministers who had "committed suicide".
He hadn't hung these photographs up out of pride, to show them. It was simply a reminder of usefulness to his superiors, present or past.
David has disappeared ...

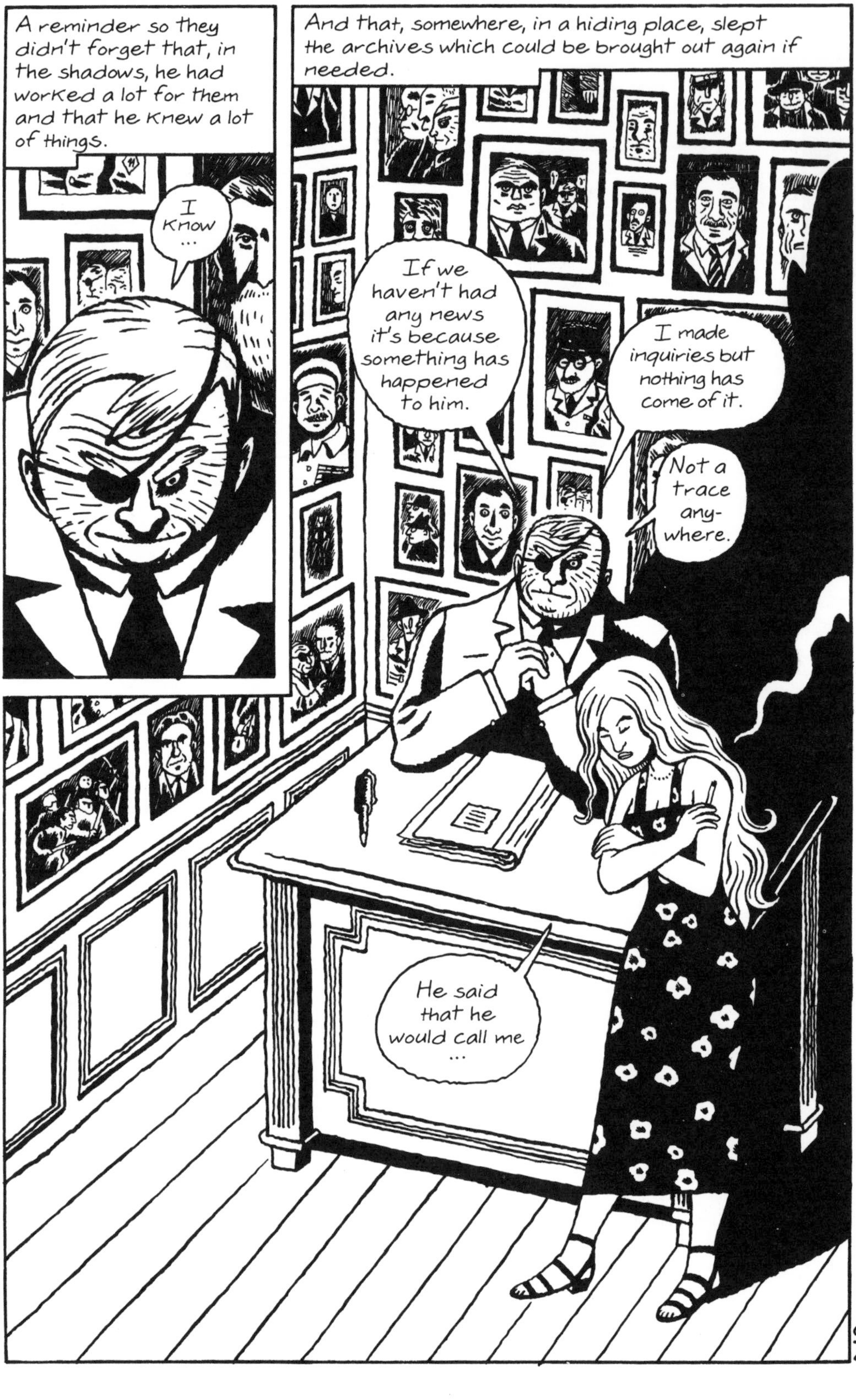
A reminder so they didn't forget that, in the shadows, he had worked a lot for them and that he knew a lot of things.
I know ...
And that, somewhere, in a hiding place, slept the archives which could be brought out again if needed.
If we haven't had any news it's because something has happened to him.
I made inquiries but nothing has come of it.
Not a trace any-where.
He said that he would call me ...

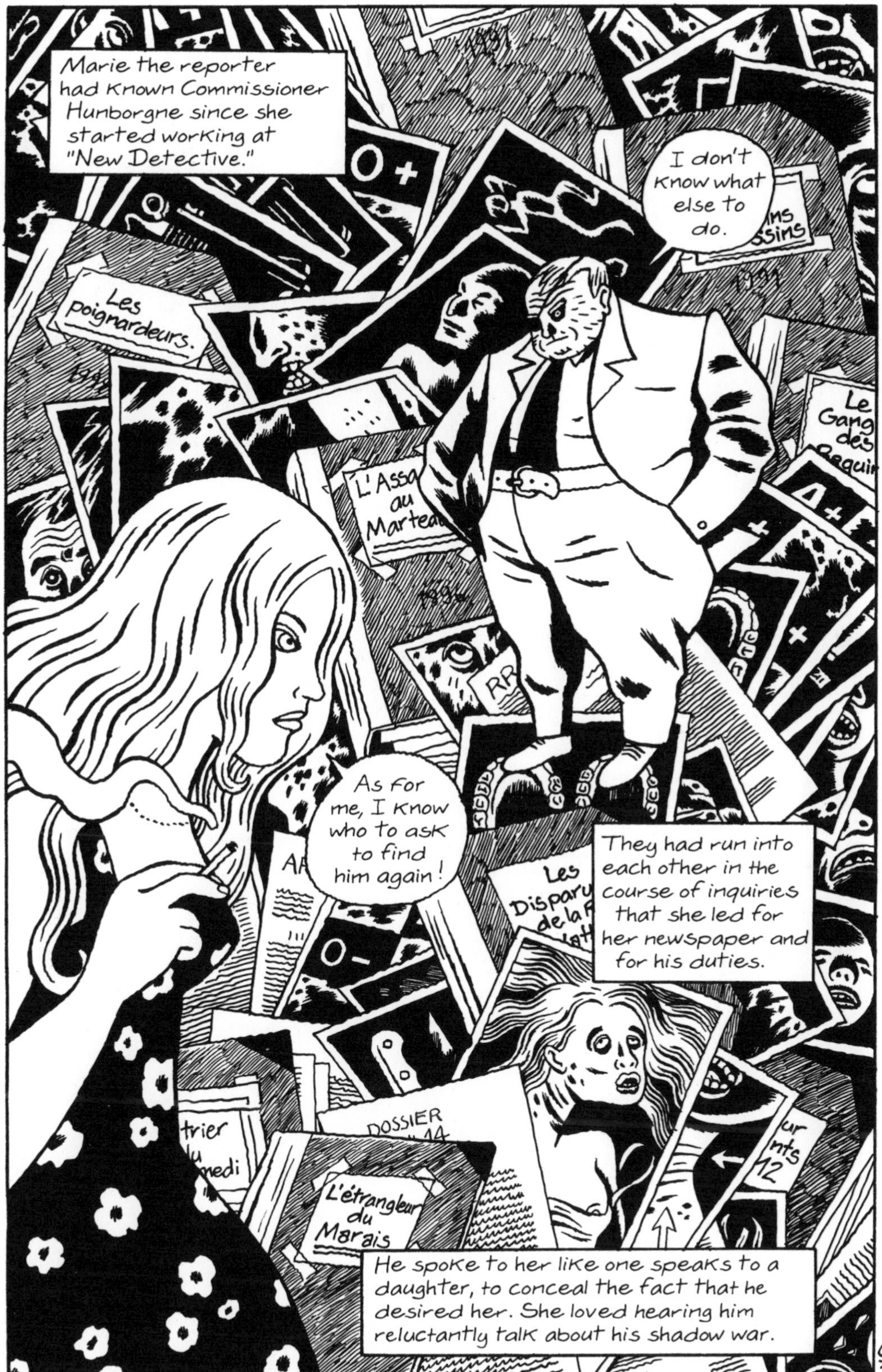
Marie the reporter had known Commissioner Hunborgne since she started working at "New Detective."
I don't know what else to do.
Les poignardeurs.
As for me, I know who to ask to find him again!
They had run into each other in the course of inquiries that she led for her newspaper and for his duties.
DOSSIER
L'étrangleur du Marais
He spoke to her like one speaks to a daughter, to conceal the fact that he desired her. She loved hearing him reluctantly talk about his shadow war.

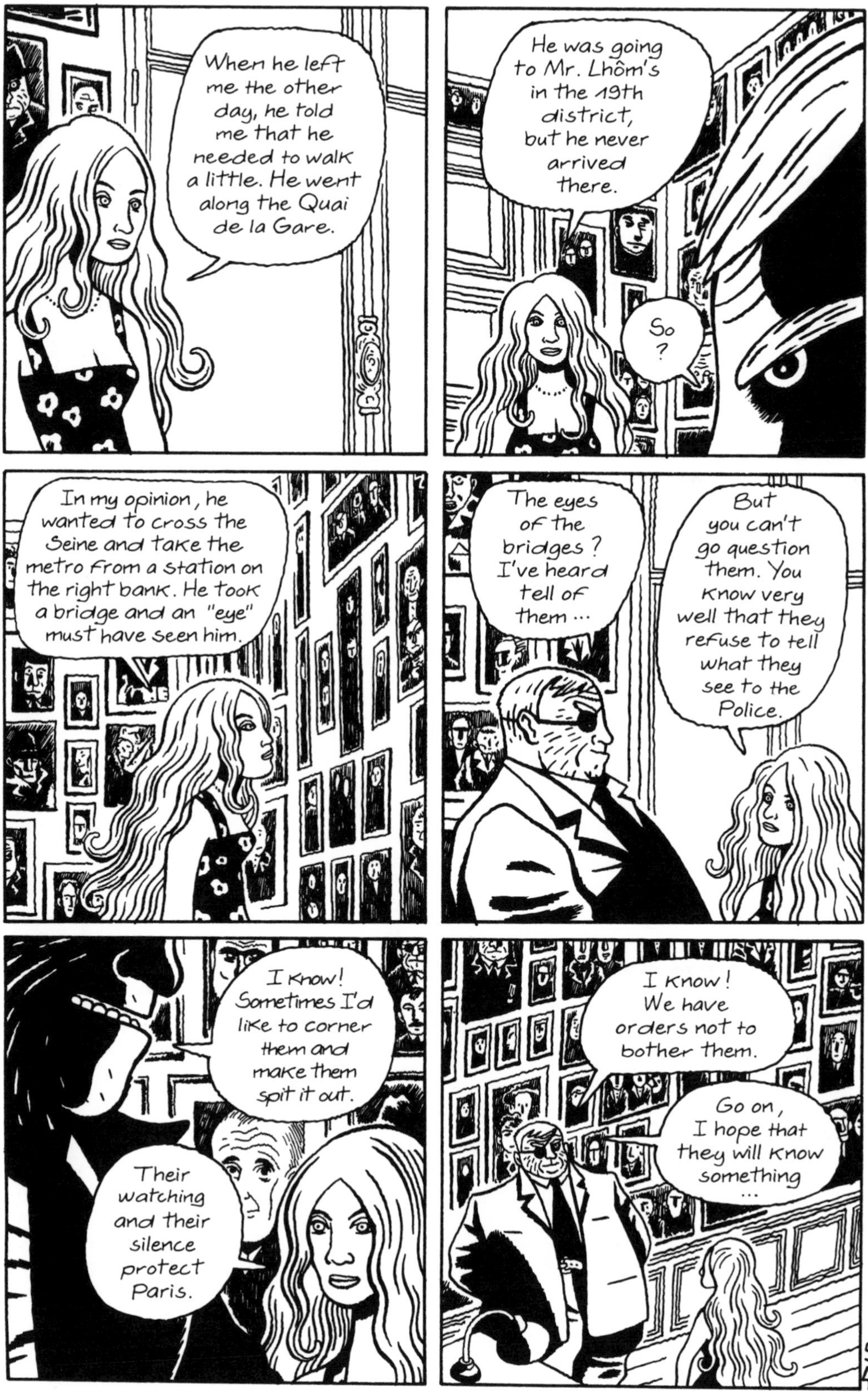
When he left me the other day, he told me that he needed to walk a little. He went along the Quai de la Gare.
He was going to Mr. Lhôm's in the 19th district, but he never arrived there.
So ?
In my opinion, he wanted to cross the Seine and take the metro from a station on the right bank. He took a bridge and an "eye" must have seen him.
The eyes of the bridges ? I've heard tell of them ...
But you can't go question them. You know very well that they refuse to tell what they see to the Police.
I know! Sometimes I'd like to corner them and make them spit it out.
Their watching and their silence protect Paris.
I know! We have orders not to bother them.
Go on, I hope that they will know something ...

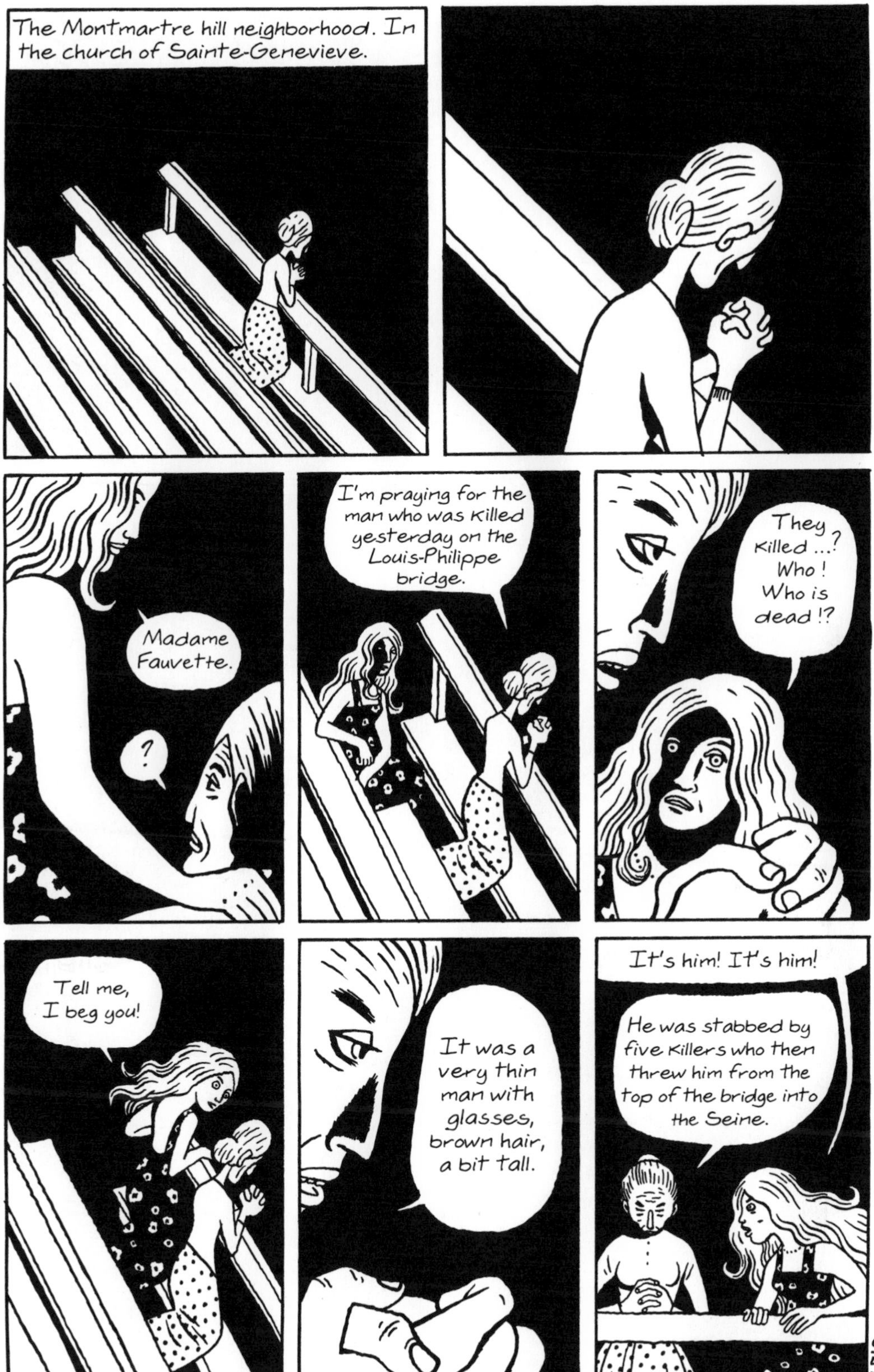
The Montmartre hill neighborhood. In the church of Sainte-Genevieve.
Madame Fauvette.
?
I'm praying for the man who was killed yesterday on the Louis-Philippe bridge.
They killed ...? Who! Who is dead!?
Tell me, I beg you!
It was a very thin man with glasses, brown hair, a bit tall.
It's him! It's him!
He was stabbed by five killers who then threw him from the top of the bridge into the Seine.

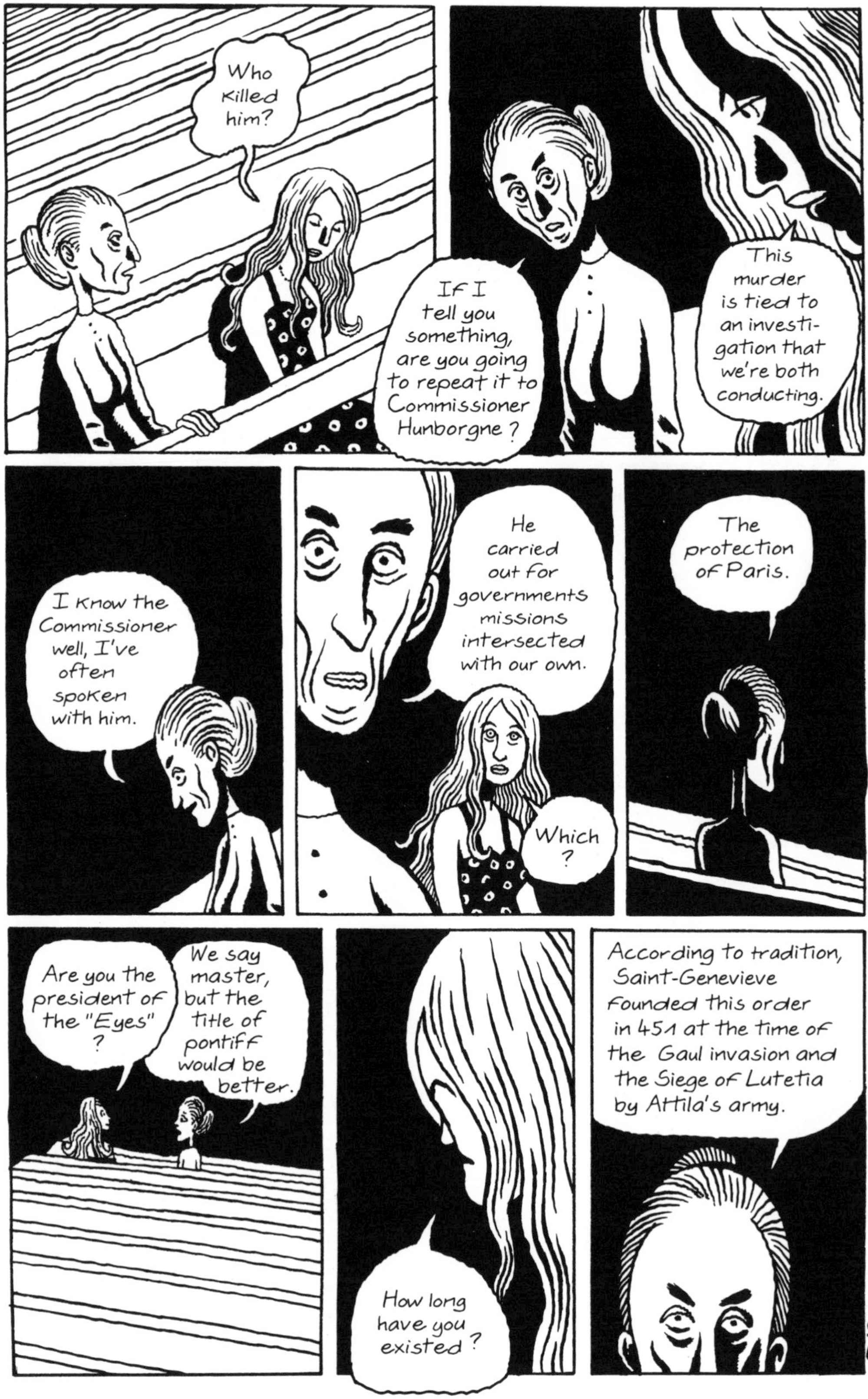
Who Killed him?
If I tell you something, are you going to repeat it to Commissioner Hunborgne?
This murder is tied to an investigation that we're both conducting.
I Know the Commissioner well, I've often spoken with him.
He carried out for governments missions intersected with our own.
Which?
The protection of Paris.
Are you the president of the "Eyes"?
We say master, but the title of pontiff would be better.
How long have you existed?
According to tradition, Saint-Genevieve founded this order in 451 at the time of the Gaul invasion and the Siege of Lutetia by Attila's army.

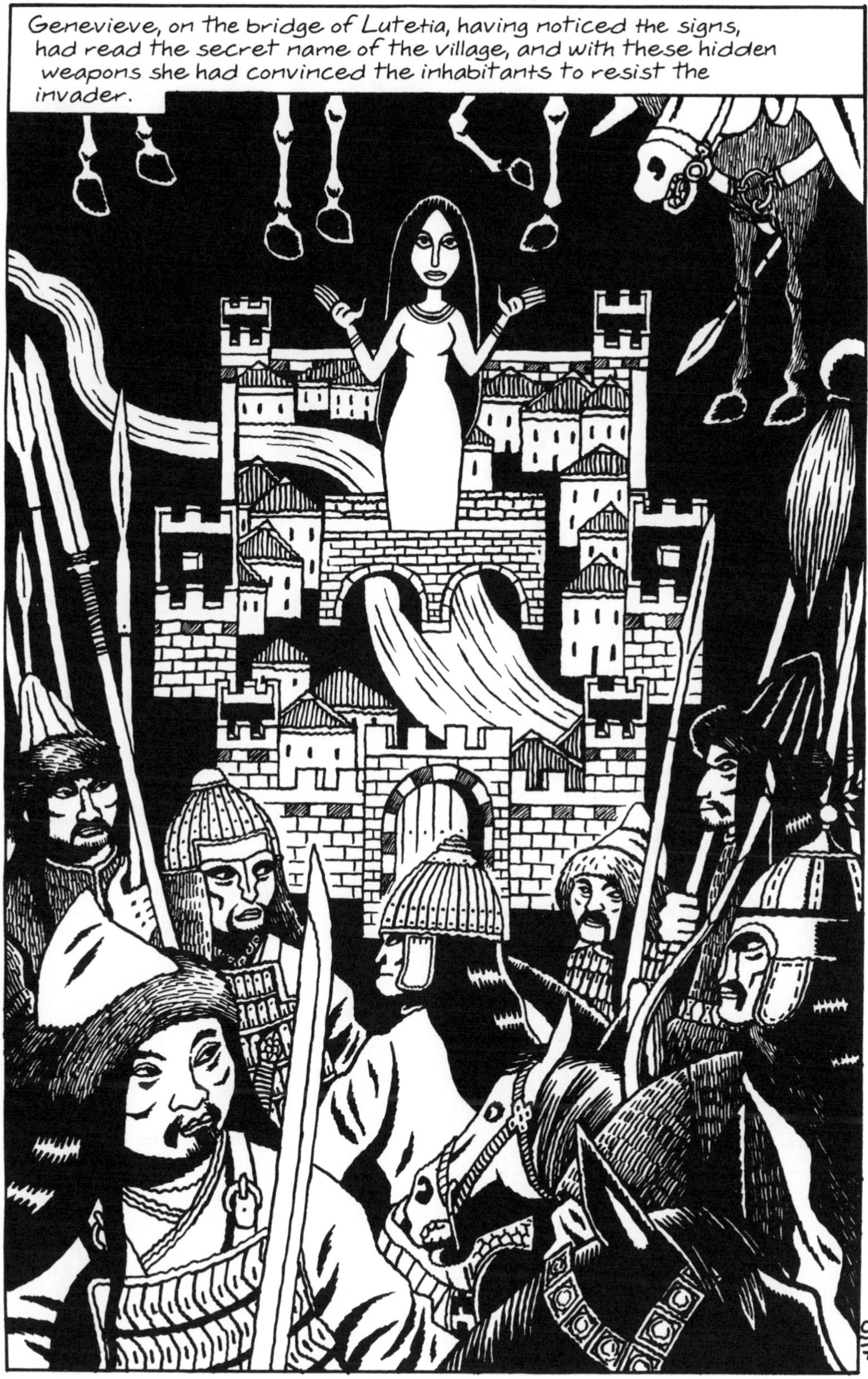
Genevieve, on the bridge of Lutetia, having noticed the signs, had read the secret name of the village, and with these hidden weapons she had convinced the inhabitants to resist the invader.

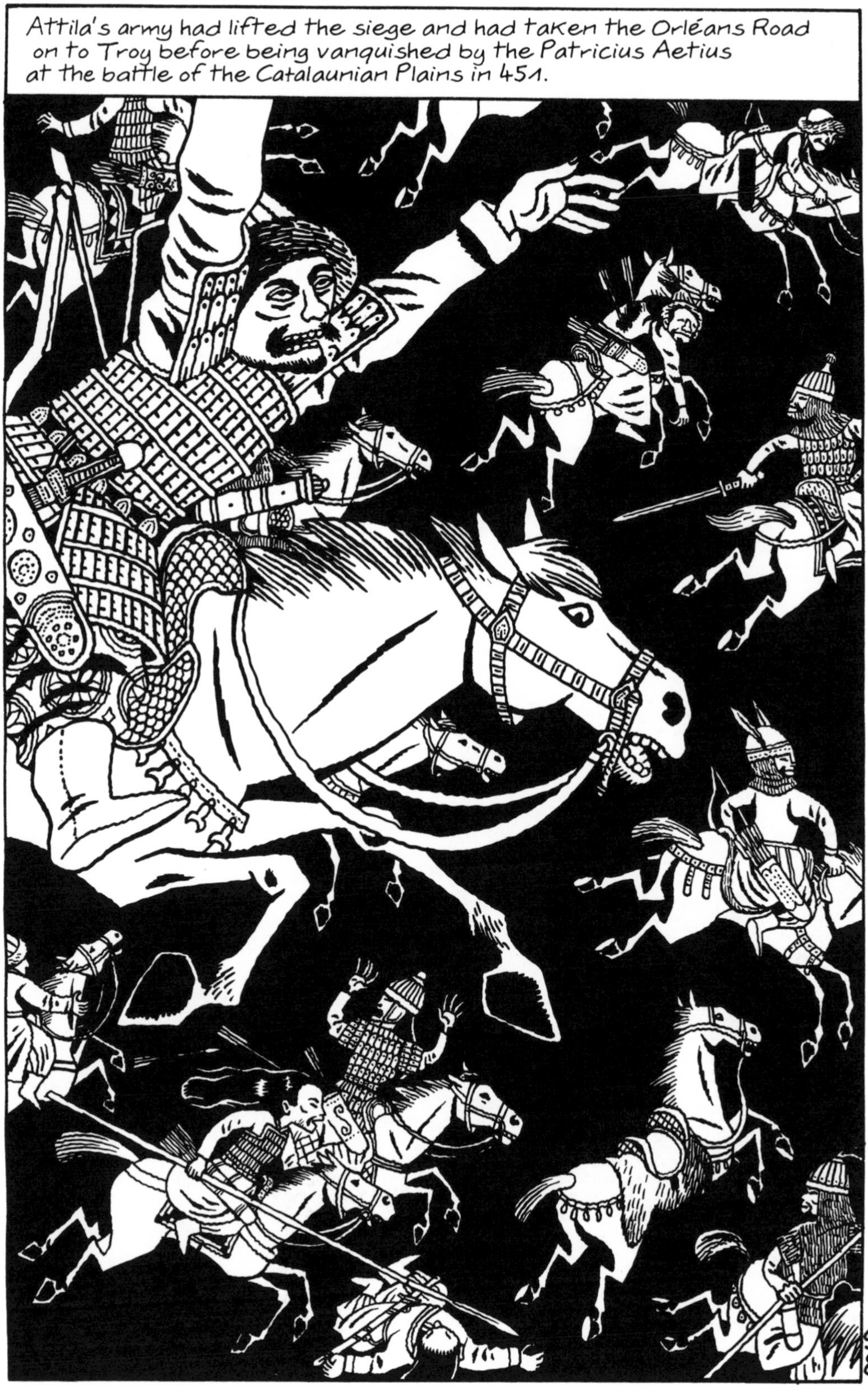
Attila's army had lifted the siege and had taken the Orléans Road on to Troy before being vanquished by the Patricius Aetius at the battle of the Catalaunian Plains in 451.

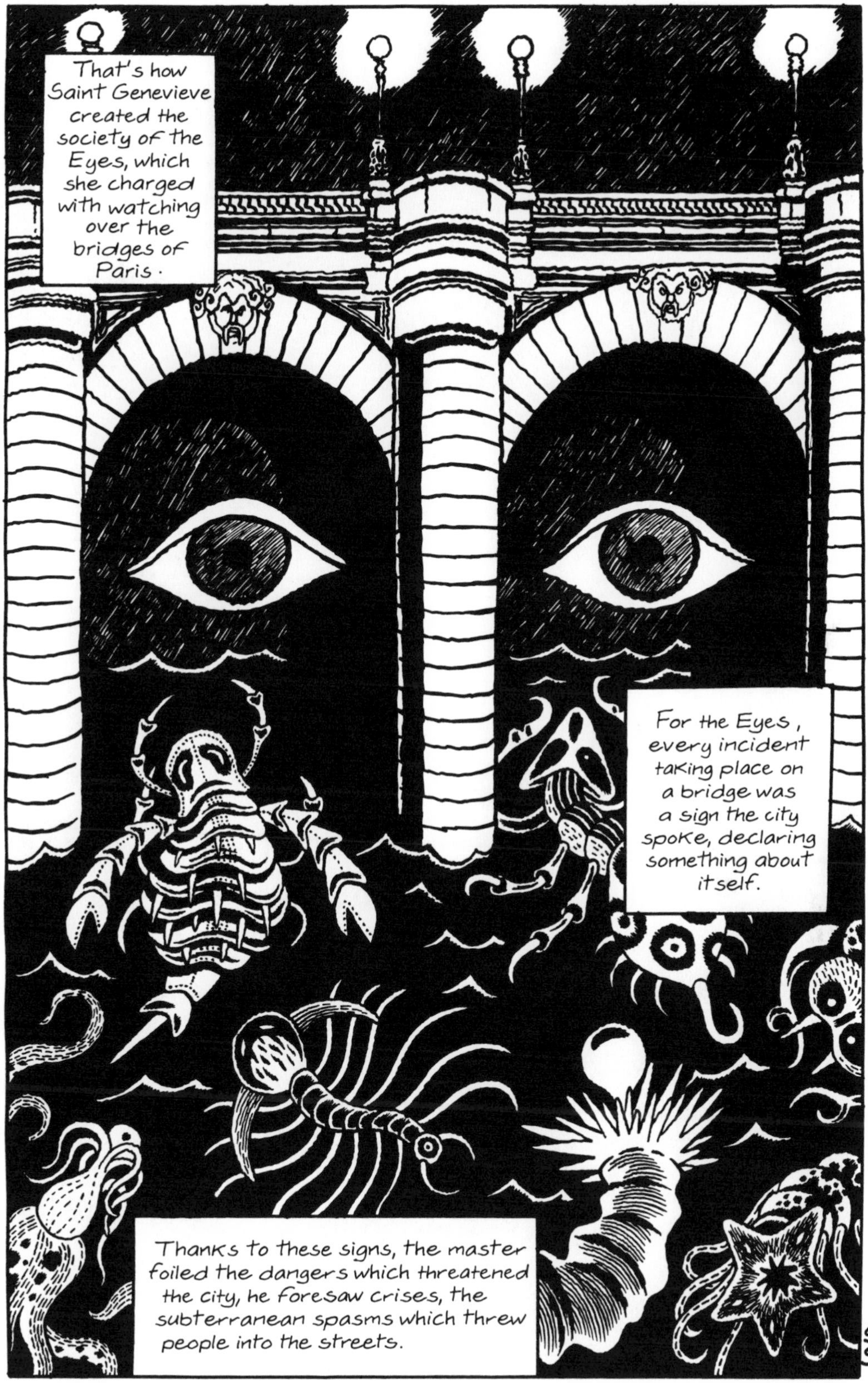
That's how Saint Genevieve created the society of the Eyes, which she charged with watching over the bridges of Paris.
For the Eyes, every incident taking place on a bridge was a sign the city spoke, declaring something about itself.
Thanks to these signs, the master foiled the dangers which threatened the city, he foresaw crises, the subterranean spasms which threw people into the streets.

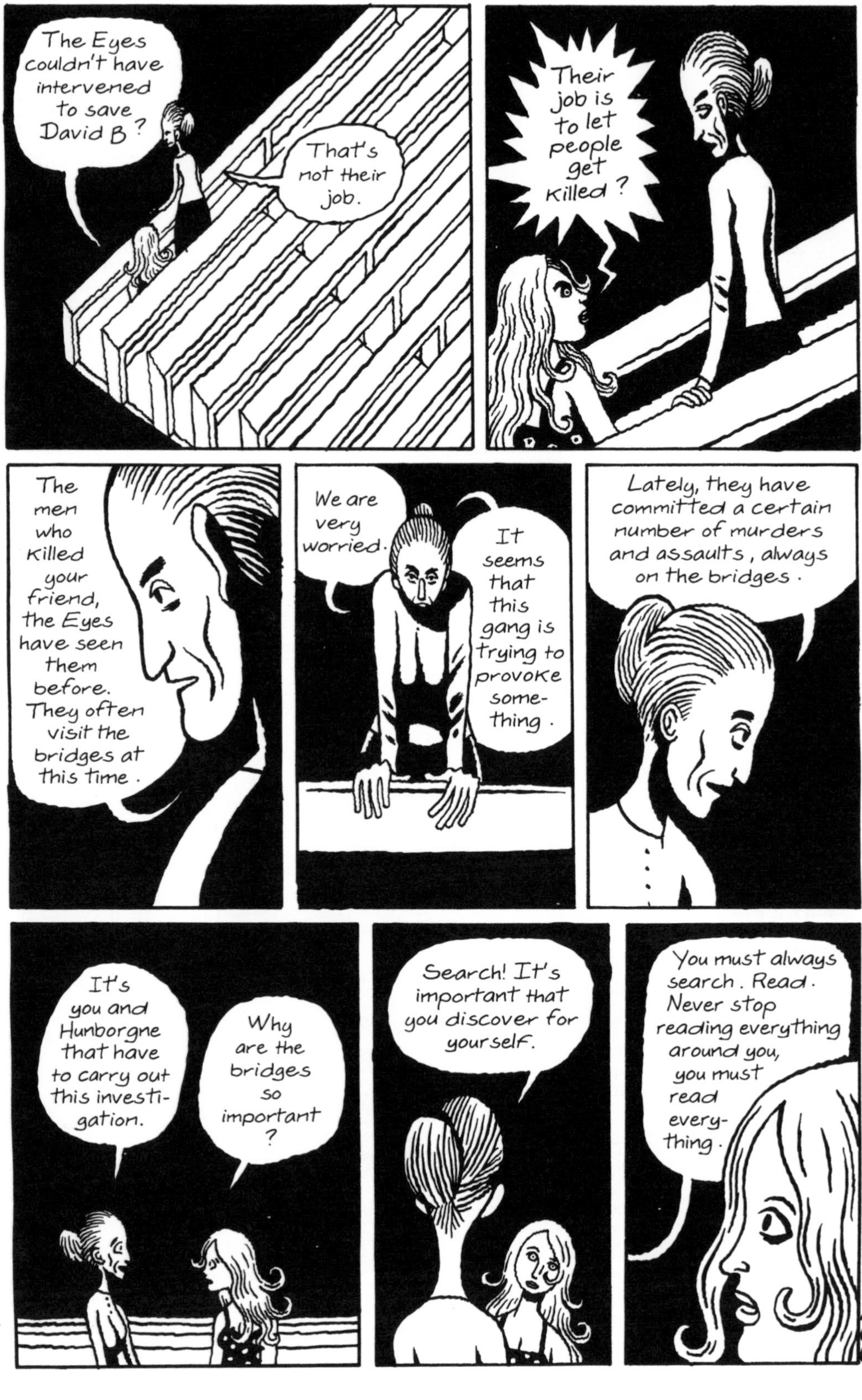
The Eyes couldn't have intervened to save David B ?
That's not their job.
Their job is to let people get killed ?
The men who killed your friend, the Eyes have seen them before. They often visit the bridges at this time.
We are very worried.
It seems that this gang is trying to provoke some-thing.
Lately, they have committed a certain number of murders and assaults, always on the bridges.
It's you and Hunborgne that have to carry out this investi-gation.
Why are the bridges so important ?
Search! It's important that you discover for yourself.
You must always search. Read. Never stop reading everything around you, you must read every-thing.

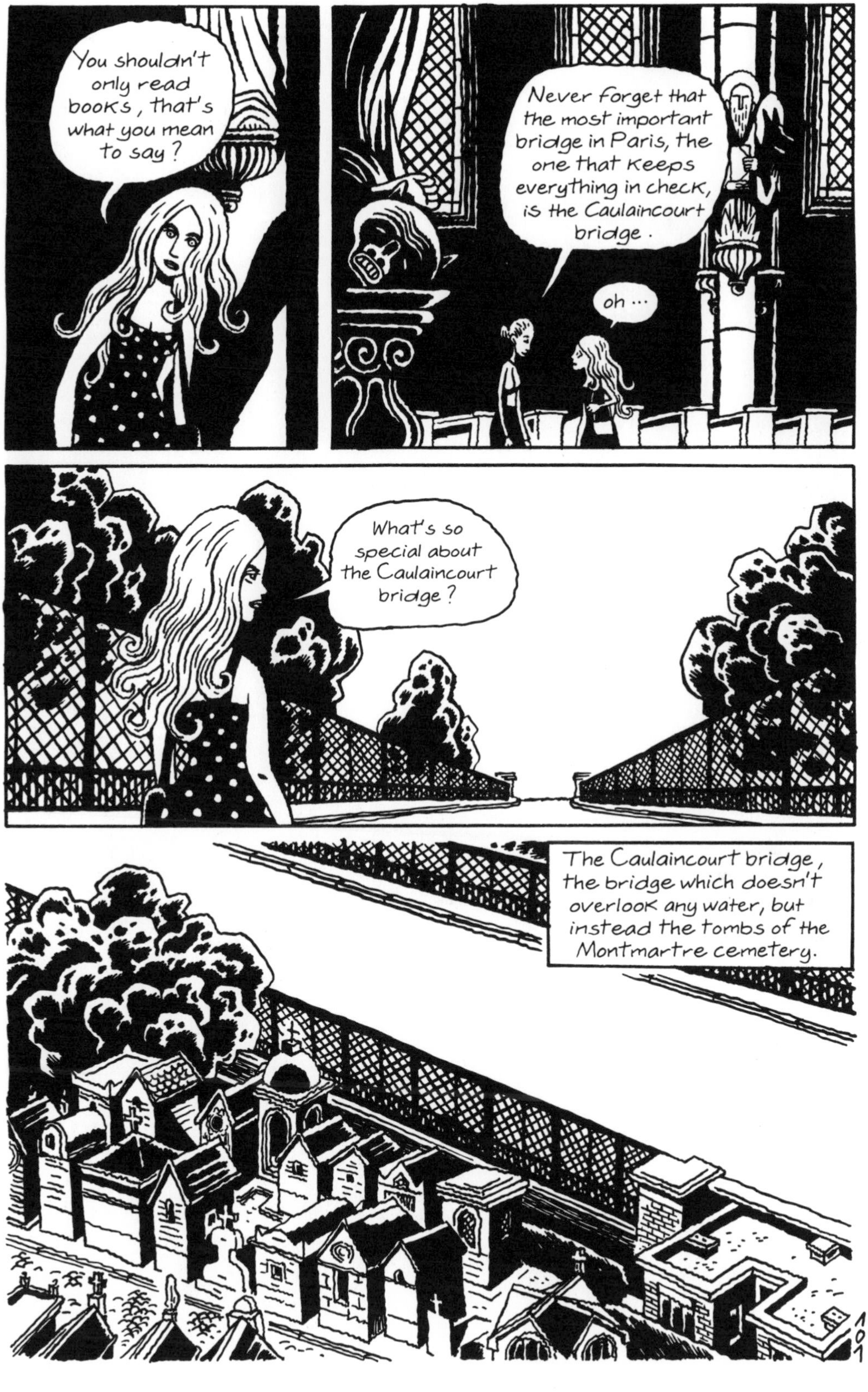
You shouldn't only read books, that's what you mean to say?
Never forget that the most important bridge in Paris, the one that keeps everything in check, is the Caulaincourt bridge.
oh ...
What's so special about the Caulaincourt bridge?
The Caulaincourt bridge, the bridge which doesn't overlook any water, but instead the tombs of the Montmartre cemetery.

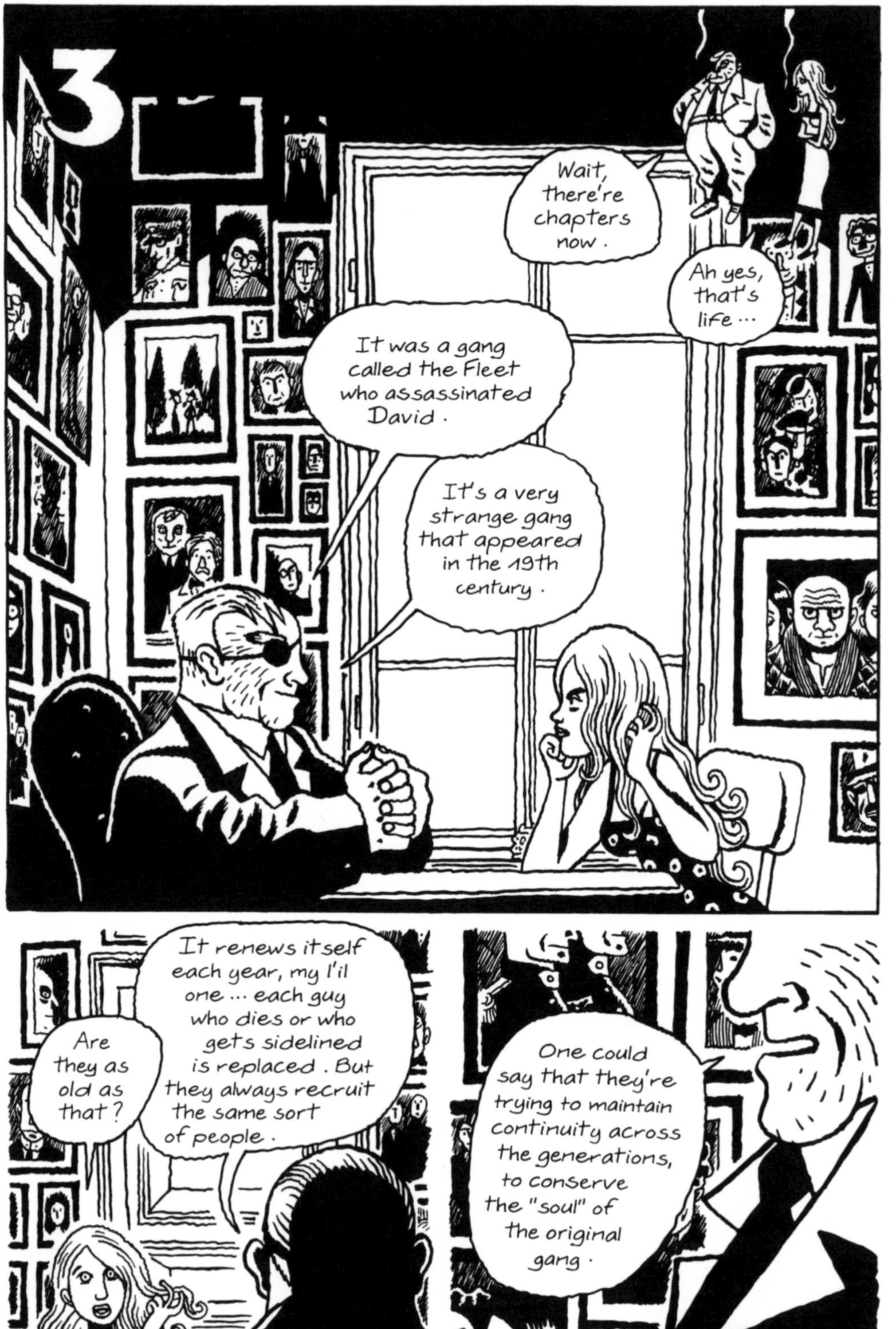
3
Wait, there're chapters now.
Ah yes, that's life...
It was a gang called the Fleet who assassinated David.
It's a very strange gang that appeared in the 19th century.
Are they as old as that?
It renews itself each year, my l'il one... each guy who dies or who gets sidelined is replaced. But they always recruit the same sort of people.
One could say that they're trying to maintain continuity across the generations, to conserve the "soul" of the original gang.

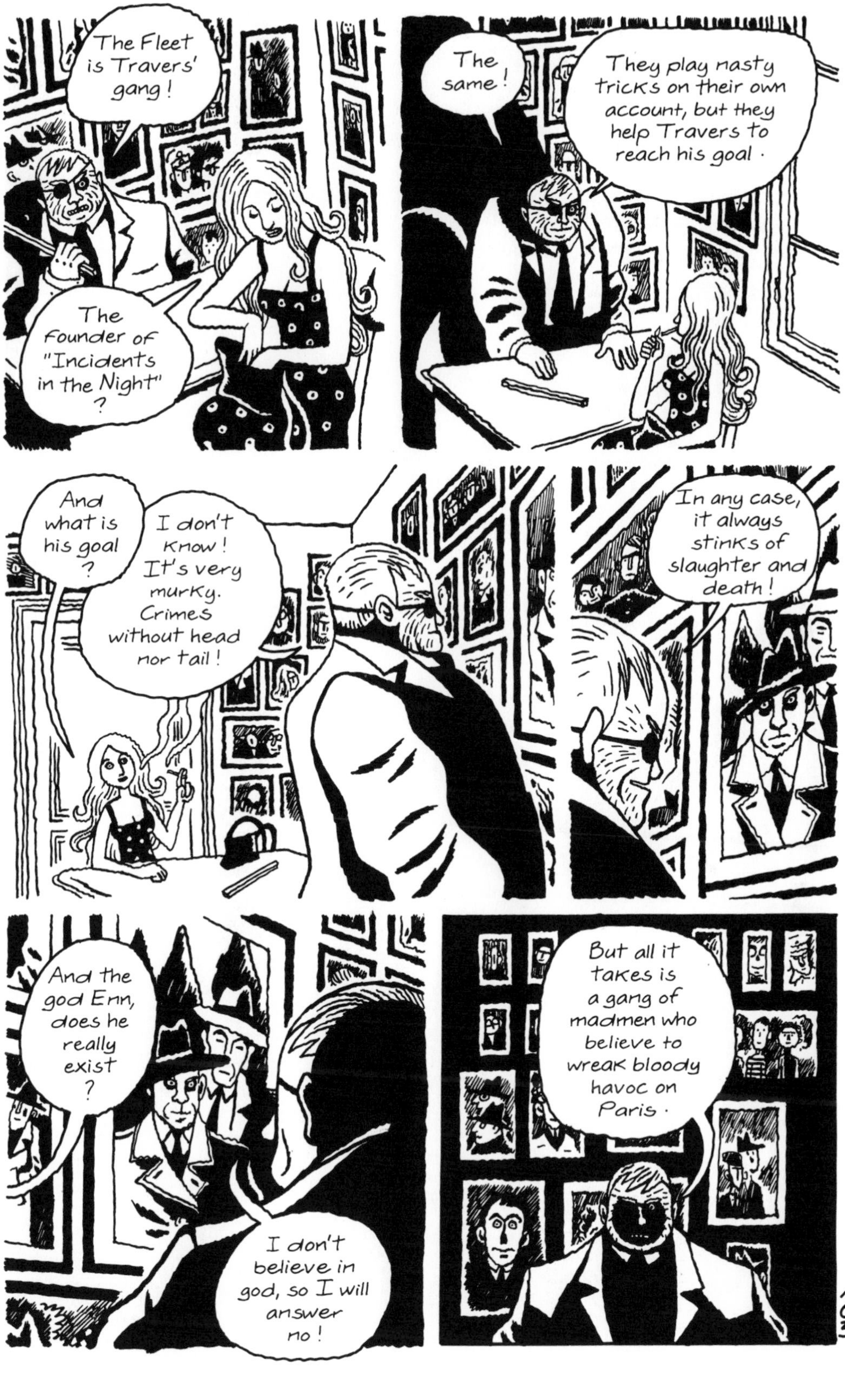
The Fleet is Travers' gang !
The founder of "Incidents in the Night" ?
The same !
They play nasty tricks on their own account, but they help Travers to reach his goal .
And what is his goal ?
I don't know ! It's very murky. Crimes without head nor tail !
In any case, it always stinks of slaughter and death !
And the god Enn, does he really exist ?
I don't believe in god, so I will answer no !
But all it takes is a gang of madmen who believe to wreak bloody havoc on Paris .

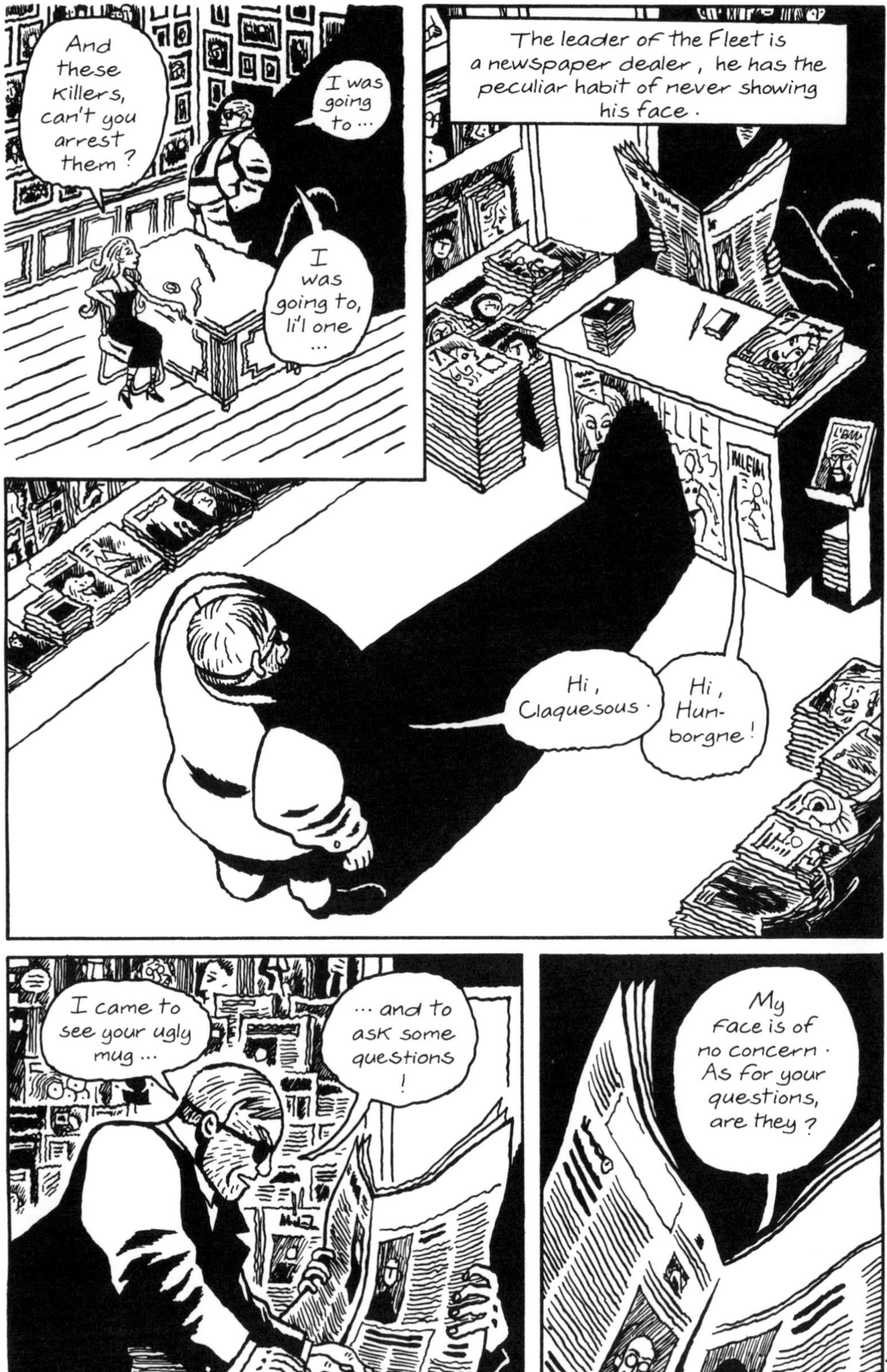
And these killers, can't you arrest them ?
I was going to ...
I was going to, li'l one ...
The leader of the Fleet is a newspaper dealer , he has the peculiar habit of never showing his face .
Hi , Claquesous .
Hi , Hunborgne !
I came to see your ugly mug ...
... and to ask some questions !
My face is of no concern . As for your questions, are they ?

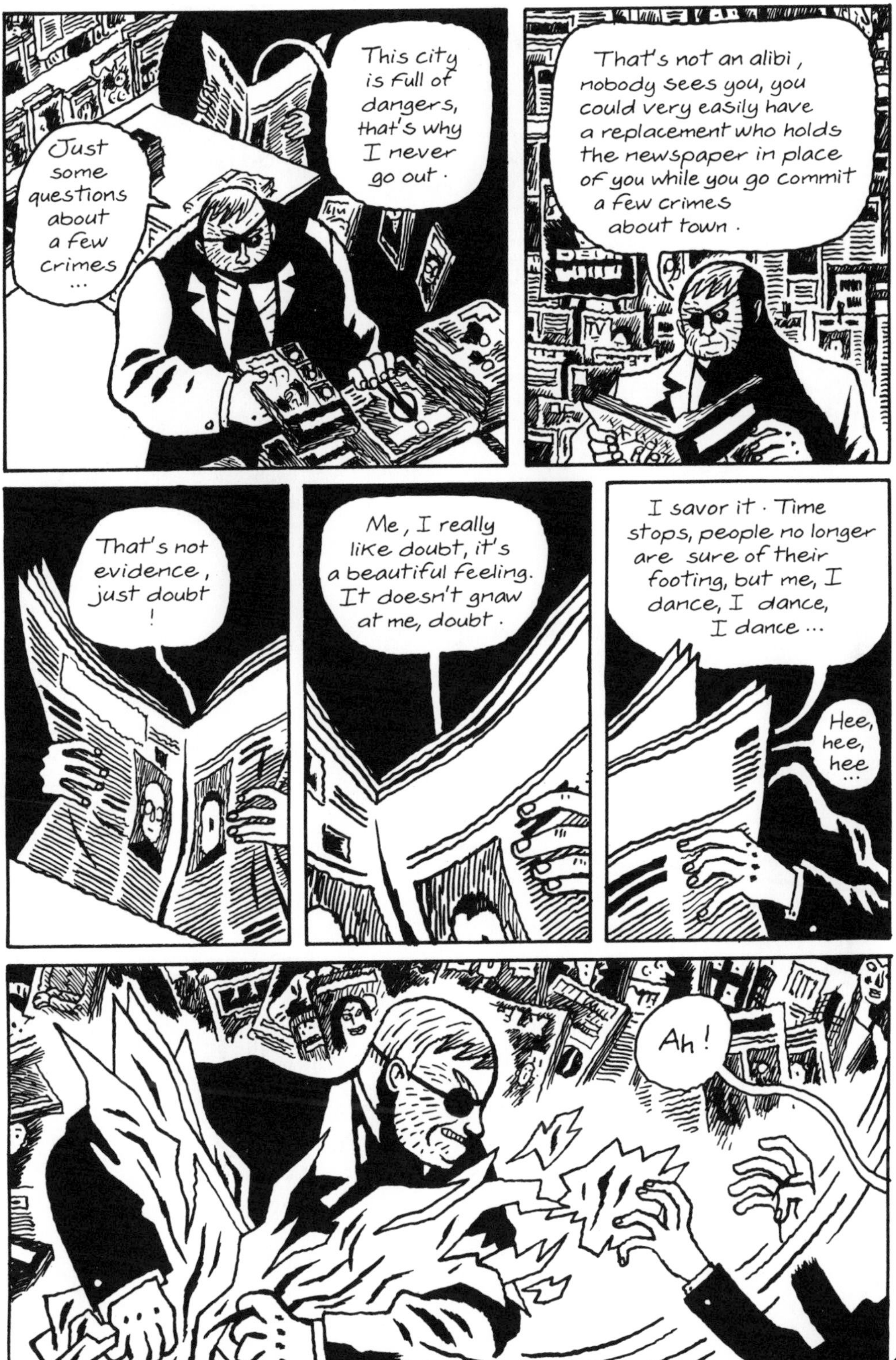
Just some questions about a few crimes ...
This city is full of dangers, that's why I never go out.
That's not an alibi, nobody sees you, you could very easily have a replacement who holds the newspaper in place of you while you go commit a few crimes about town.
That's not evidence, just doubt!
Me, I really like doubt, it's a beautiful feeling. It doesn't gnaw at me, doubt.
I savor it. Time stops, people no longer are sure of their footing, but me, I dance, I dance, I dance ...
Hee, hee, hee ...
Ah!

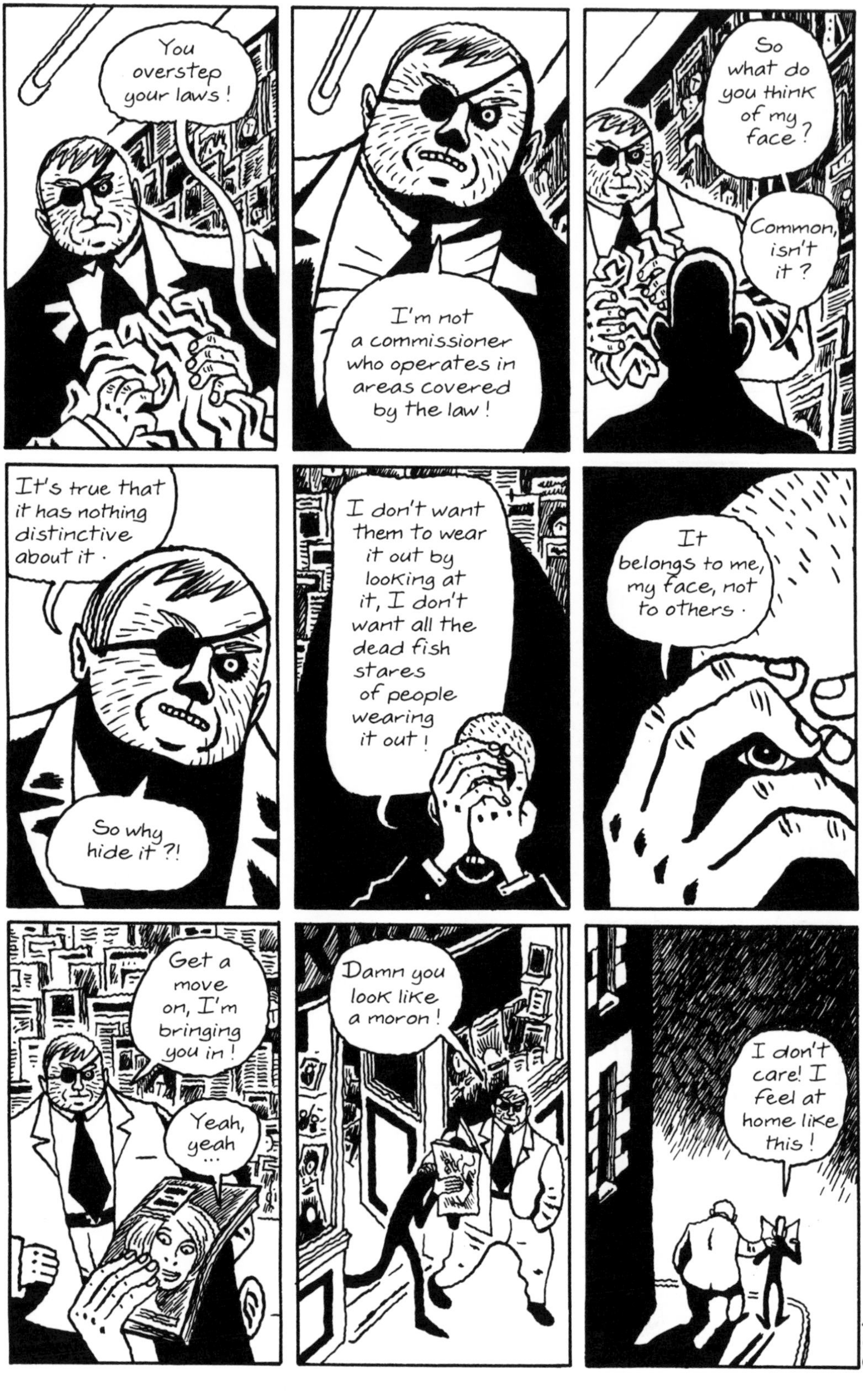
You overstep your laws!
I'm not a commissioner who operates in areas covered by the law!
So what do you think of my face?
Common, isn't it?
It's true that it has nothing distinctive about it.
So why hide it?!
I don't want them to wear it out by looking at it, I don't want all the dead fish stares of people wearing it out!
It belongs to me, my face, not to others.
Get a move on, I'm bringing you in!
Yeah, yeah...
Damn you look like a moron!
I don't care! I feel at home like this!

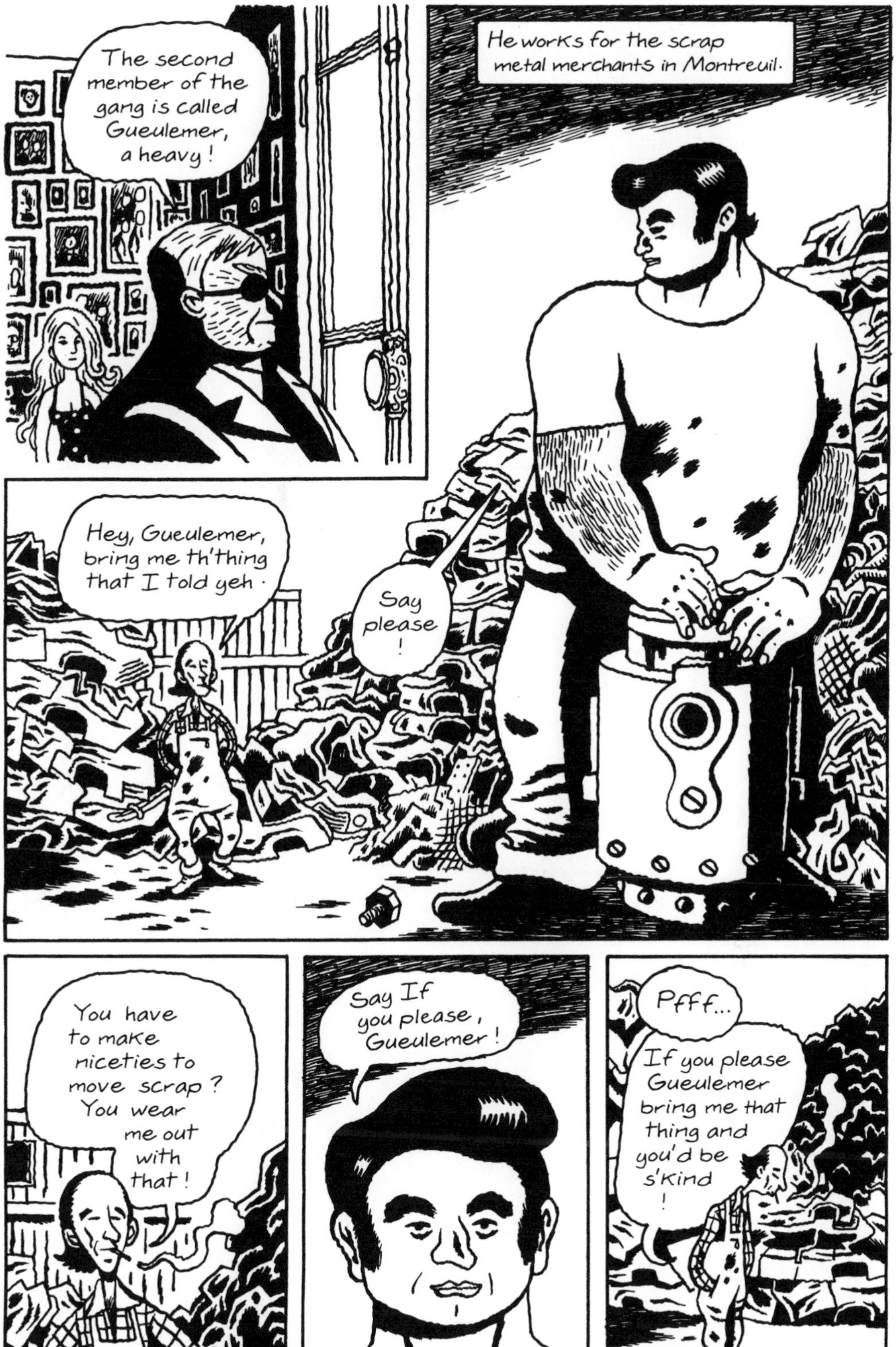
The second member of the gang is called Gueulemer, a heavy !
He works for the scrap metal merchants in Montreuil.
Hey, Gueulemer, bring me th'thing that I told yeh.
Say please !
You have to make niceties to move scrap ? You wear me out with that !
Say If you please, Gueulemer !
Pfff...
If you please Gueulemer bring me that thing and you'd be s'Kind !

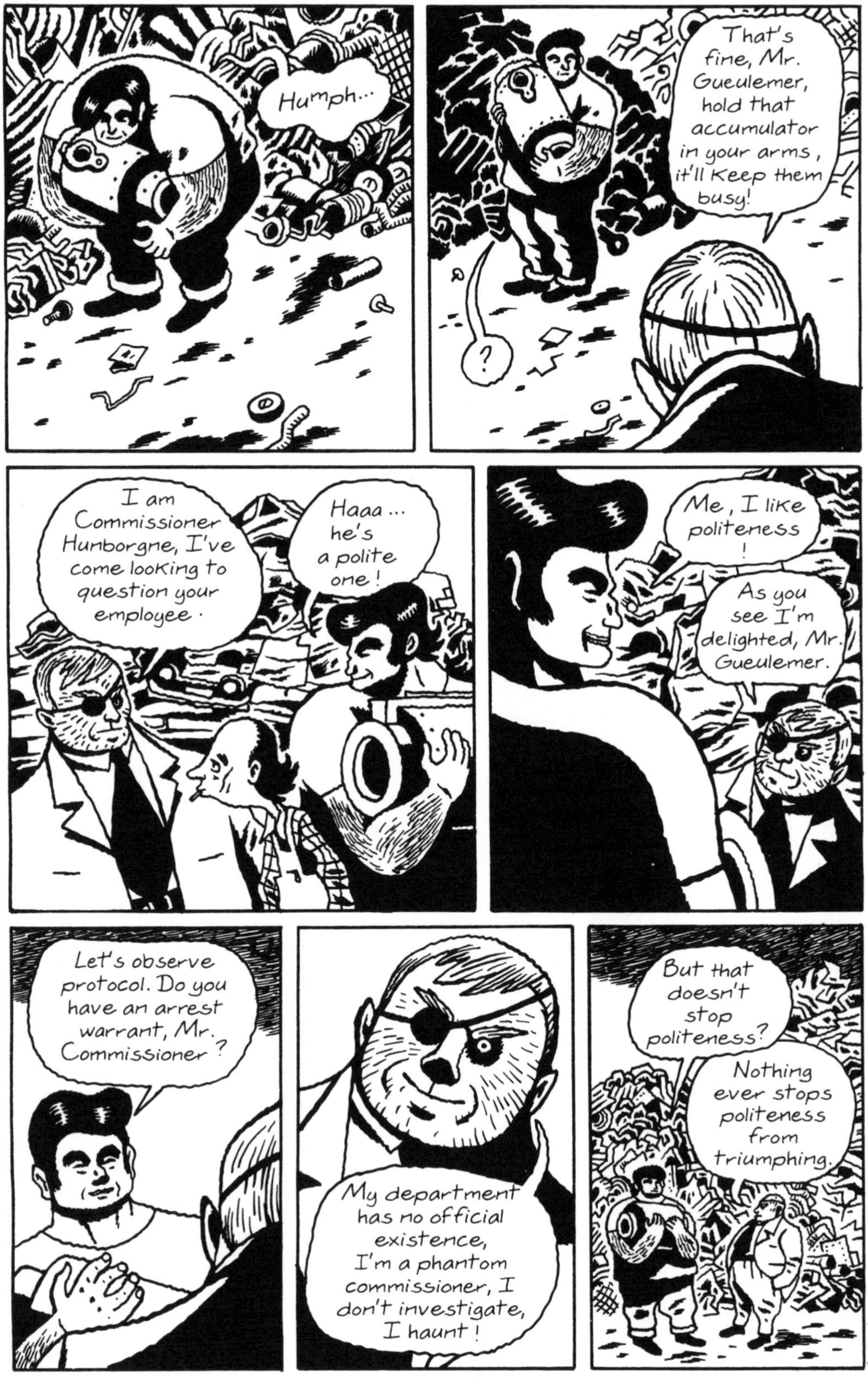
Humph...
That's fine, Mr. Gueulemer, hold that accumulator in your arms, it'll Keep them busy!
?
I am Commissioner Hunborgne, I've come looking to question your employee.
Haaa... he's a polite one!
Me, I like politeness!
As you see I'm delighted, Mr. Gueulemer.
Let's observe protocol. Do you have an arrest warrant, Mr. Commissioner?
My department has no official existence, I'm a phantom commissioner, I don't investigate, I haunt!
But that doesn't stop politeness?
Nothing ever stops politeness from triumphing.

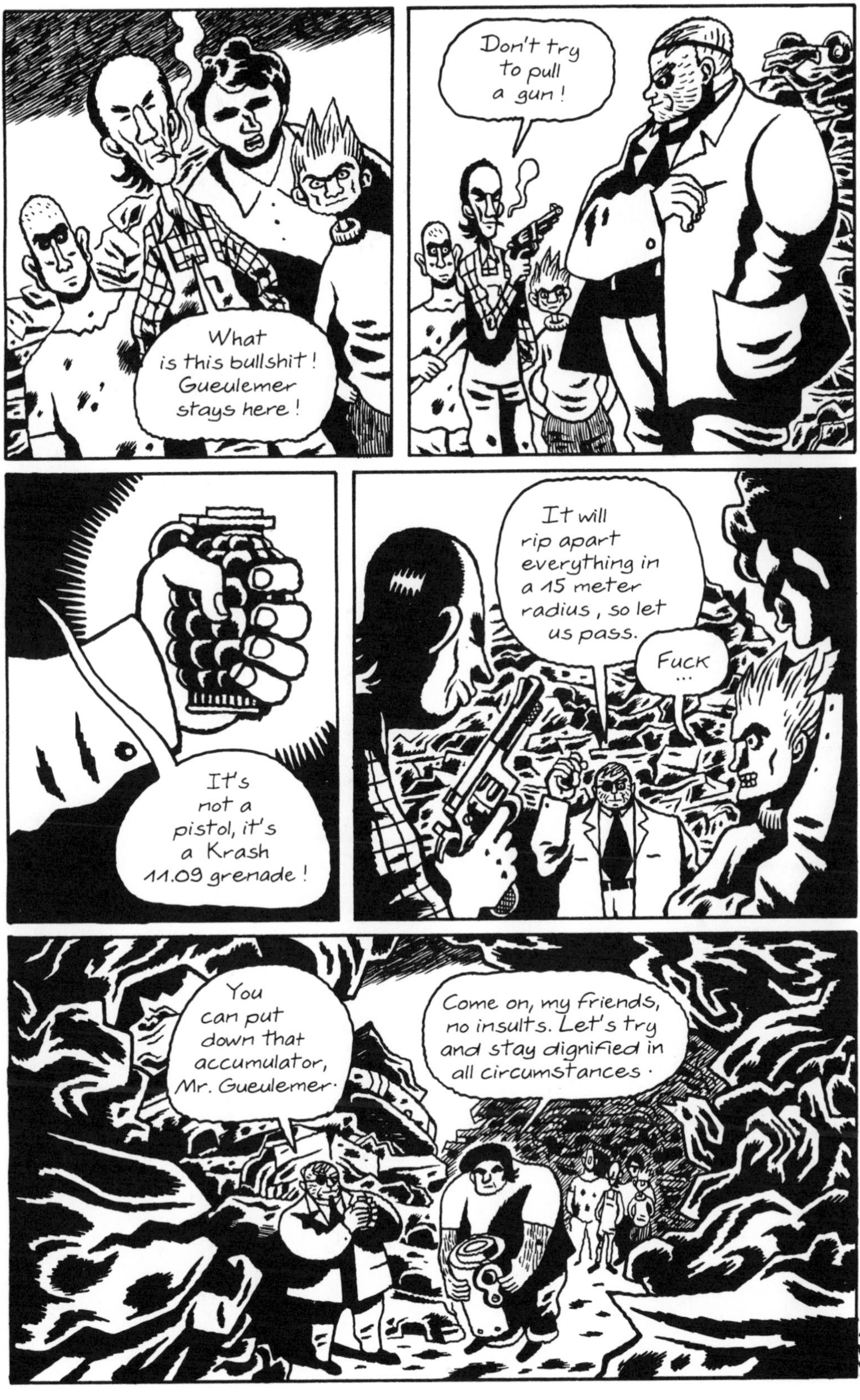
What is this bullshit! Gueulemer stays here!
Don't try to pull a gun!
It's not a pistol, it's a Krash 11.09 grenade!
It will rip apart everything in a 15 meter radius, so let us pass.
Fuck ...
You can put down that accumulator, Mr. Gueulemer.
Come on, my friends, no insults. Let's try and stay dignified in all circumstances.

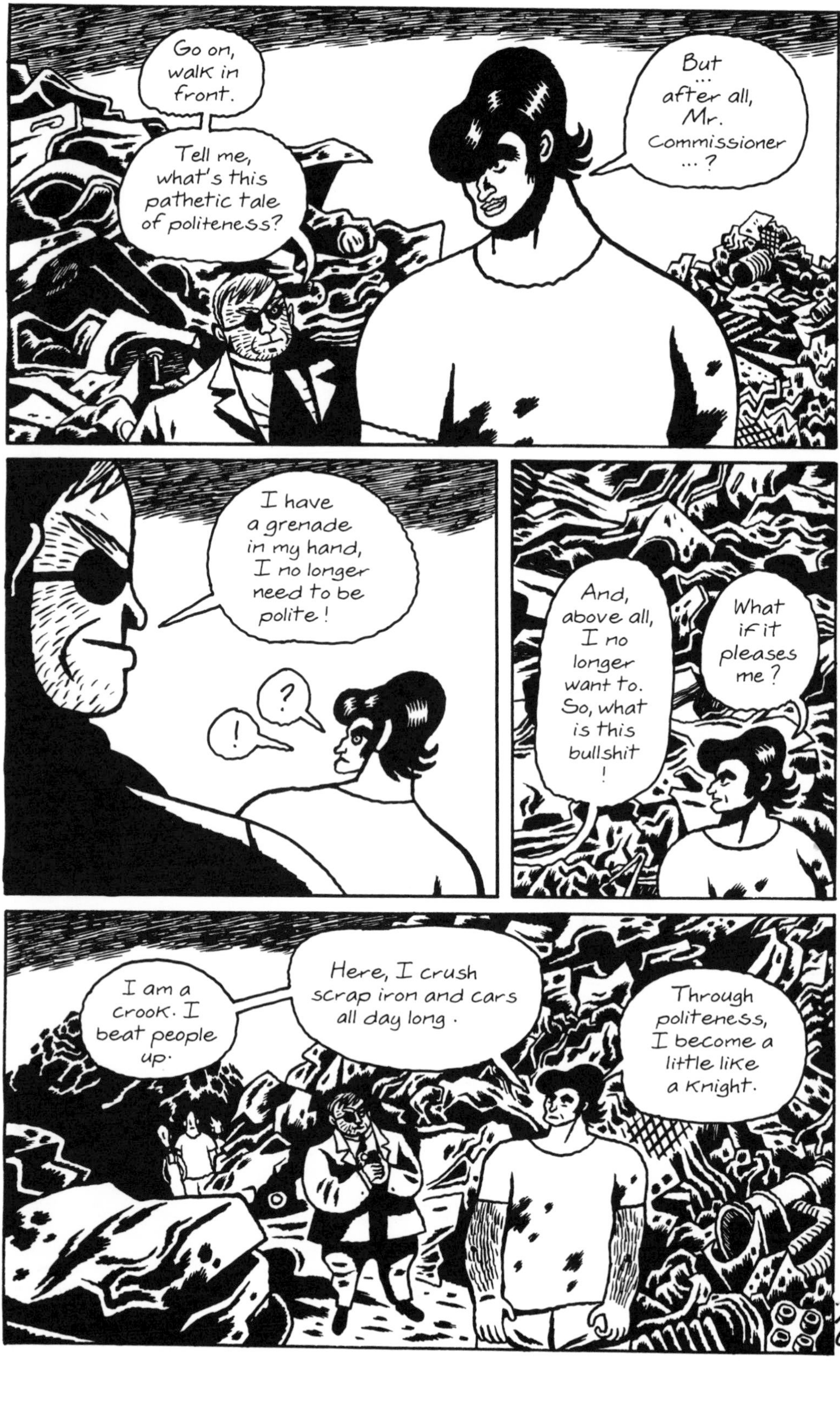

Go on, walk in front.
Tell me, what's this pathetic tale of politeness?
But ... after all, Mr. Commissioner ...?
I have a grenade in my hand, I no longer need to be polite!
?
!
And, above all, I no longer want to. So, what is this bullshit!
What if it pleases me?
I am a crook. I beat people up.
Here, I crush scrap iron and cars all day long.
Through politeness, I become a little like a Knight.

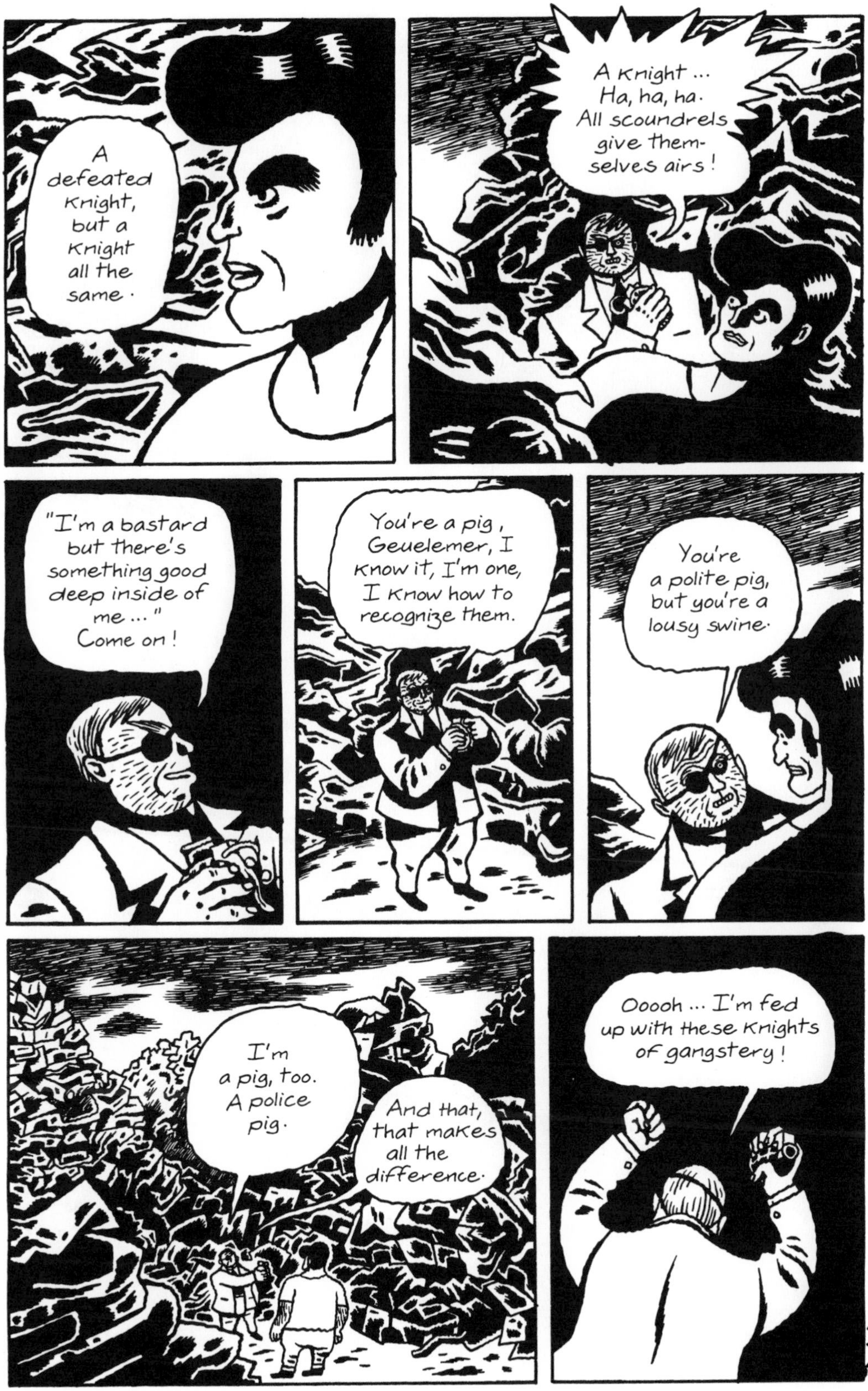
A defeated Knight, but a Knight all the same.
A Knight ... Ha, ha, ha. All scoundrels give themselves airs!
"I'm a bastard but there's something good deep inside of me ..." Come on!
You're a pig, Geuelemer, I know it, I'm one, I know how to recognize them.
You're a polite pig, but you're a lousy swine.
I'm a pig, too. A police pig.
And that, that makes all the difference.
Ooooh ... I'm fed up with these Knights of gangstery!

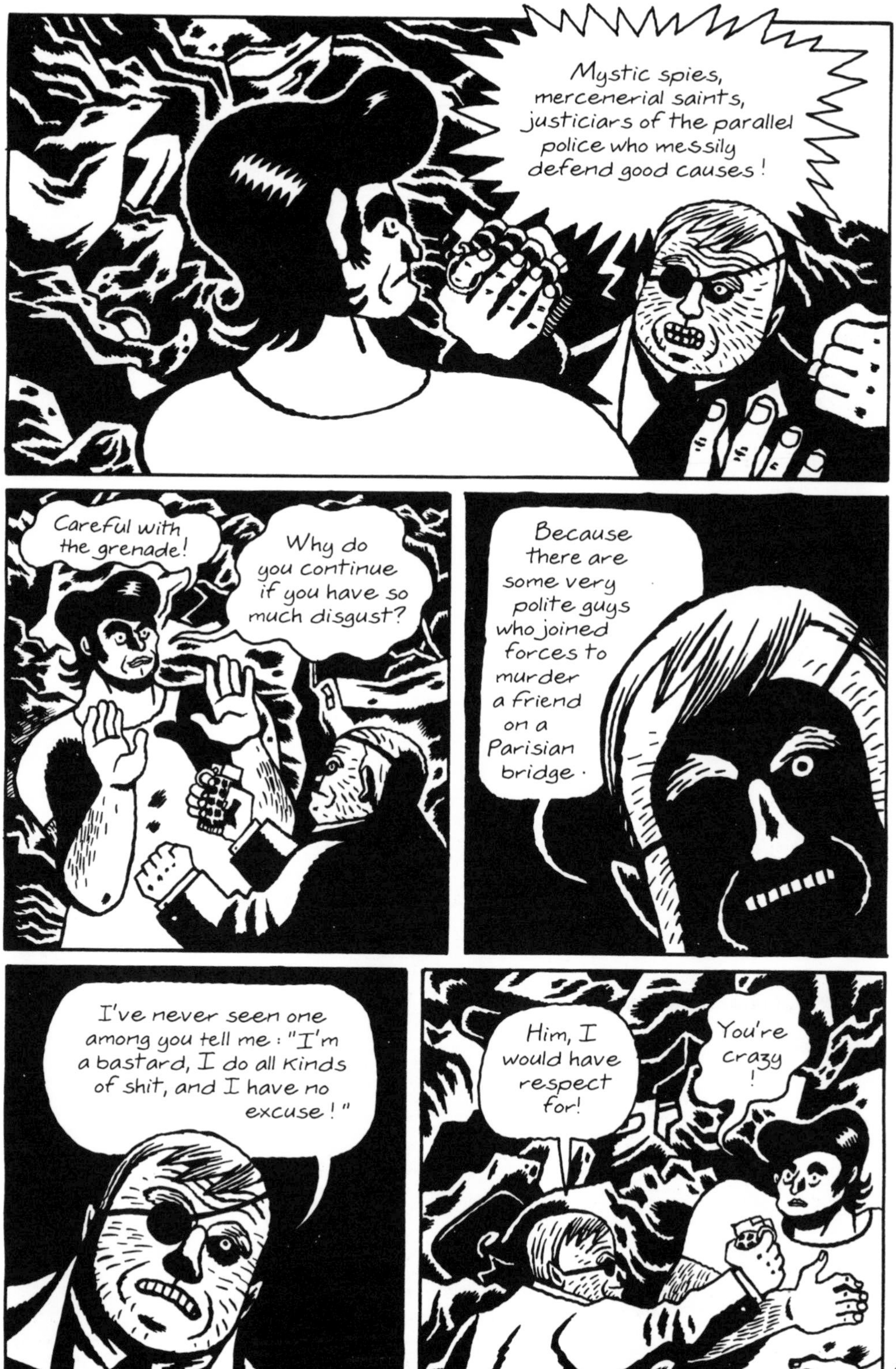
Mystic spies, mercenerial saints, justiciars of the parallel police who messily defend good causes!
Careful with the grenade!
Why do you continue if you have so much disgust?
Because there are some very polite guys who joined forces to murder a friend on a Parisian bridge.
I've never seen one among you tell me: "I'm a bastard, I do all kinds of shit, and I have no excuse!"
Him, I would have respect for!
You're crazy!

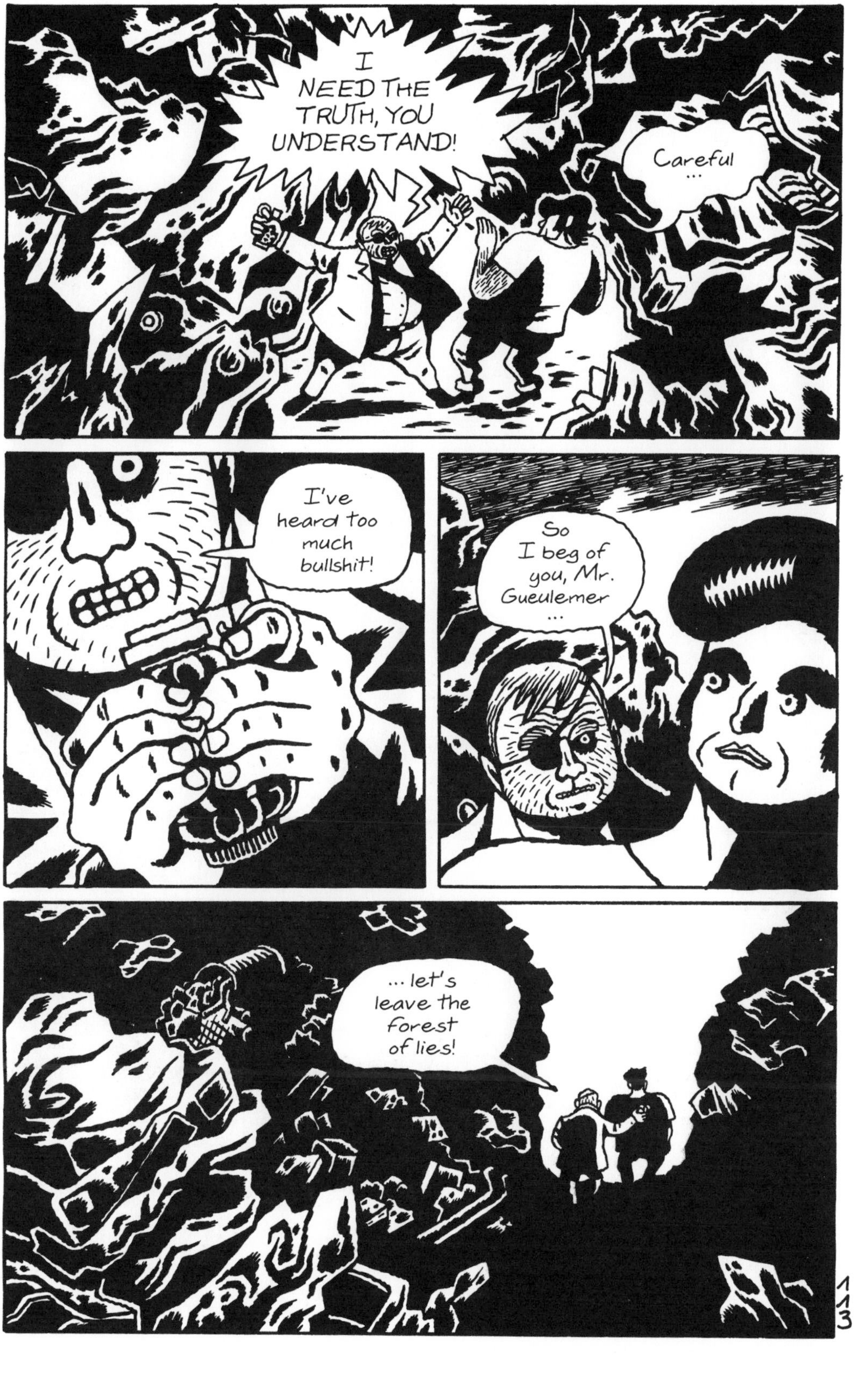
I NEED THE TRUTH, YOU UNDERSTAND!
Careful ...
I've heard too much bullshit!
So I beg of you, Mr. Gueulemer ...
... let's leave the forest of lies!

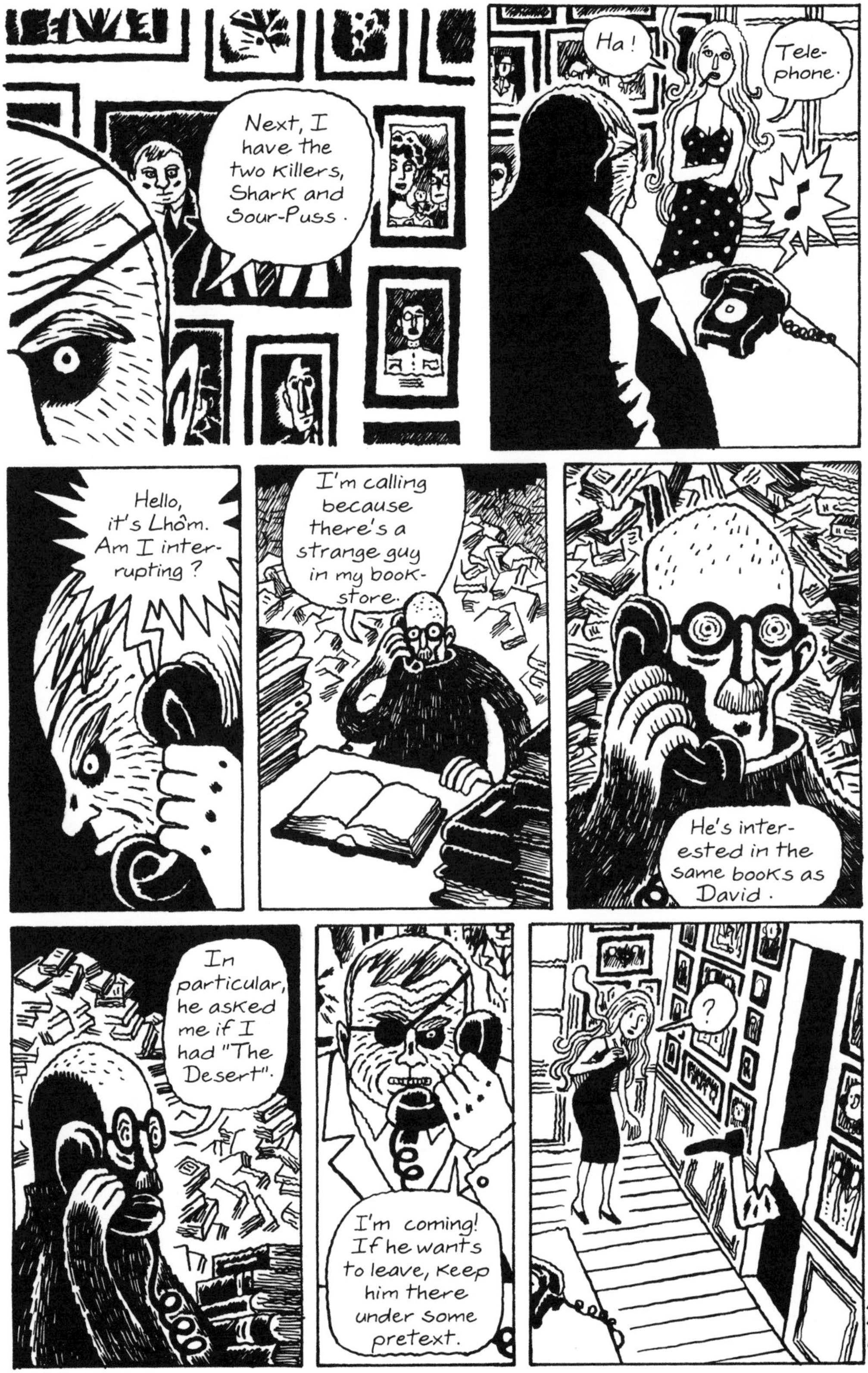

Next, I have the two killers, Shark and Sour-Puss.
Ha!
Telephone.
Hello, it's Lhôm. Am I interrupting?
I'm calling because there's a strange guy in my bookstore.
He's interested in the same books as David.
In particular, he asked me if I had "The Desert".
I'm coming! If he wants to leave, keep him there under some pretext.
?

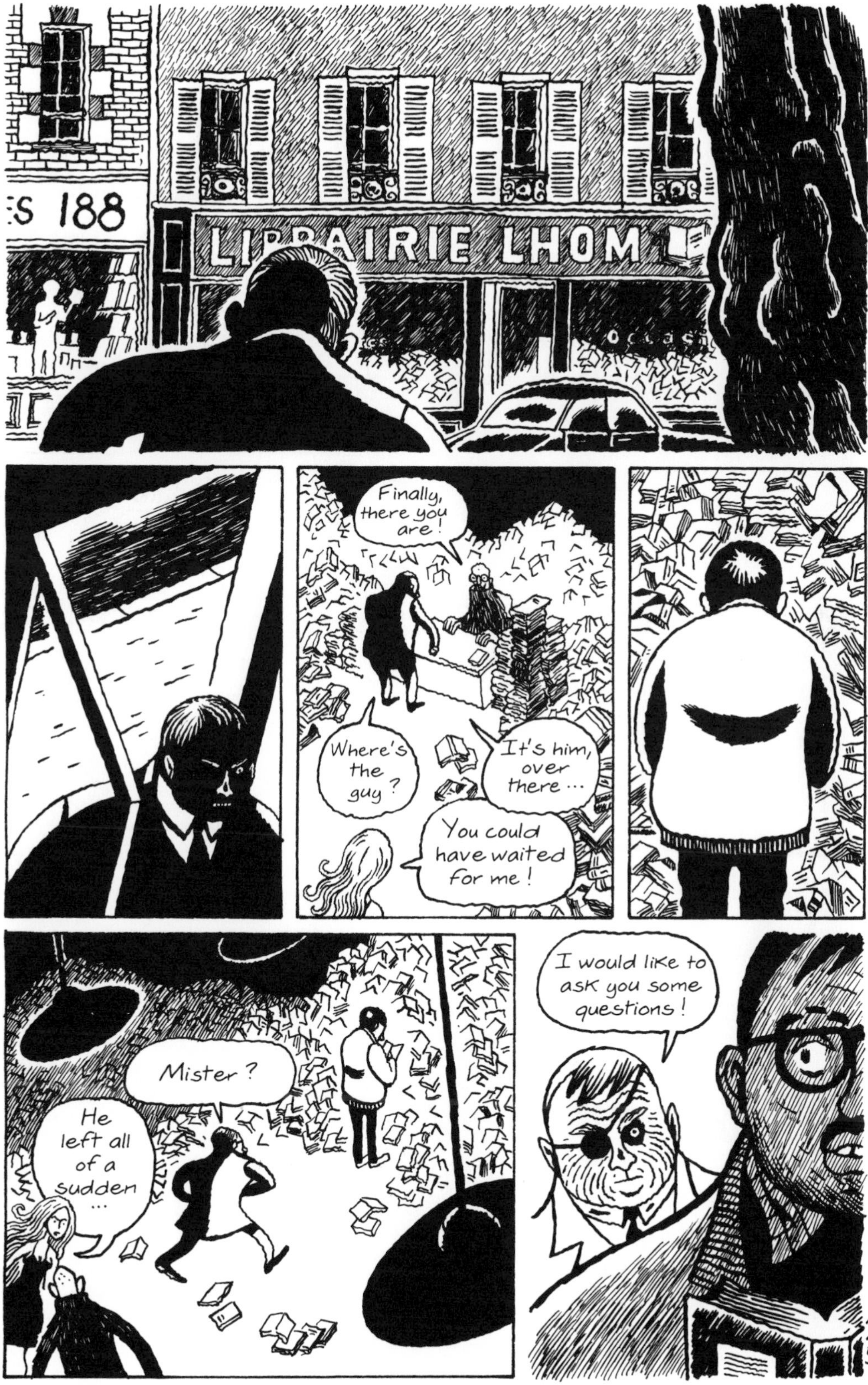
ES 188
LIBRAIRIE LHOM
Finally, there you are!
Where's the guy?
It's him, over there...
You could have waited for me!
Mister?
He left all of a sudden ...
I would like to ask you some questions!

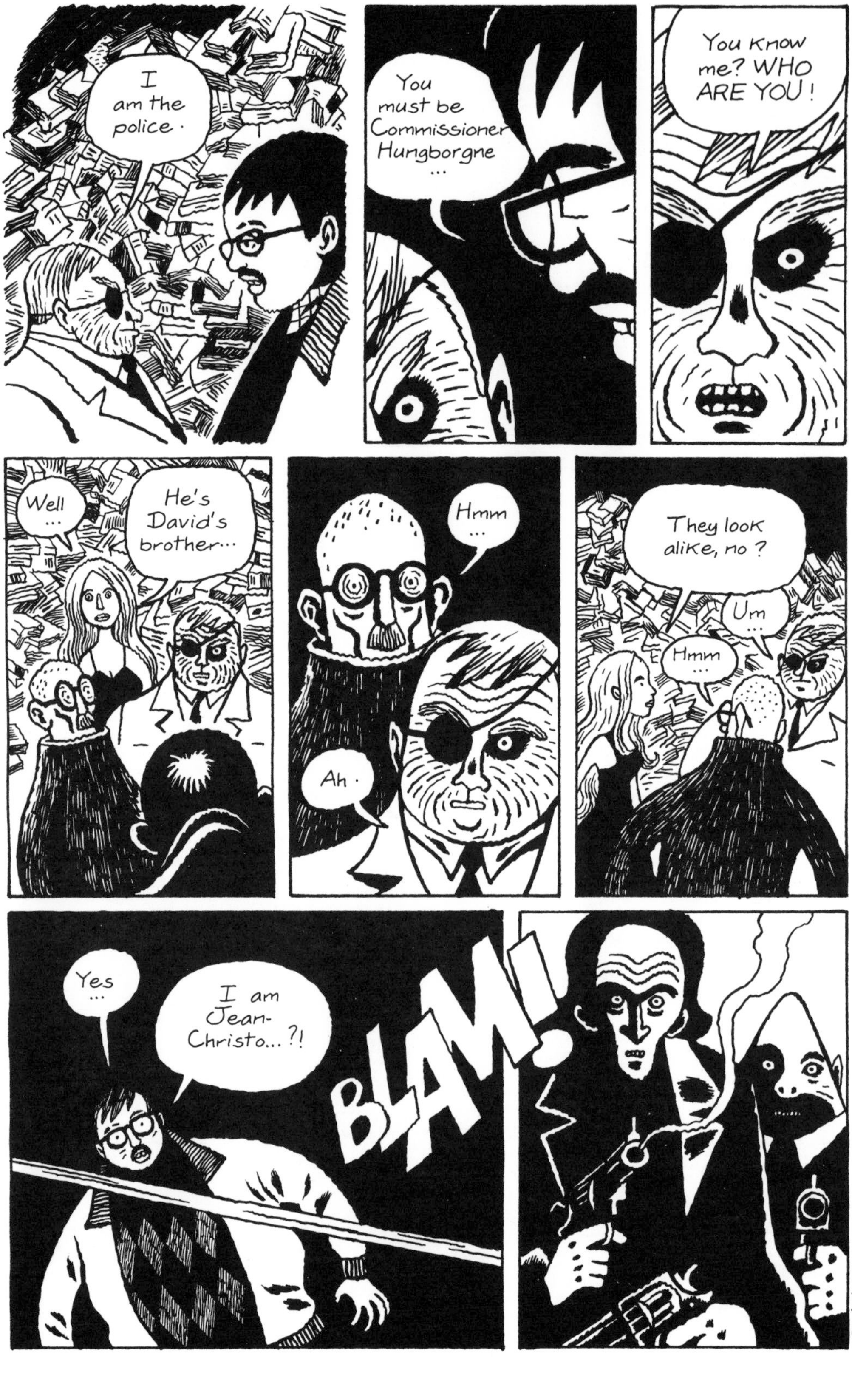
I am the police.
You must be Commissioner Hungborgne ...
You know me? WHO ARE YOU!
Well ...
He's David's brother...
Hmm ...
Ah.
They look alike, no?
Um ...
Hmm ...
Yes ...
I am Jean-Christo... ?!
BLAM!

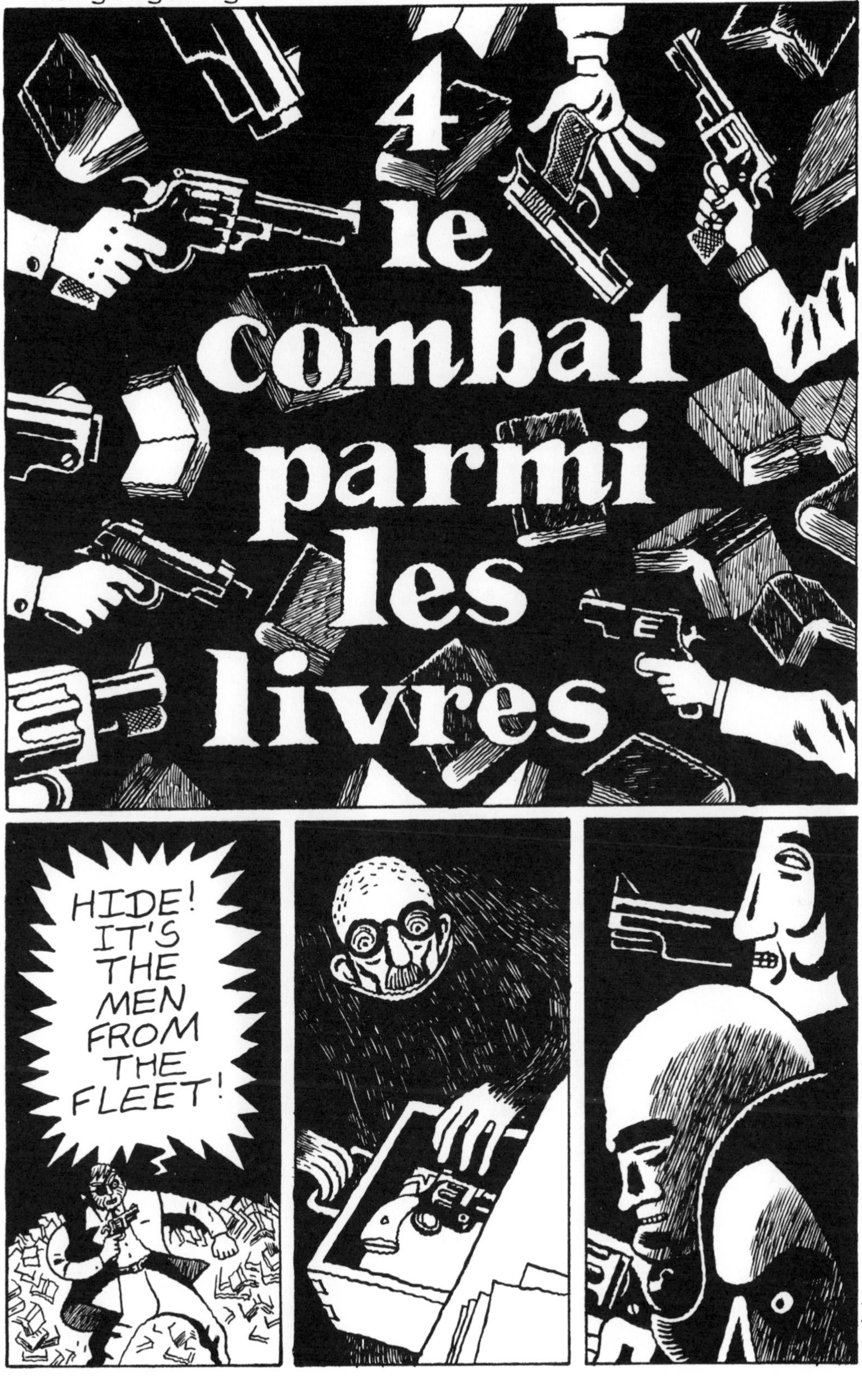
4
le
combat
parmi
les
livres
HIDE! IT'S THE MEN FROM THE FLEET!

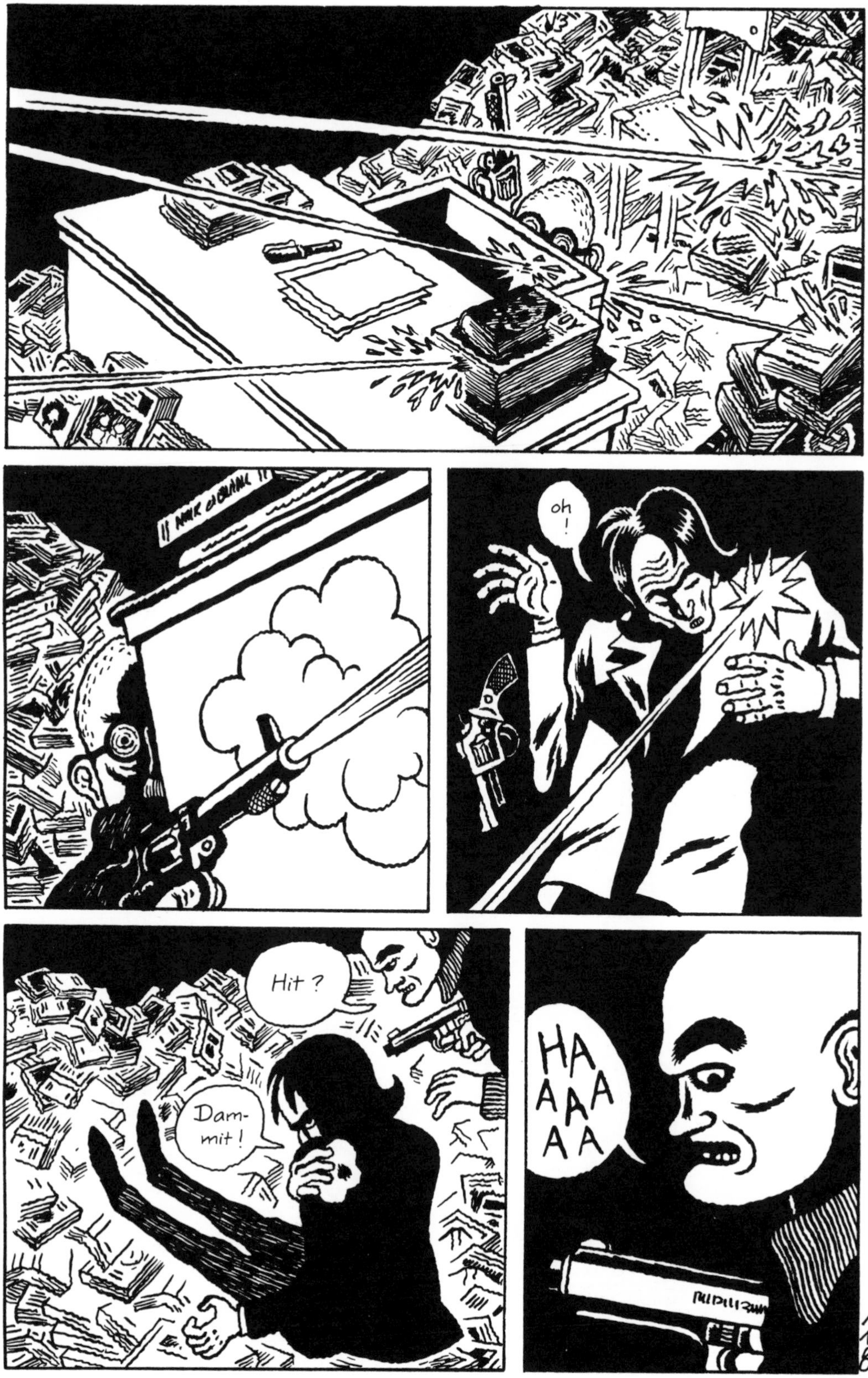
oh !
Hit ?
Dam-
mit !
HA
AAA
AA

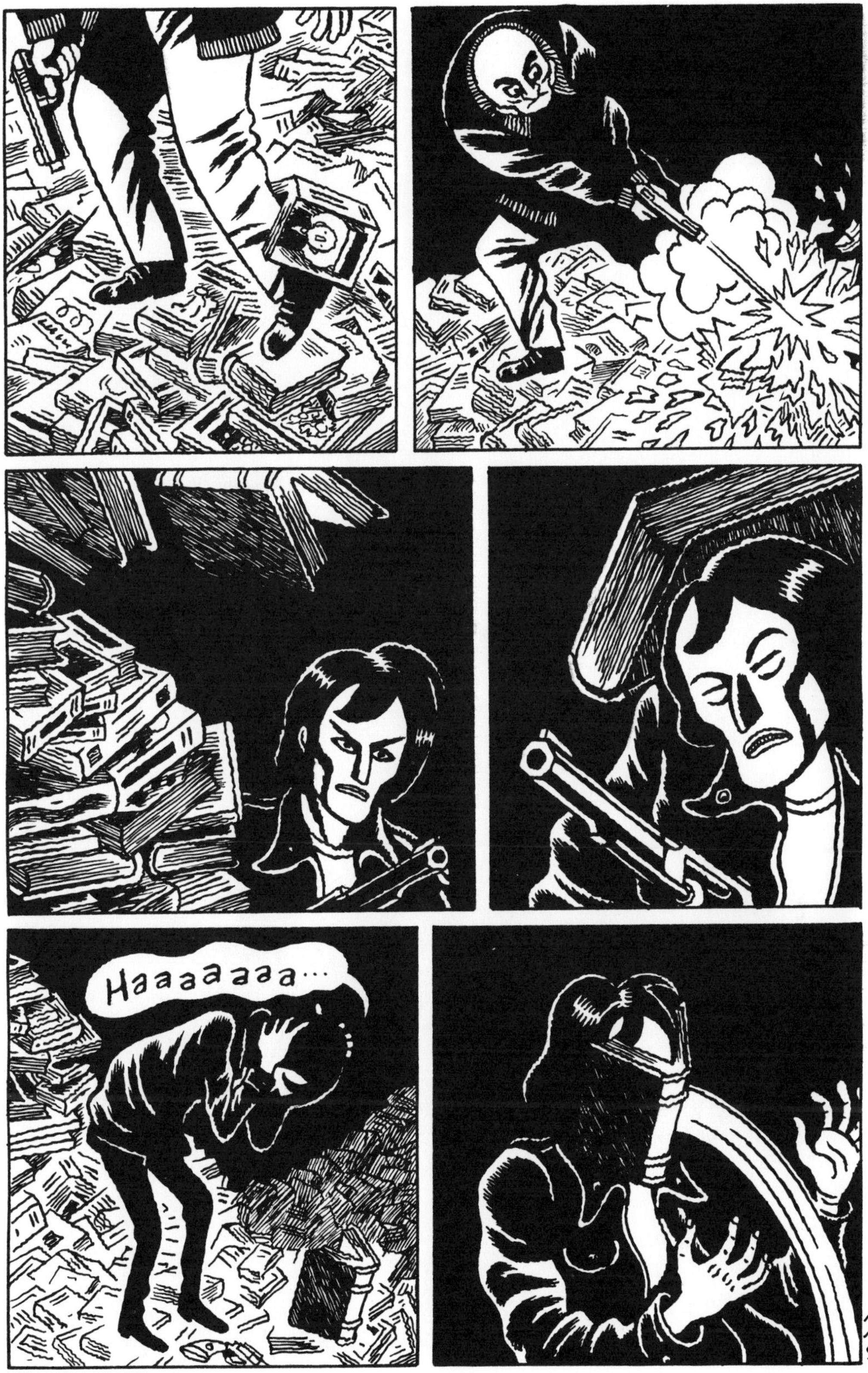
Haaaaaaa...

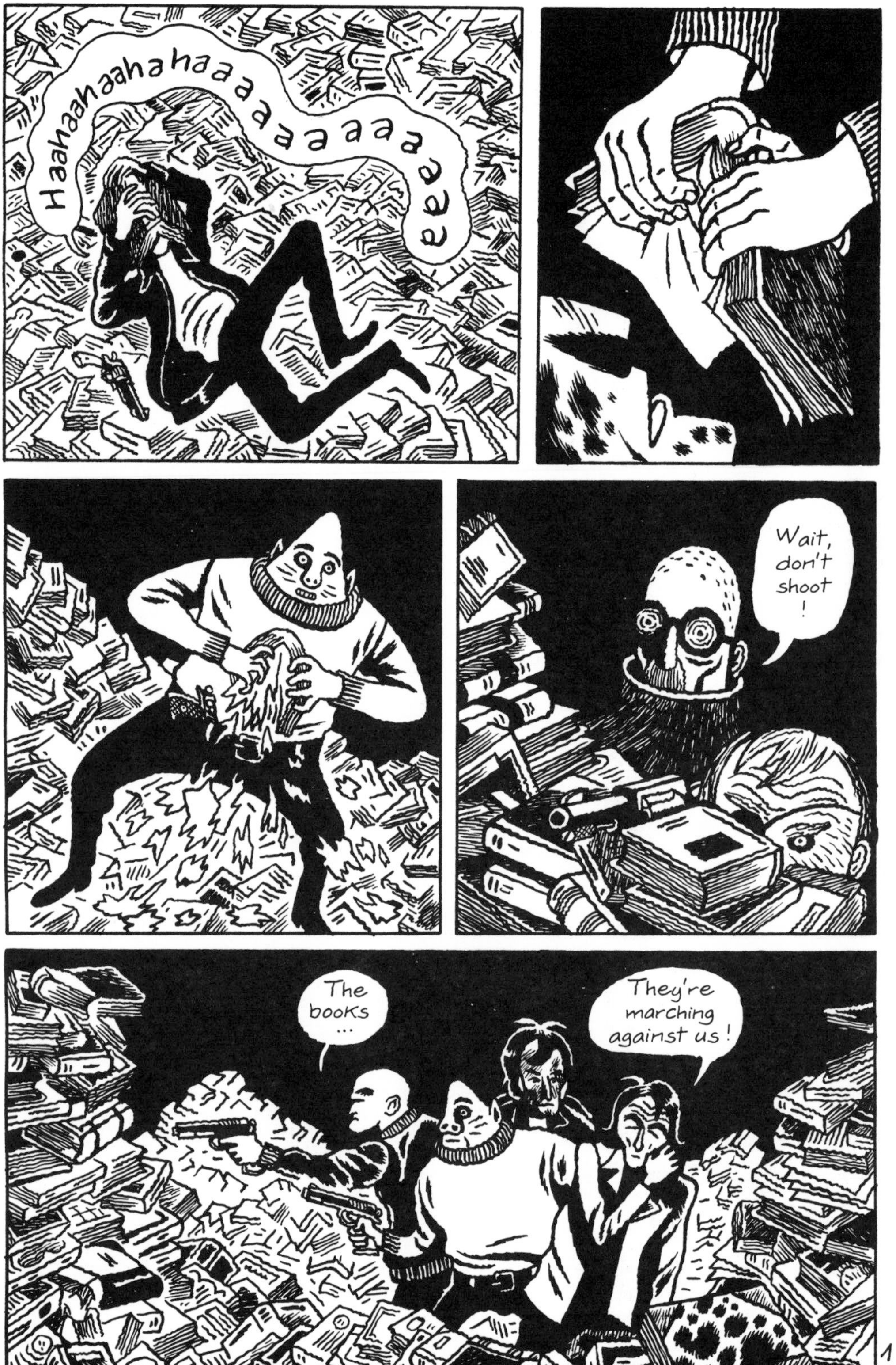
Haahaahaahahaaaaaaaaaaaeeee
Wait, don't shoot !
The books ...
They're marching against us !

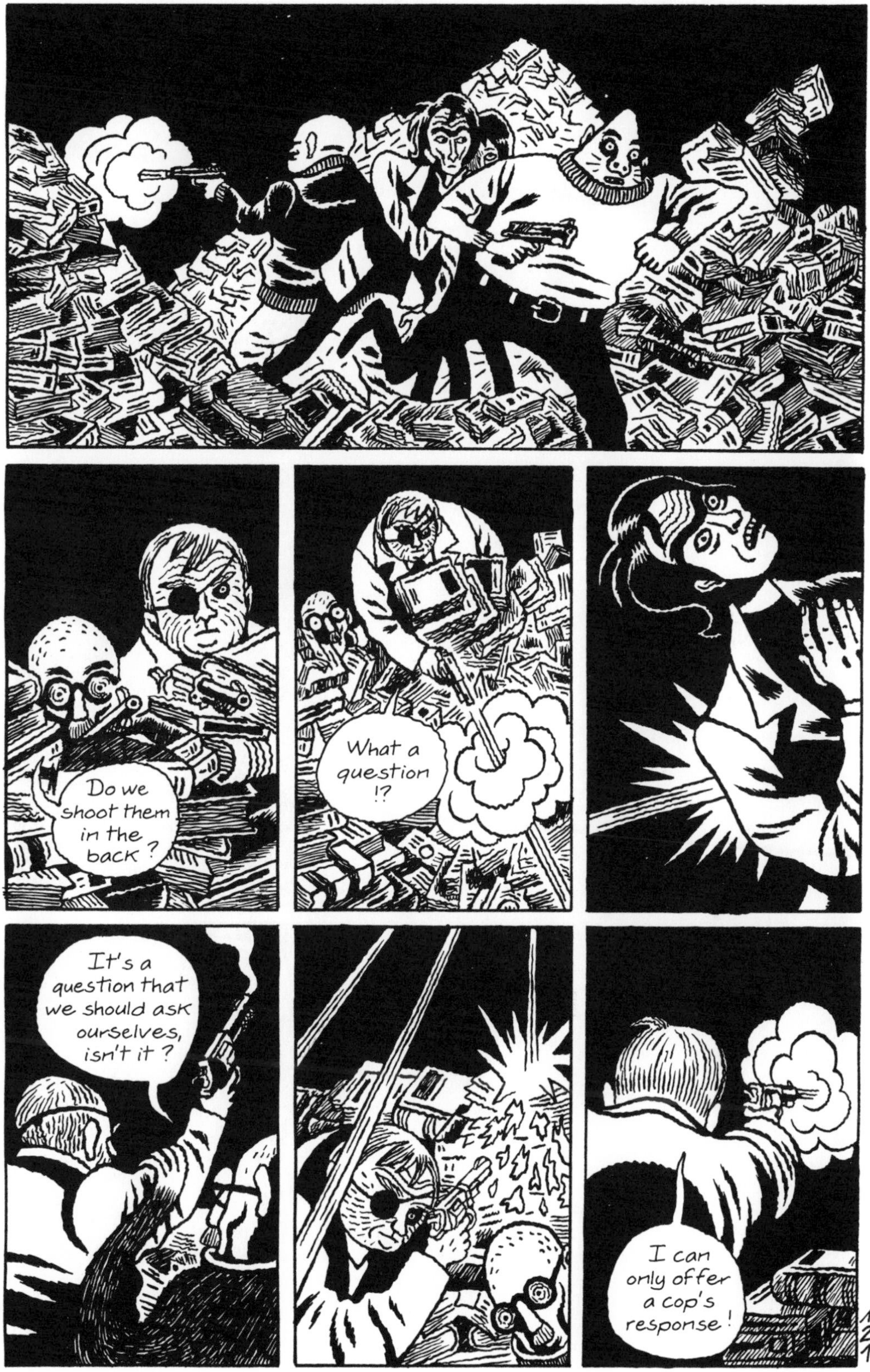
Do we shoot them in the back ?
What a question !?
It's a question that we should ask ourselves, isn't it ?
I can only offer a cop's response !

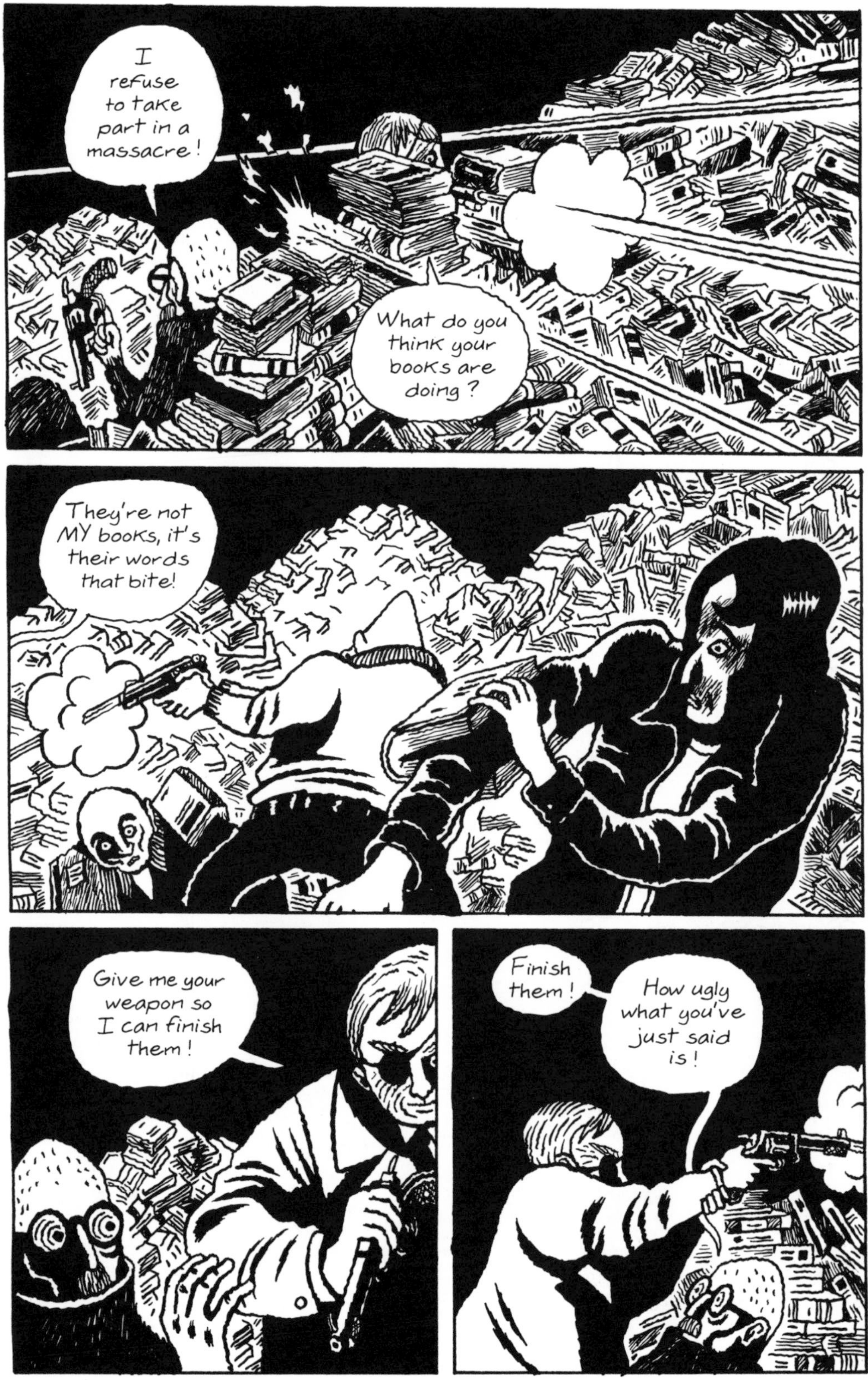
I refuse to take part in a massacre!
What do you think your books are doing?
They're not MY books, it's their words that bite!
Give me your weapon so I can finish them!
Finish them!
How ugly what you've just said is!

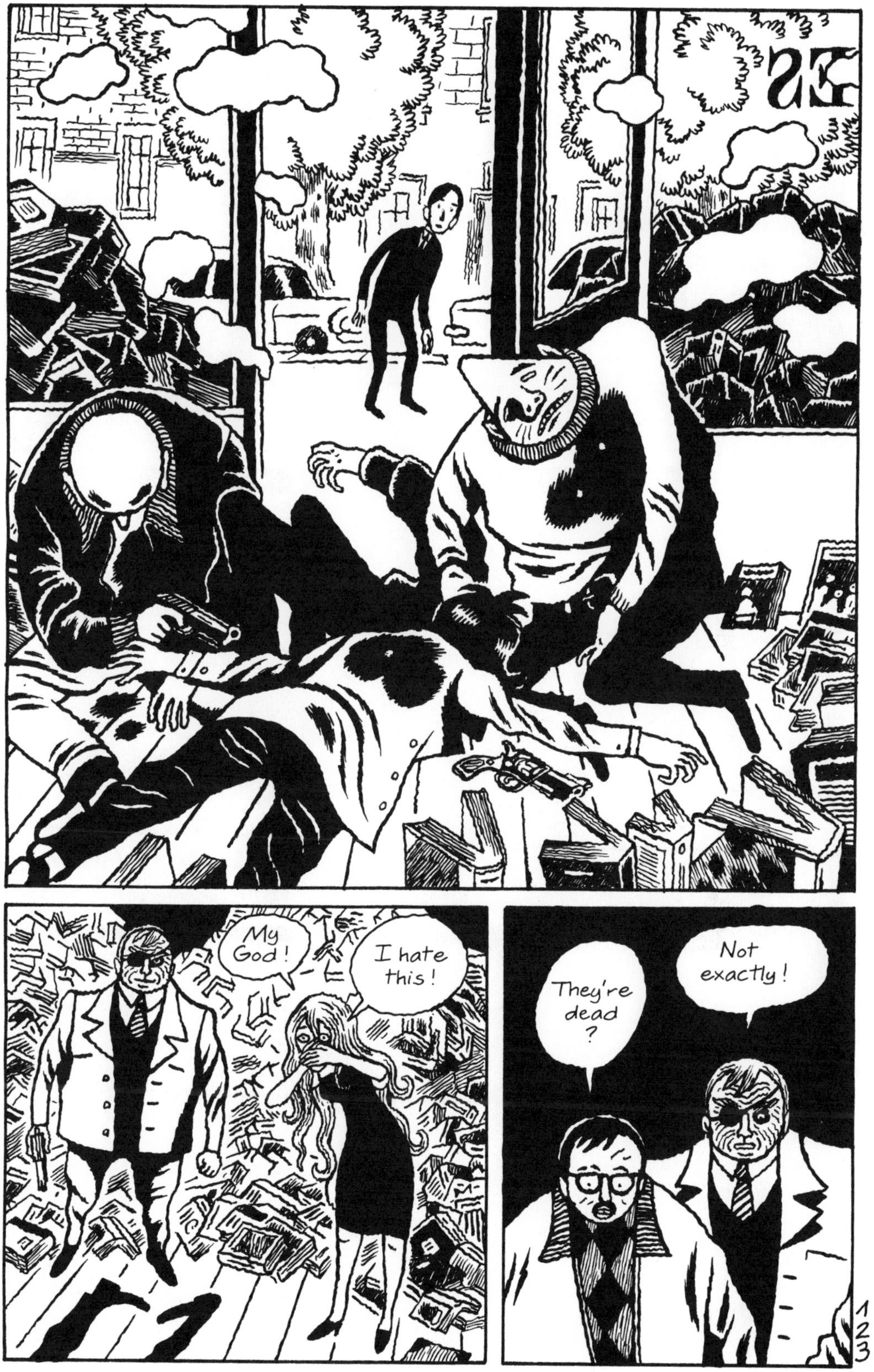
My God!
I hate this!
They're dead?
Not exactly!

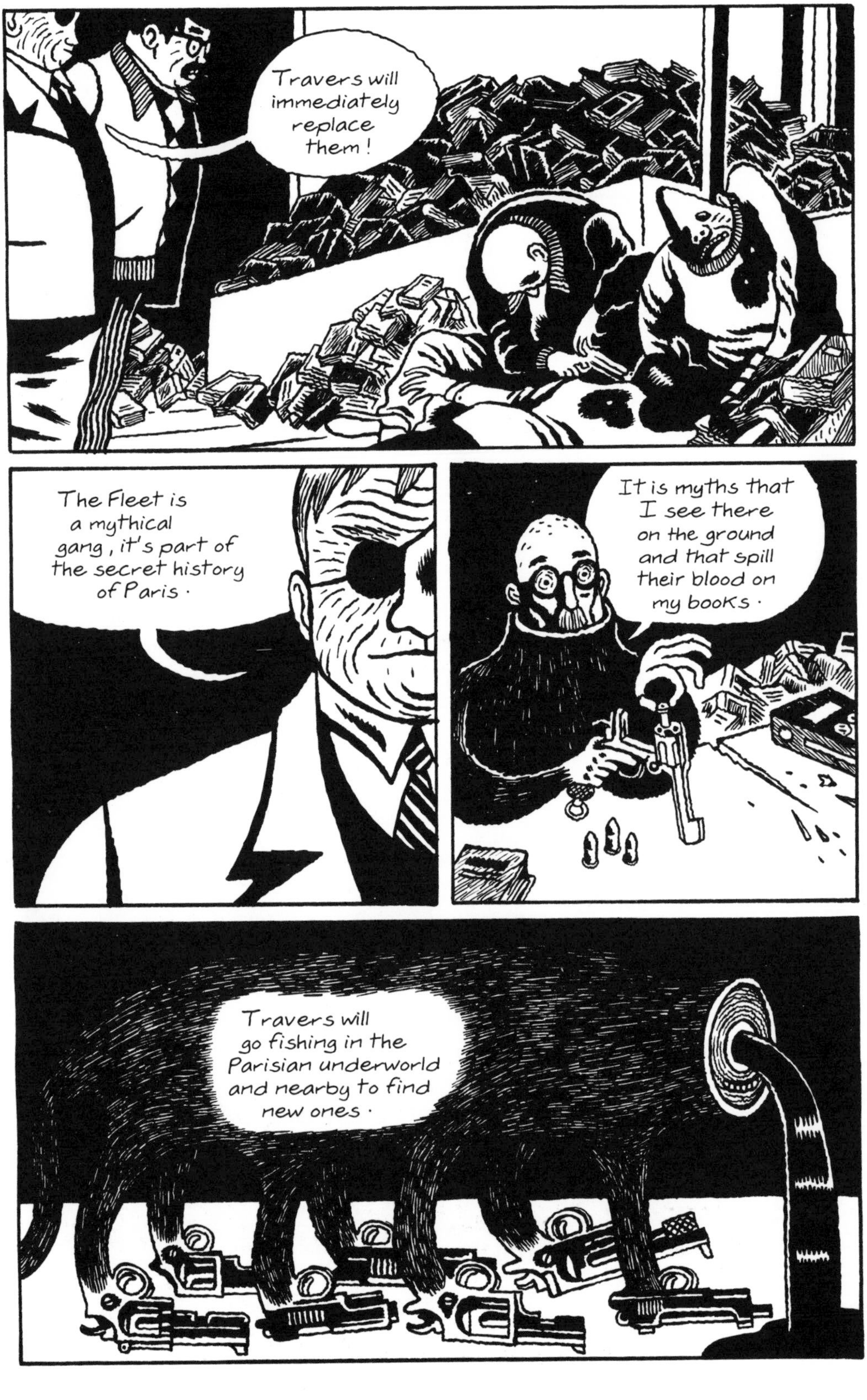
Travers will immediately replace them!
The Fleet is a mythical gang, it's part of the secret history of Paris.
It is myths that I see there on the ground and that spill their blood on my books.
Travers will go fishing in the Parisian underworld and nearby to find new ones.

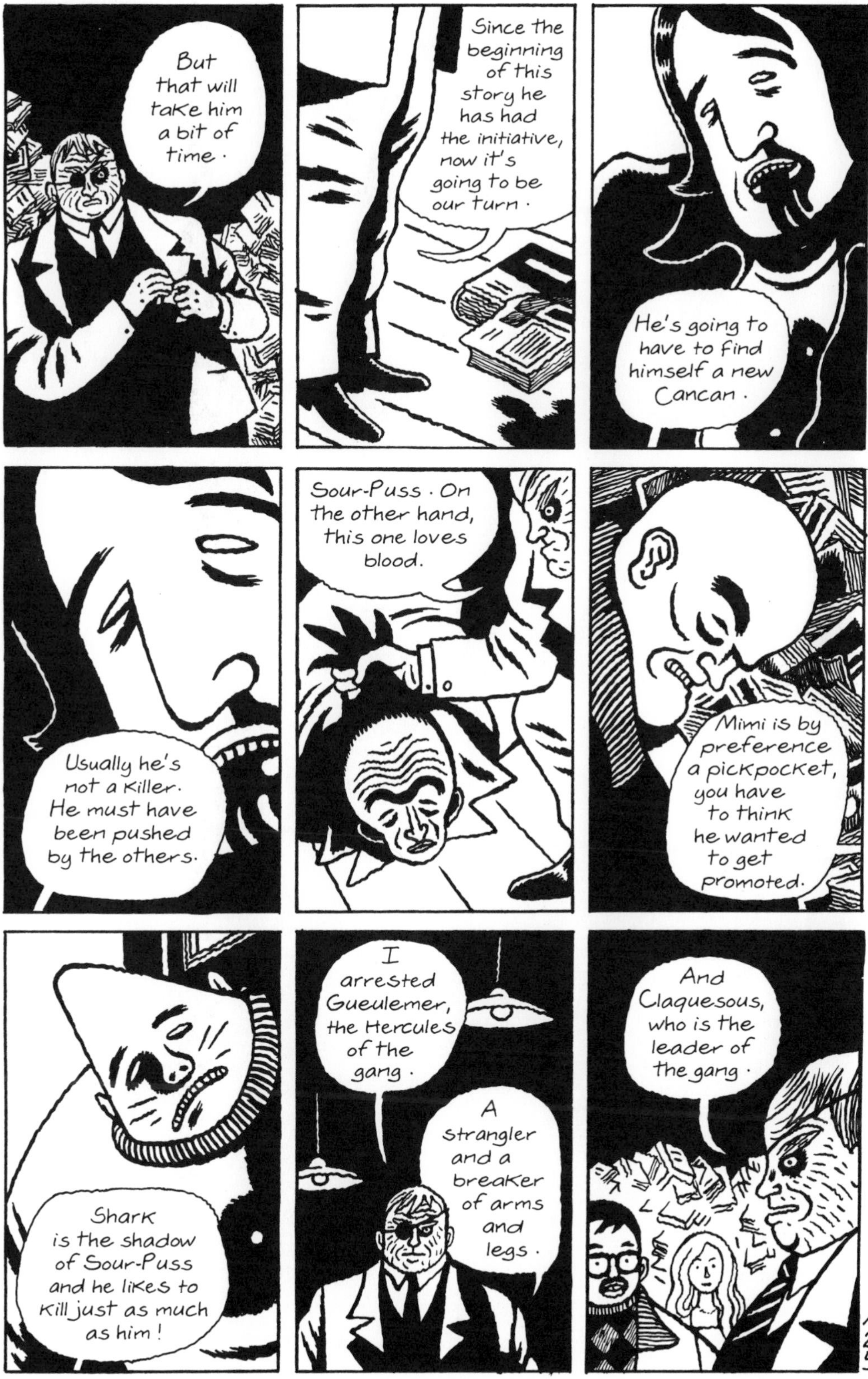
But that will take him a bit of time.
Since the beginning of this story he has had the initiative, now it's going to be our turn.
He's going to have to find himself a new Cancan.
Usually he's not a killer. He must have been pushed by the others.
Sour-Puss. On the other hand, this one loves blood.
Mimi is by preference a pickpocket, you have to think he wanted to get promoted.
Shark is the shadow of Sour-Puss and he likes to kill just as much as him!
I arrested Gueulemer, the Hercules of the gang.
A strangler and a breaker of arms and legs.
And Claquesous, who is the leader of the gang.

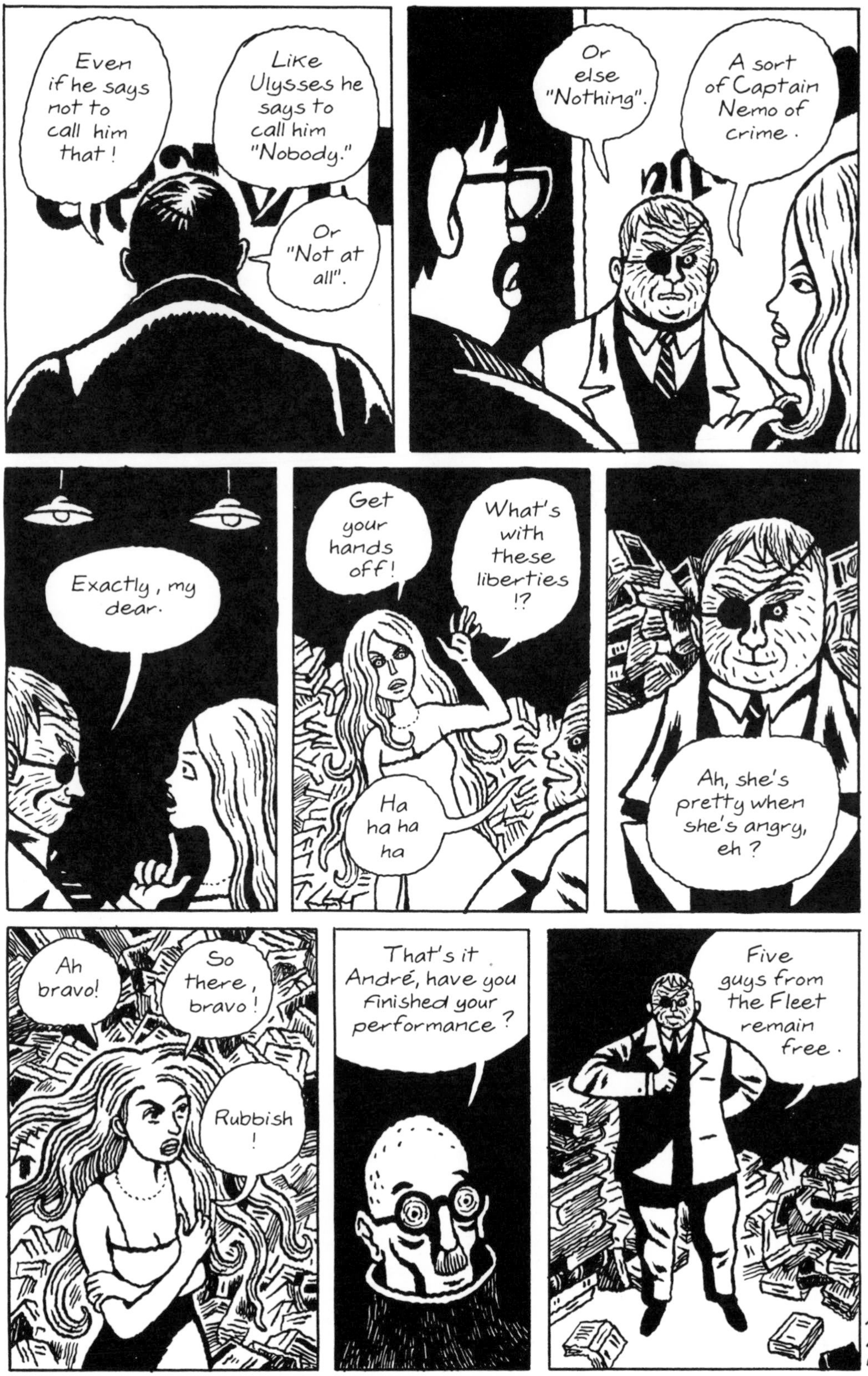

Even if he says not to call him that!
Like Ulysses he says to call him "Nobody."
Or "Not at all".
Or else "Nothing".
A sort of Captain Nemo of crime.
Exactly, my dear.
Get your hands off!
What's with these liberties !?
Ha ha ha ha
Ah, she's pretty when she's angry, eh?
Ah bravo!
So there, bravo!
Rubbish!
That's it André, have you finished your performance?
Five guys from the Fleet remain free.

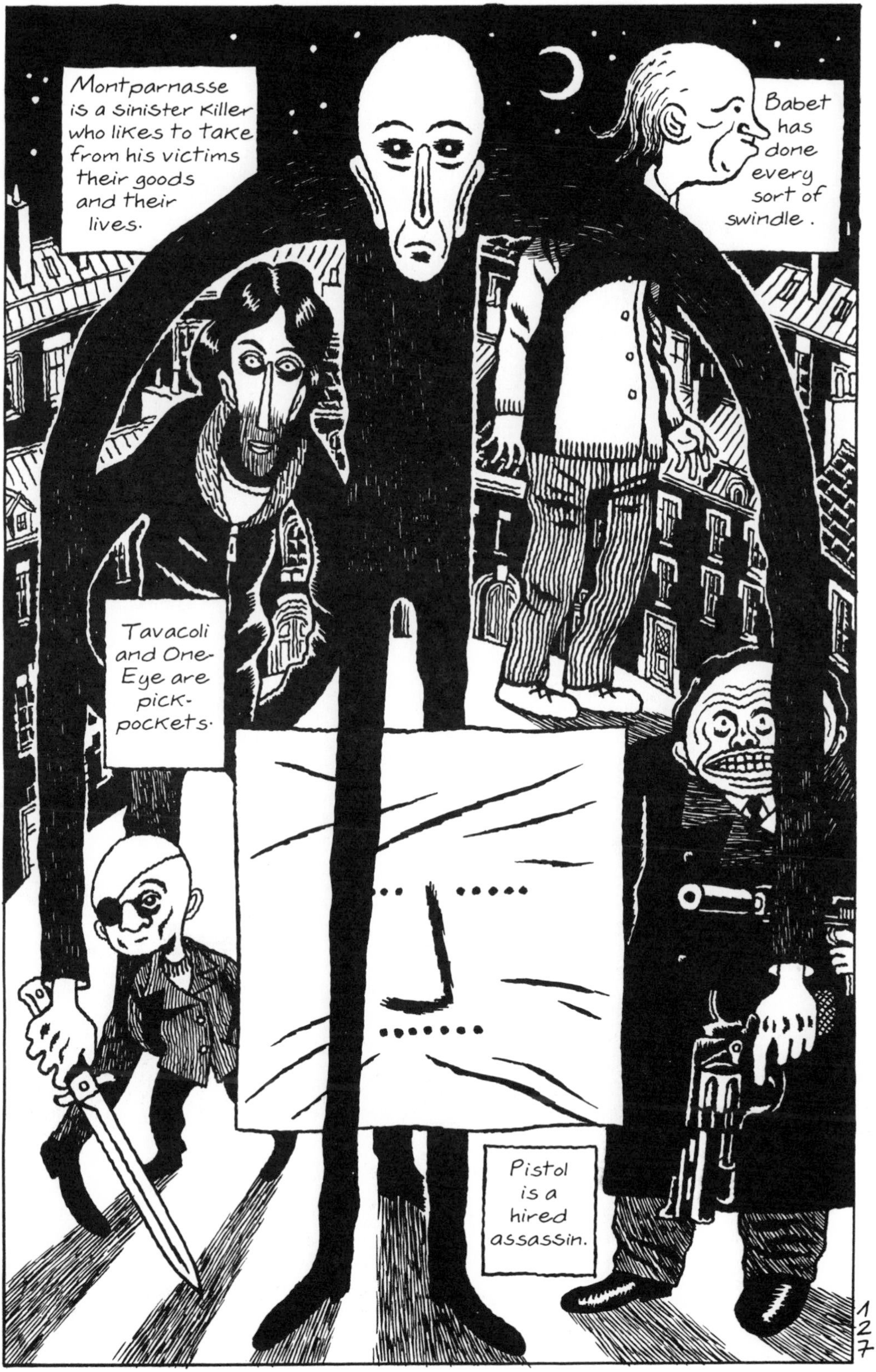

Montparnasse is a sinister killer who likes to take from his victims their goods and their lives.
Babet has done every sort of swindle.
Tavacoli and One-Eye are pick-pockets.
Pistol is a hired assassin.

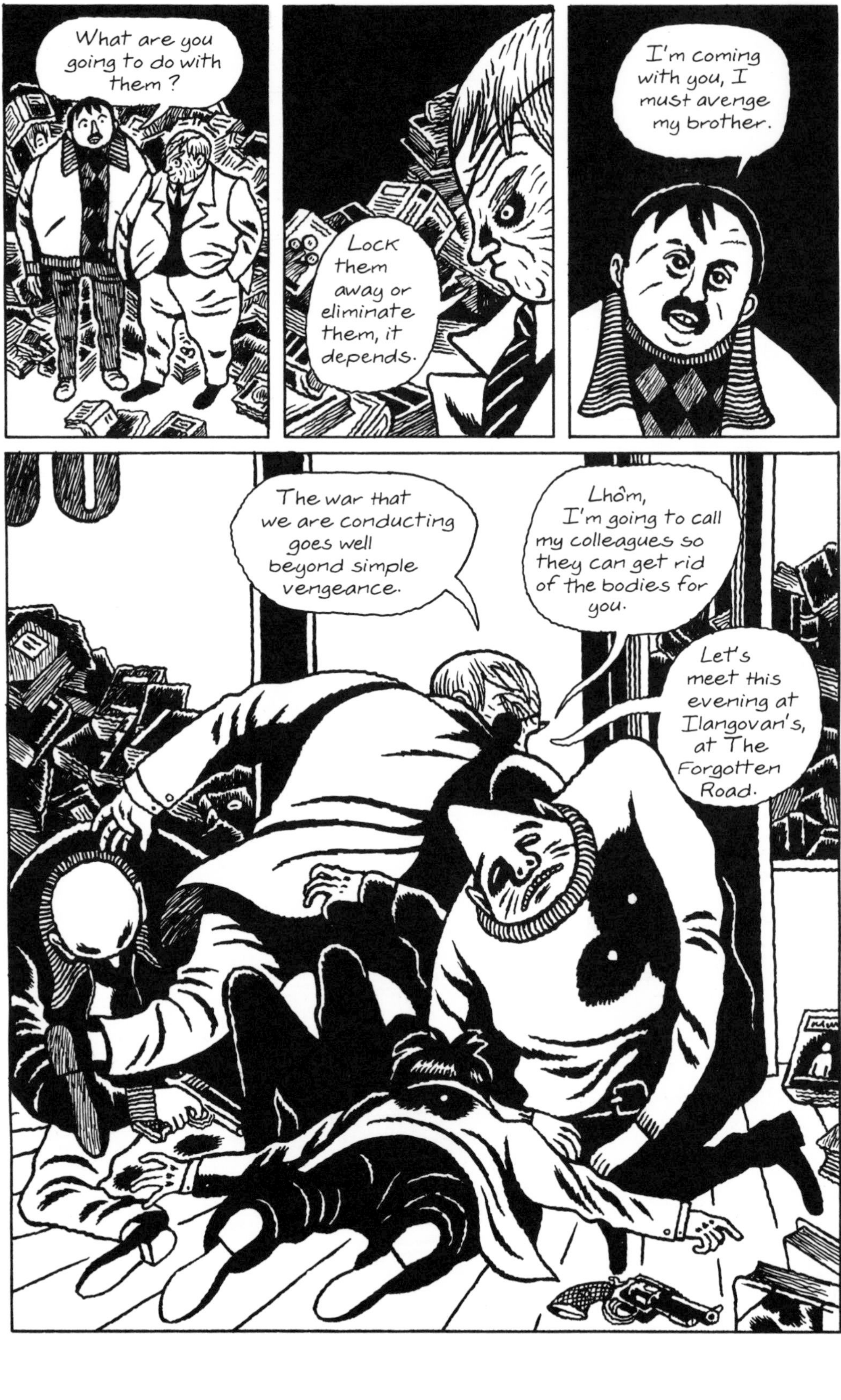
What are you going to do with them ?
Lock them away or eliminate them, it depends.
I'm coming with you, I must avenge my brother.
The war that we are conducting goes well beyond simple vengeance.
Lhôm, I'm going to call my colleagues so they can get rid of the bodies for you.
Let's meet this evening at Ilangovan's, at The Forgotten Road.

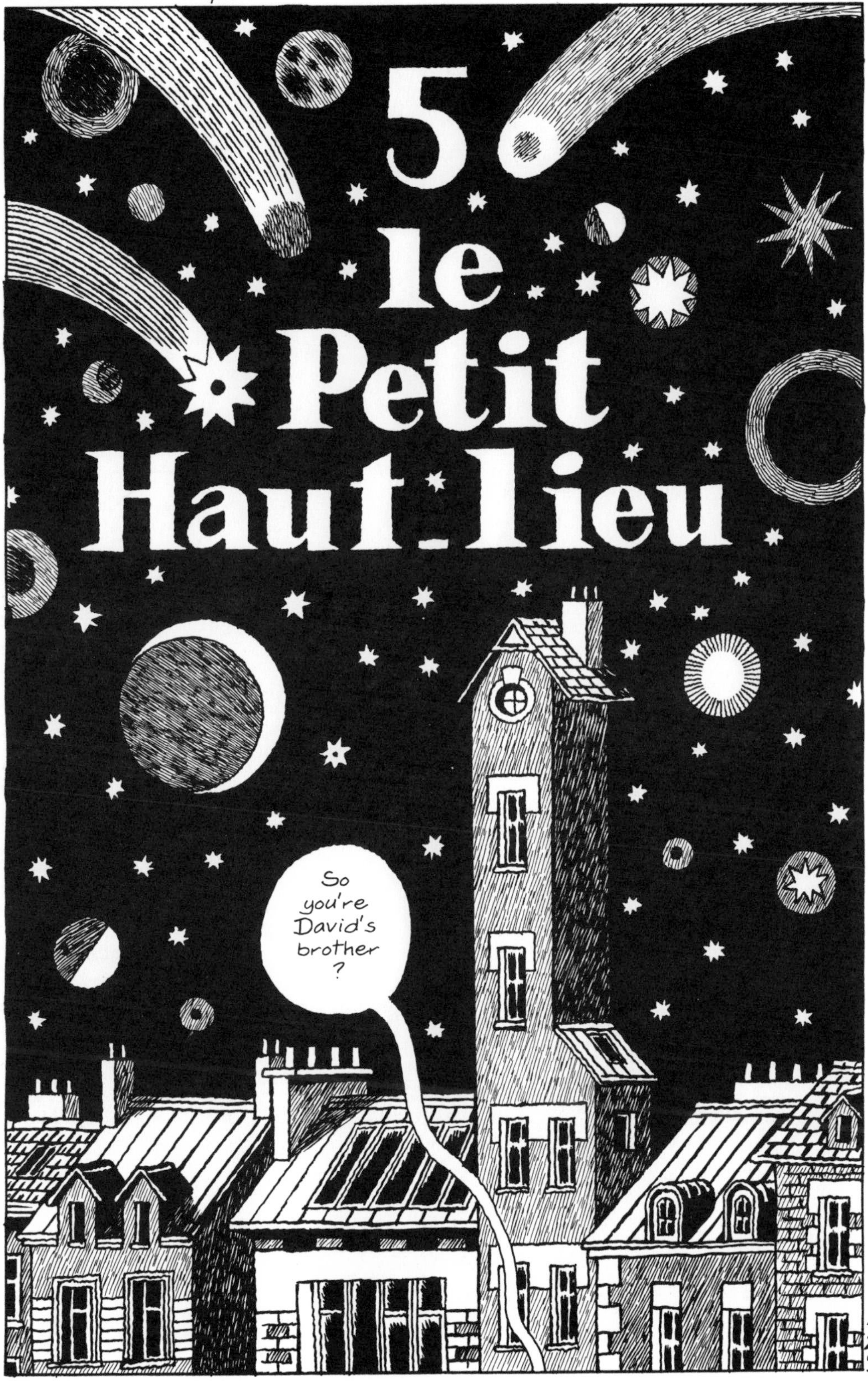
5
le
Petit
Haut-lieu
So you're David's brother ?

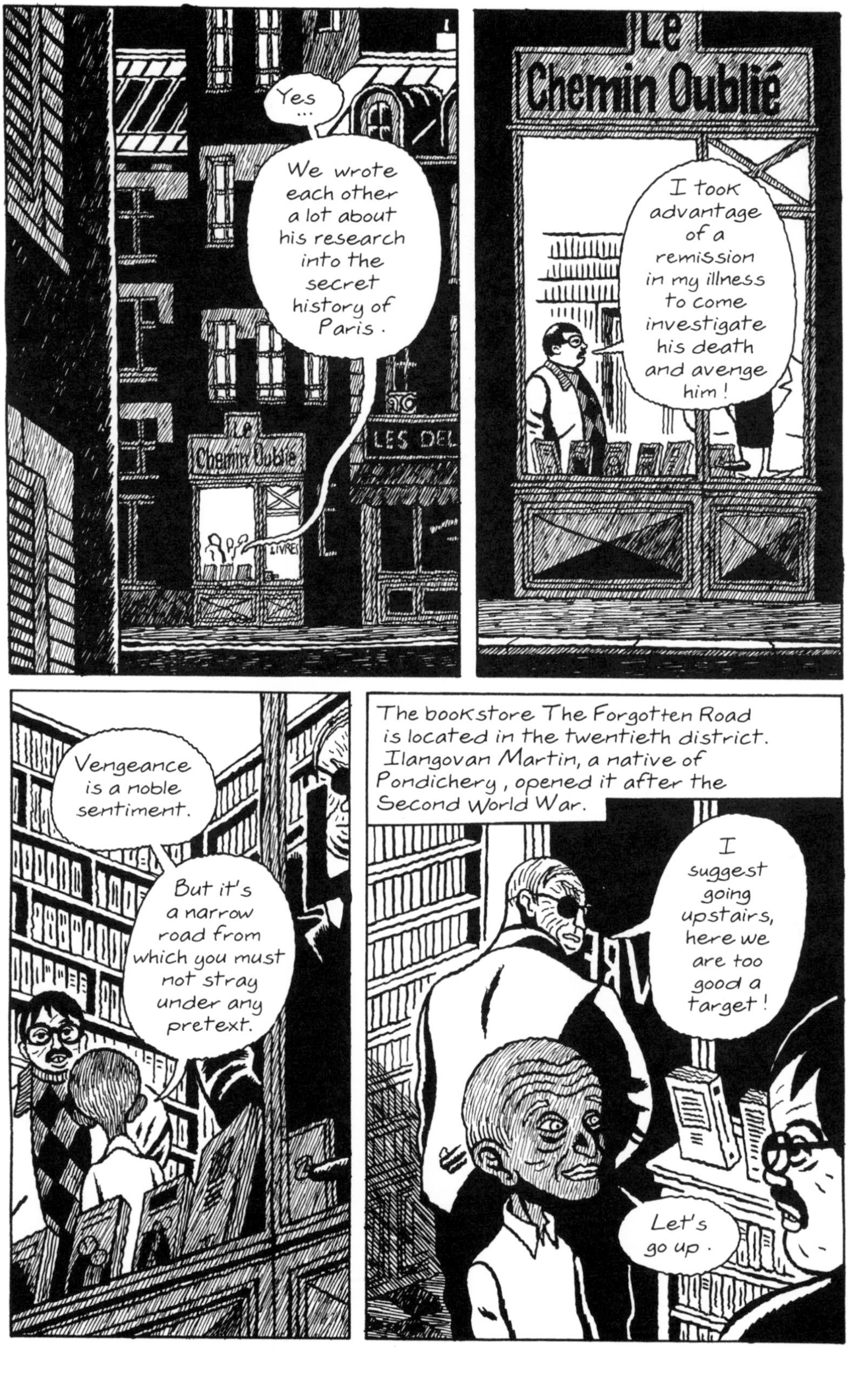
Yes ...
We wrote each other a lot about his research into the secret history of Paris.
Le Chemin Oublié
LES DEL
LIVRES
Le Chemin Oublié
I took advantage of a remission in my illness to come investigate his death and avenge him!
Vengeance is a noble sentiment.
But it's a narrow road from which you must not stray under any pretext.
The bookstore The Forgotten Road is located in the twentieth district. Ilangovan Martin, a native of Pondichery, opened it after the Second World War.
I suggest going upstairs, here we are too good a target!
Let's go up.

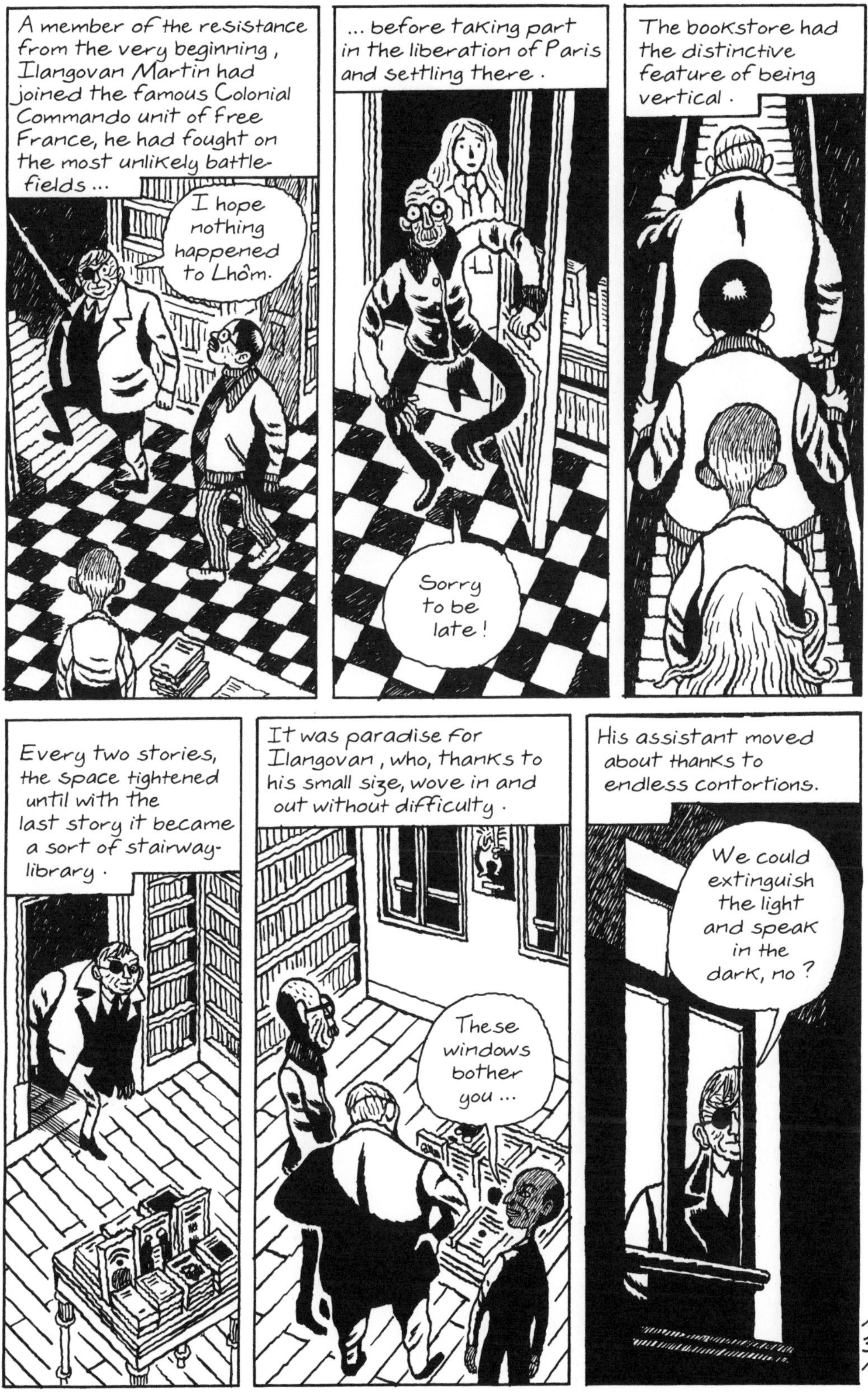
A member of the resistance from the very beginning, Ilangovan Martin had joined the famous Colonial Commando unit of Free France, he had fought on the most unlikely battle-fields ...
I hope nothing happened to Lhôm.
... before taking part in the liberation of Paris and settling there.
Sorry to be late!
The bookstore had the distinctive feature of being vertical.
Every two stories, the space tightened until with the last story it became a sort of stairway-library.
It was paradise for Ilangovan, who, thanks to his small size, wove in and out without difficulty.
These windows bother you ...
His assistant moved about thanks to endless contortions.
We could extinguish the light and speak in the dark, no?

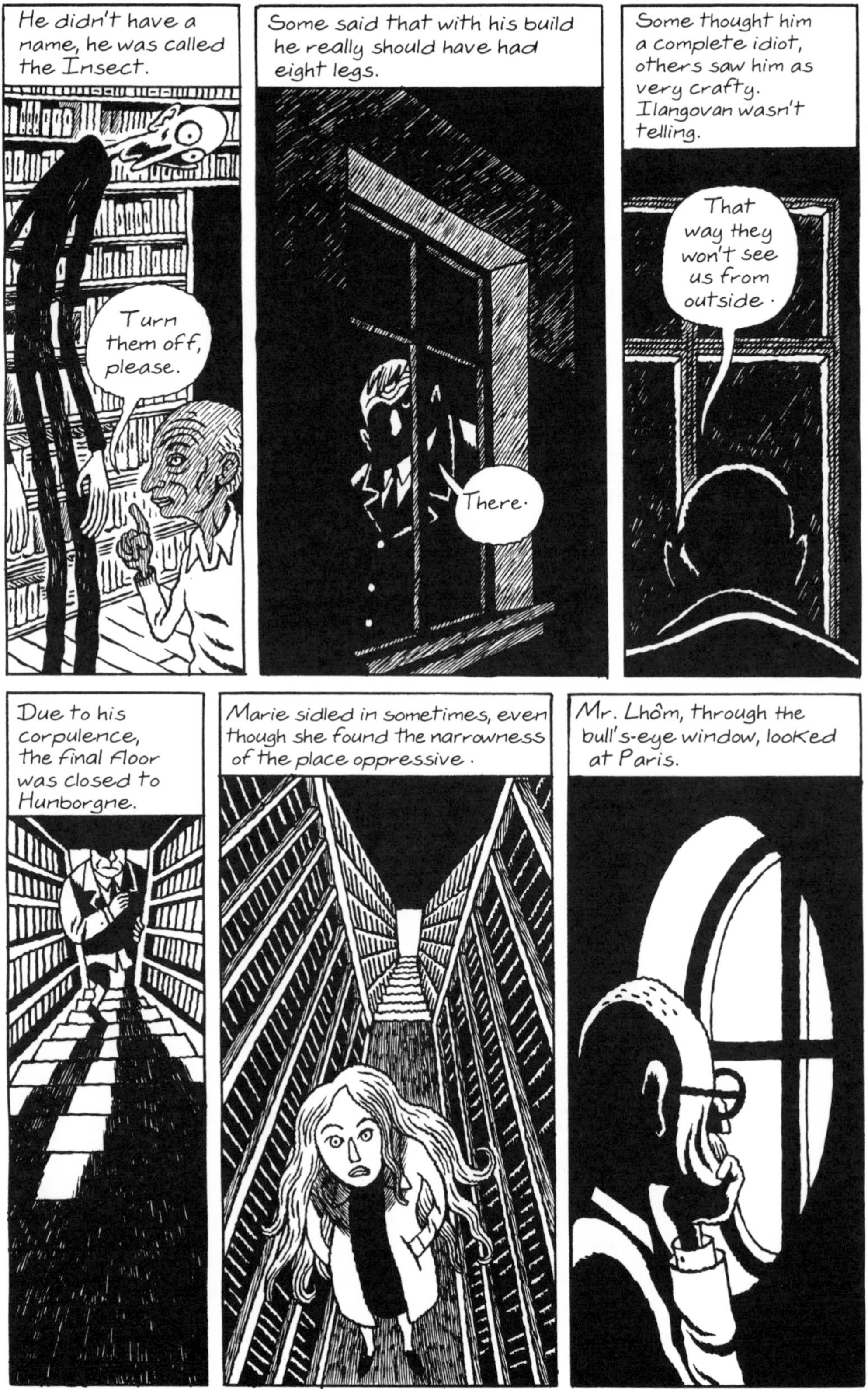
He didn't have a name, he was called the Insect.
Turn them off, please.
Some said that with his build he really should have had eight legs.
There.
Some thought him a complete idiot, others saw him as very crafty. Ilangovan wasn't telling.
That way they won't see us from outside.
Due to his corpulence, the final floor was closed to Hunborgne.
Marie sidled in sometimes, even though she found the narrowness of the place oppressive.
Mr. Lhôm, through the bull's-eye window, looked at Paris.

Situated on the heights of Ménilmontant, the bookstore The Forgotten Road overlooked the city.

The gaze of Mr. Lhôm perceived under the roofs the nineteen other bookstores that are part of the city's secret geography.

In each district of the game of the goose which constitutes Paris is located a bookstore which is nothing less than a "foundation pin".

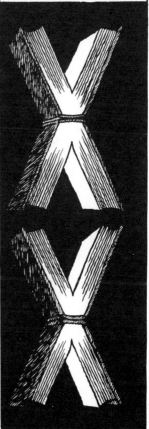

The Babylonians planted at the base of their city walls nails in the image of their gods; the Parisians opened twenty bookstores.

1
33

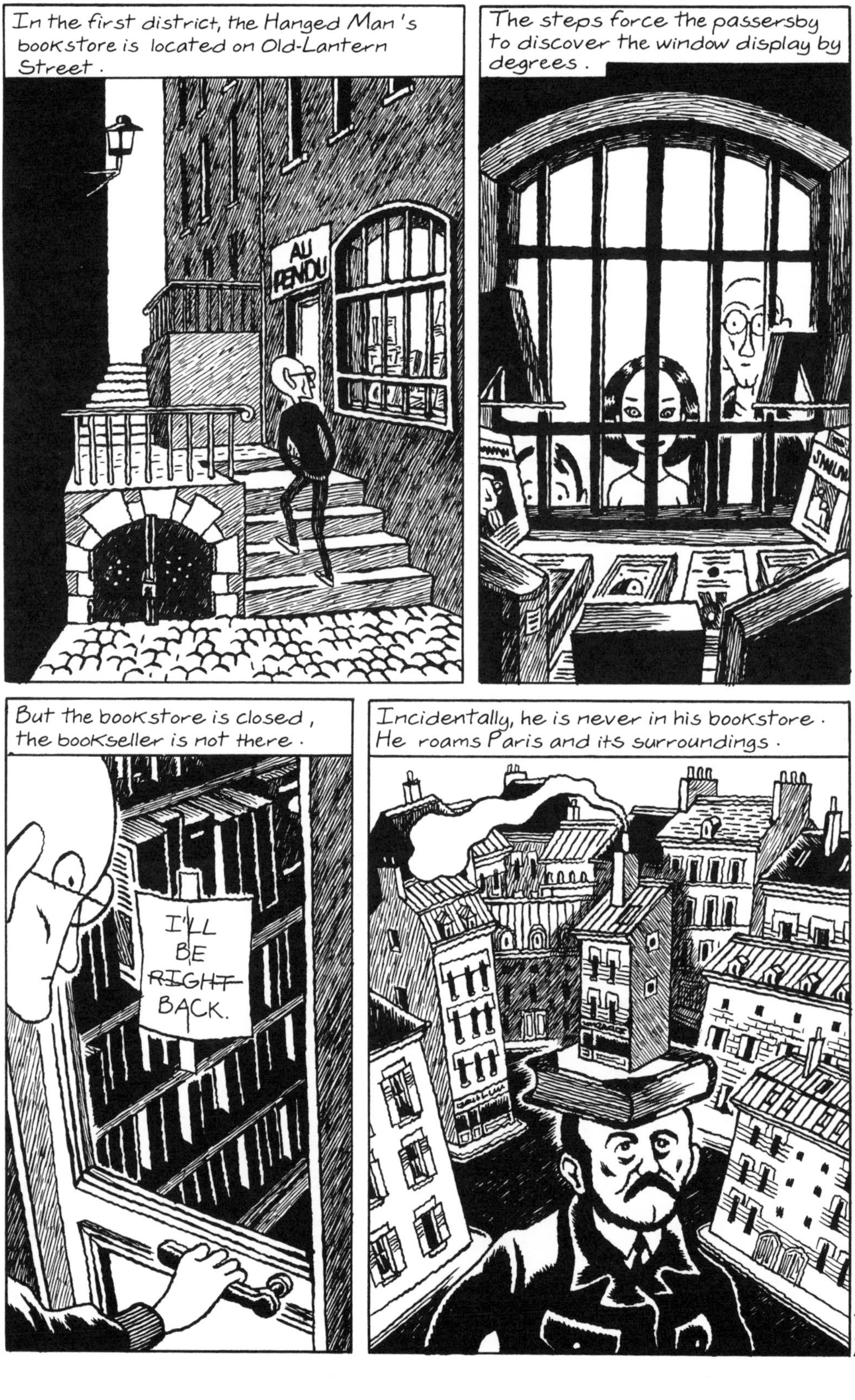
In the first district, the Hanged Man's bookstore is located on Old-Lantern Street.
AU PENDU
The steps force the passersby to discover the window display by degrees.
But the bookstore is closed, the bookseller is not there.
I'LL BE RIGHT BACK.
Incidentally, he is never in his bookstore. He roams Paris and its surroundings.

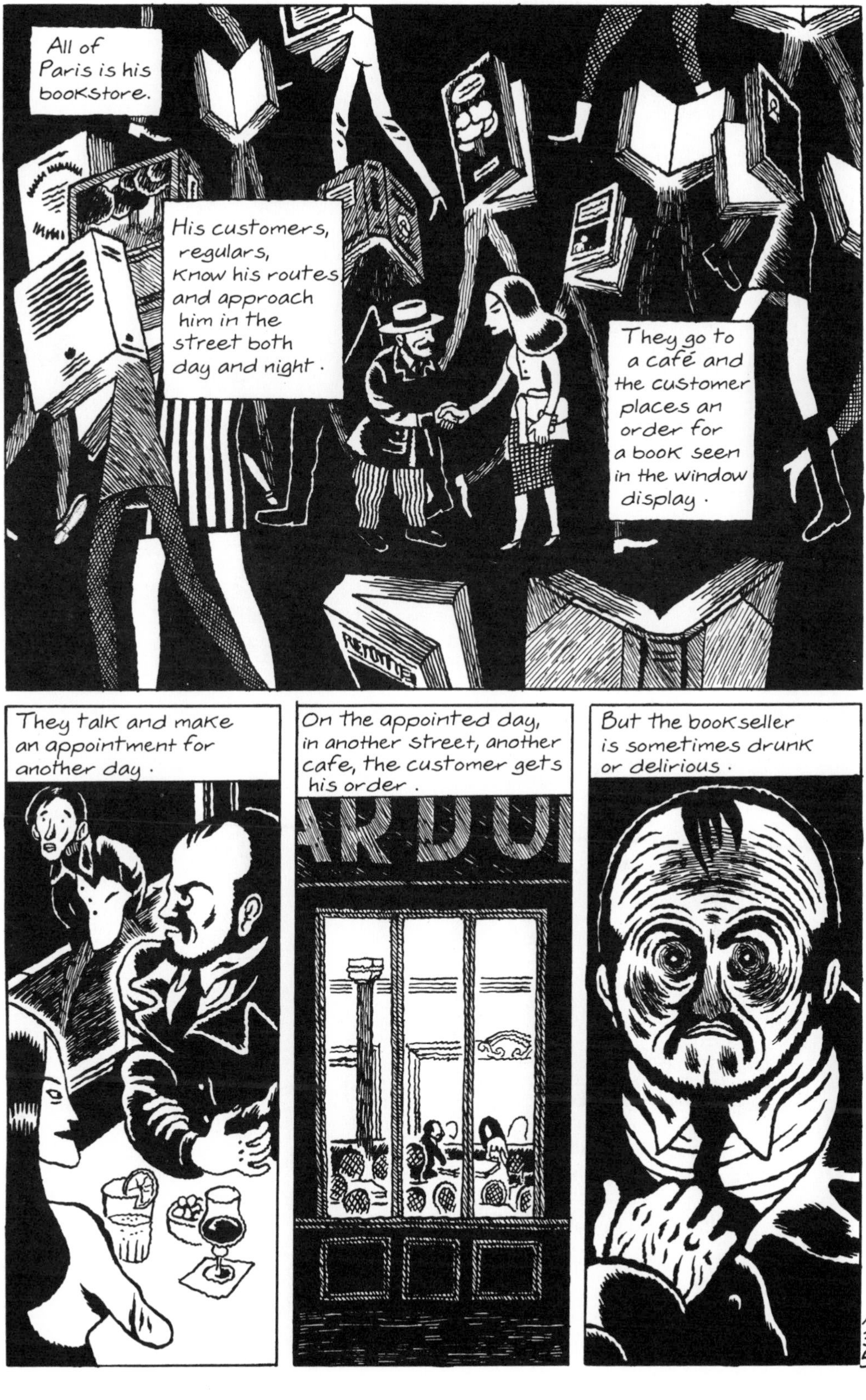
All of Paris is his bookstore.
His customers, regulars, know his routes and approach him in the street both day and night.
They go to a café and the customer places an order for a book seen in the window display.
They talk and make an appointment for another day.
On the appointed day, in another street, another cafe, the customer gets his order.
But the bookseller is sometimes drunk or delirious.

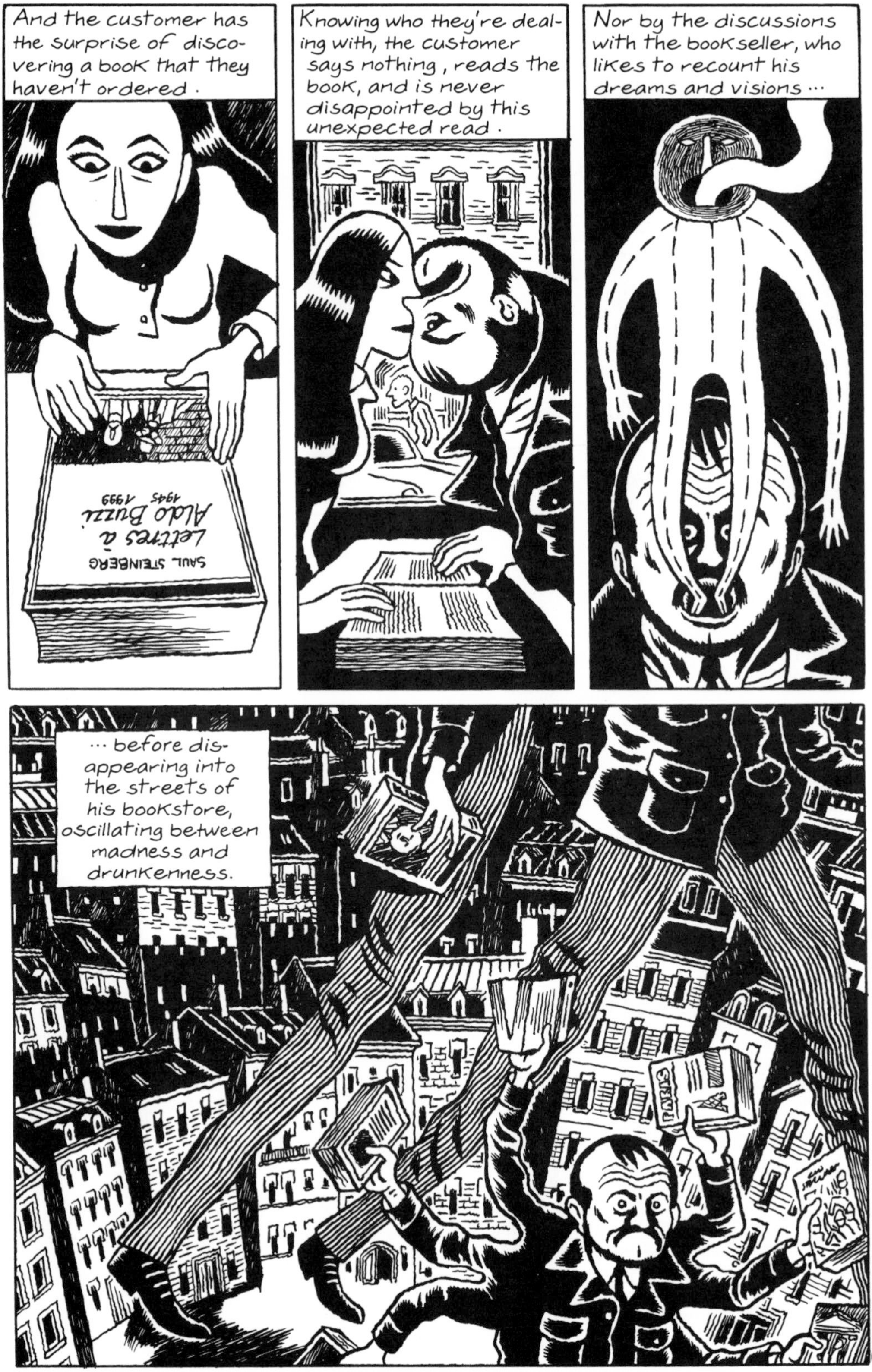
And the customer has the surprise of discovering a book that they haven't ordered.
SAUL STEINBERG
Lettres à Aldo Buzzi
1945 1999
Knowing who they're dealing with, the customer says nothing, reads the book, and is never disappointed by this unexpected read.
Nor by the discussions with the bookseller, who likes to recount his dreams and visions...
... before disappearing into the streets of his bookstore, oscillating between madness and drunkenness.

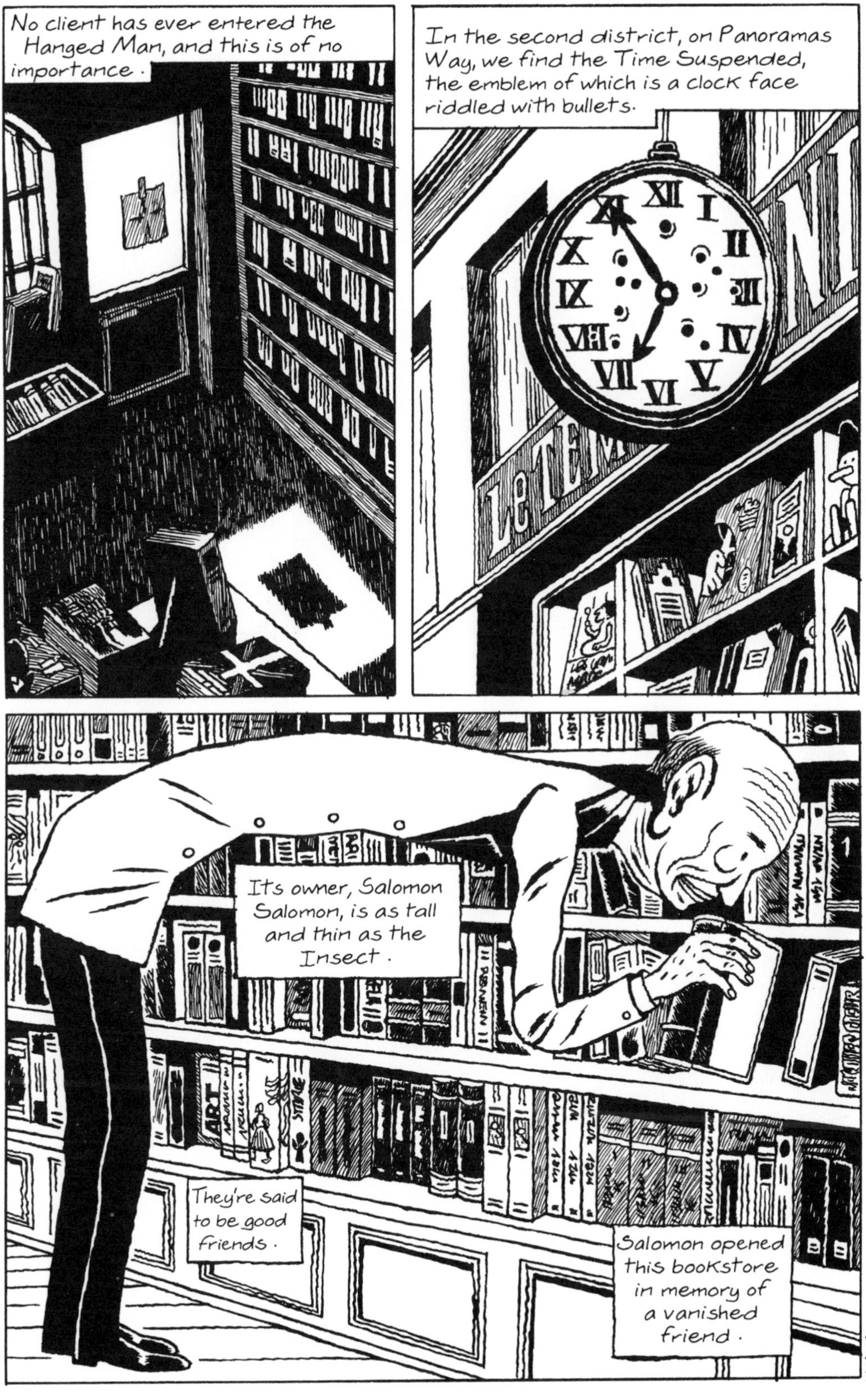
No client has ever entered the Hanged Man, and this is of no importance.
In the second district, on Panoramas Way, we find the Time Suspended, the emblem of which is a clock face riddled with bullets.
It's owner, Salomon Salomon, is as tall and thin as the Insect.
They're said to be good friends.
Salomon opened this bookstore in memory of a vanished friend.

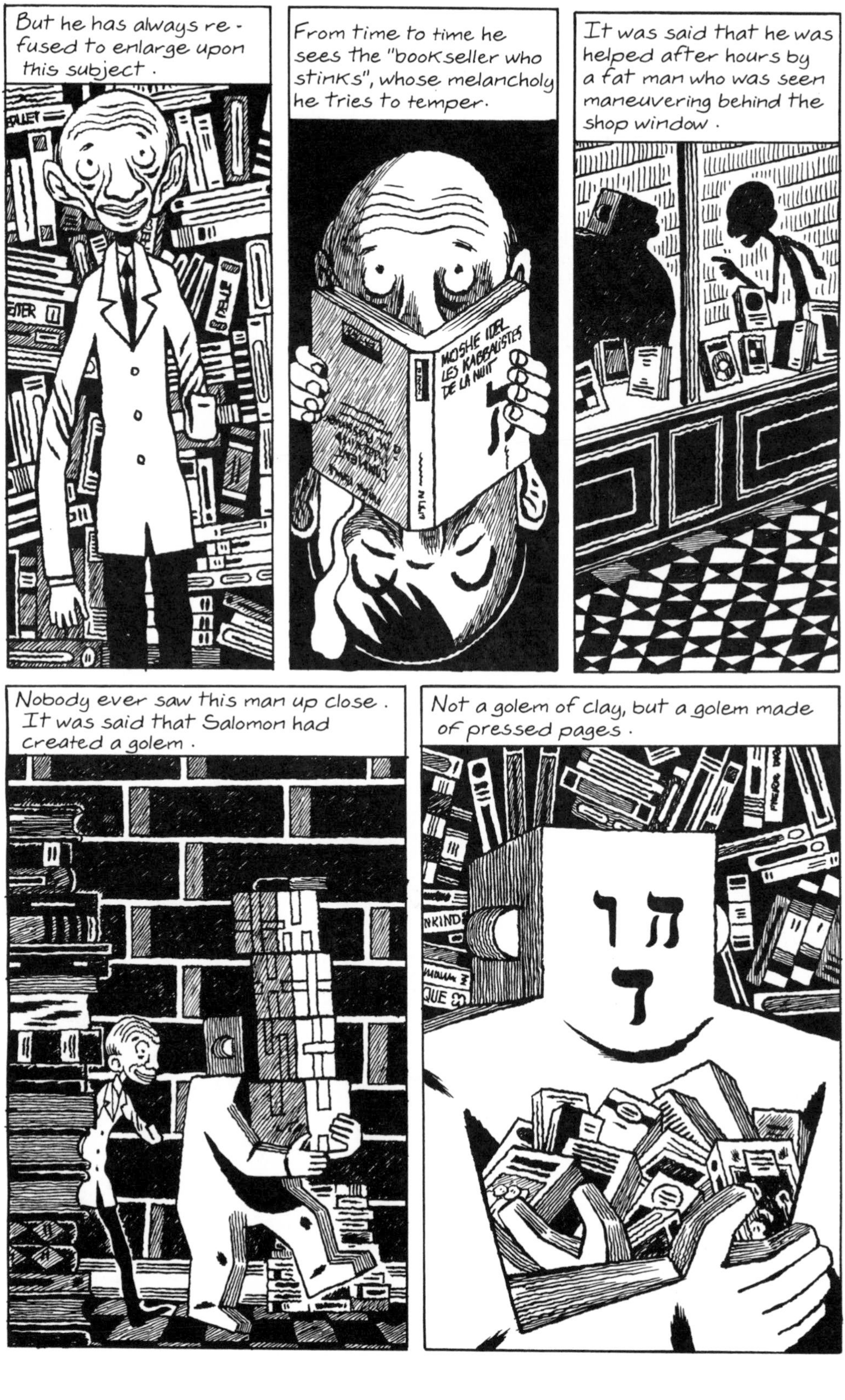
But he has always re-fused to enlarge upon this subject.
From time to time he sees the "bookseller who stinks", whose melancholy he tries to temper.
MOSHE IDEL LES KABBALISTES DE LA NUIT
It was said that he was helped after hours by a fat man who was seen maneuvering behind the shop window.
Nobody ever saw this man up close. It was said that Salomon had created a golem.
Not a golem of clay, but a golem made of pressed pages.

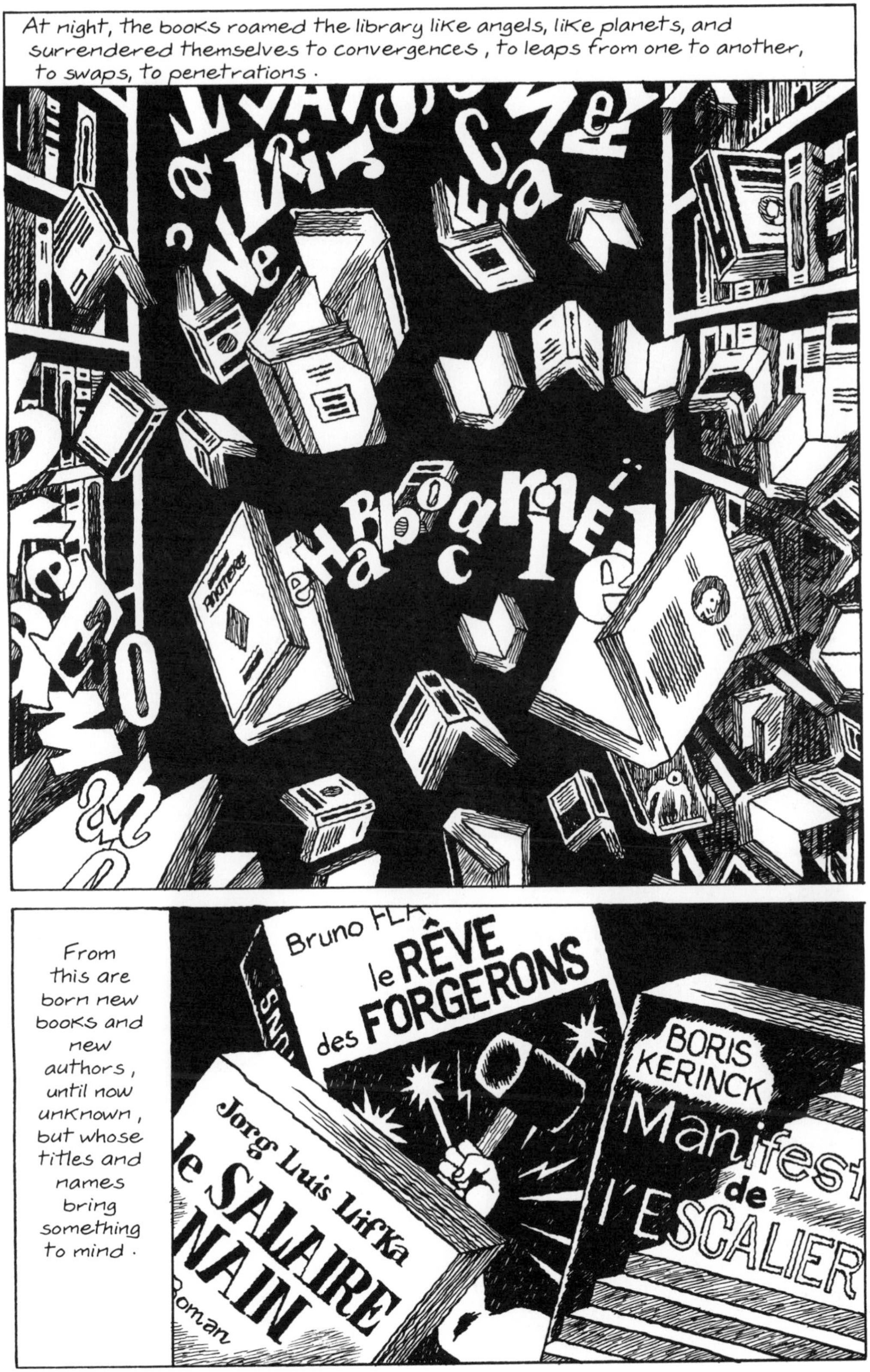
At night, the books roamed the library like angels, like planets, and surrendered themselves to convergences, to leaps from one to another, to swaps, to penetrations.
From this are born new books and new authors, until now unknown, but whose titles and names bring something to mind.
Bruno FLA
le RÊVE des FORGERONS
BORIS KERINCK
Manifest de l'ESCALIER
Jorg Luis Uifka
le SALAIRE NAIN
Roman

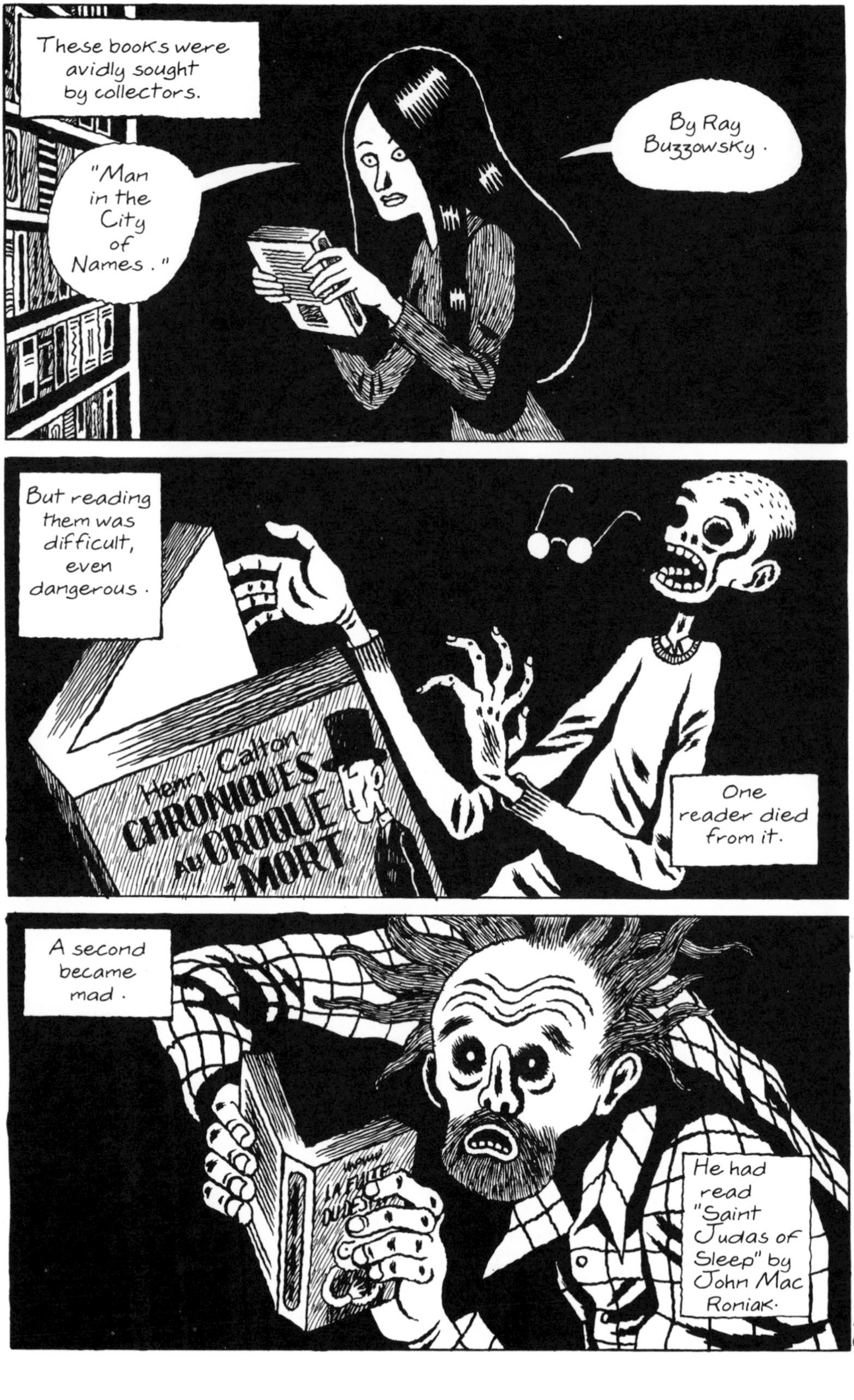
These books were avidly sought by collectors.
"Man in the City of Names."
By Ray Buzzowsky.
But reading them was difficult, even dangerous.
Henri Calton
CHRONIQUES AU CROQUE-MORT
One reader died from it.
A second became mad.
He had read "Saint Judas of Sleep" by John Mac Roniak.

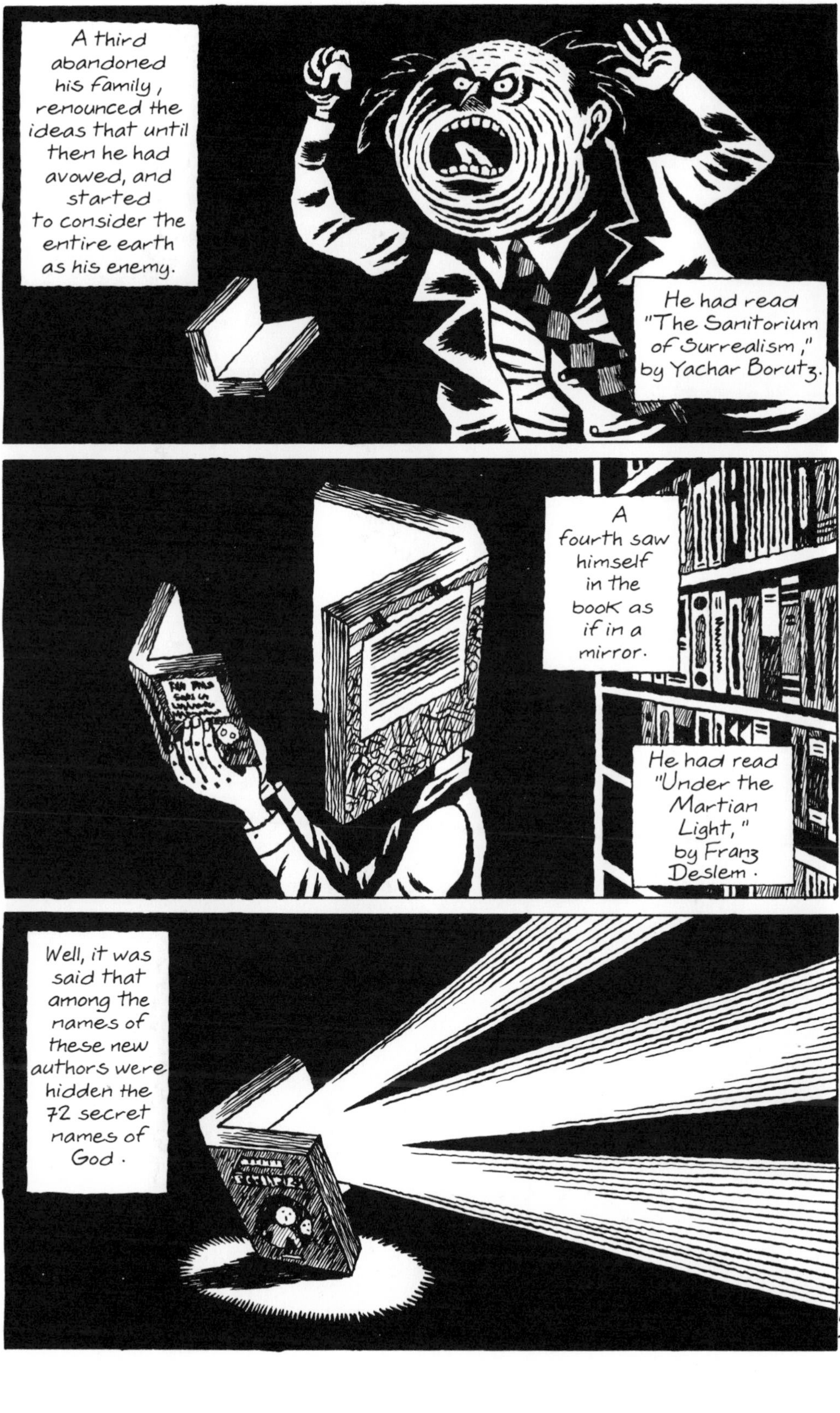
A third abandoned his family, renounced the ideas that until then he had avowed, and started to consider the entire earth as his enemy.
He had read "The Sanitorium of Surrealism," by Yachar Borutz.
A fourth saw himself in the book as if in a mirror.
He had read "Under the Martian Light," by Franz Deslem.
Well, it was said that among the names of these new authors were hidden the 72 secret names of God.

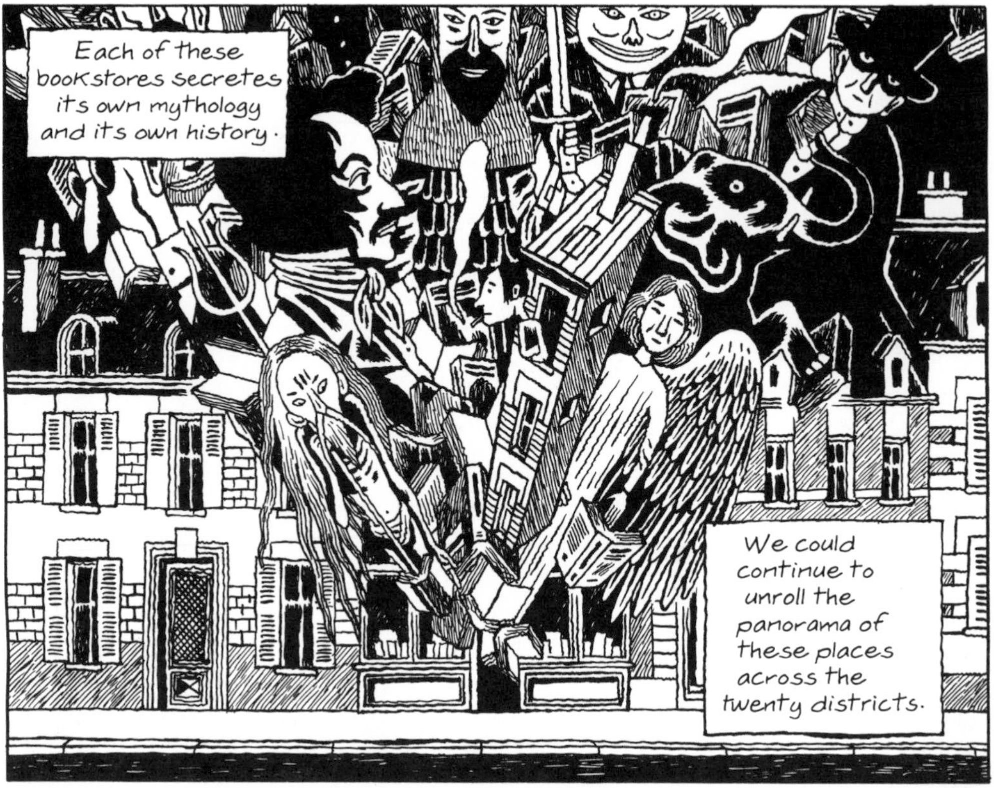
Each of these bookstores secretes its own mythology and its own history.
We could continue to unroll the panorama of these places across the twenty districts.

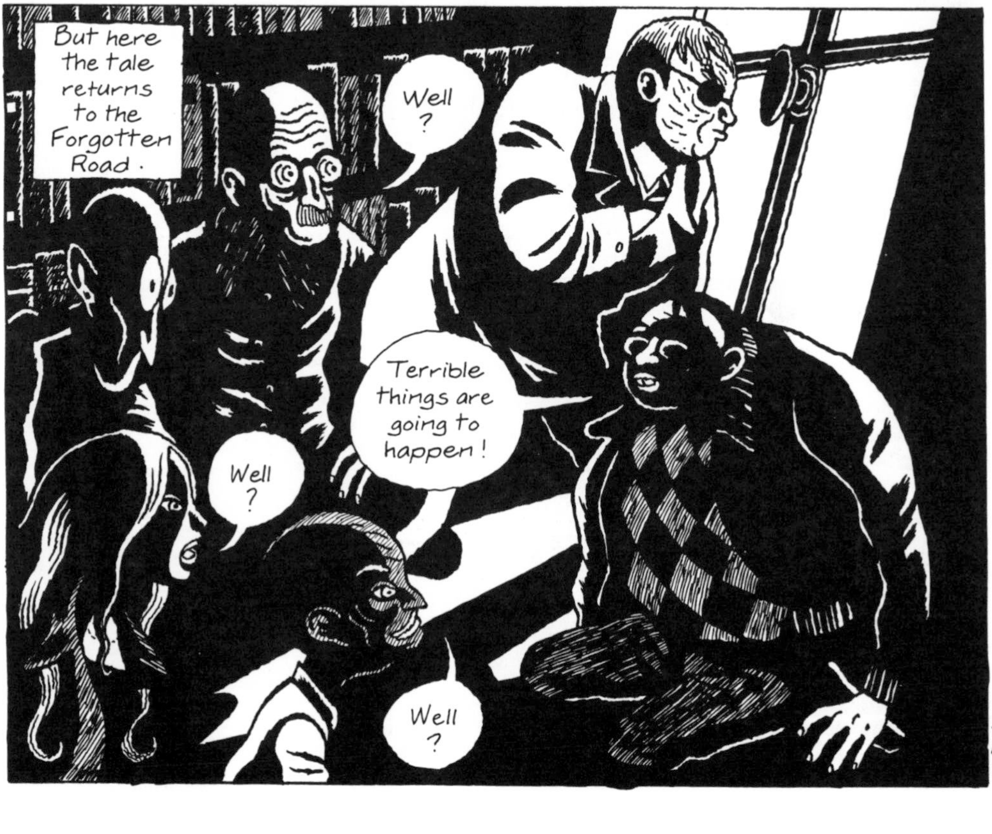
But here the tale returns to the Forgotten Road.
Well ?
Terrible things are going to happen !
Well ?
Well ?

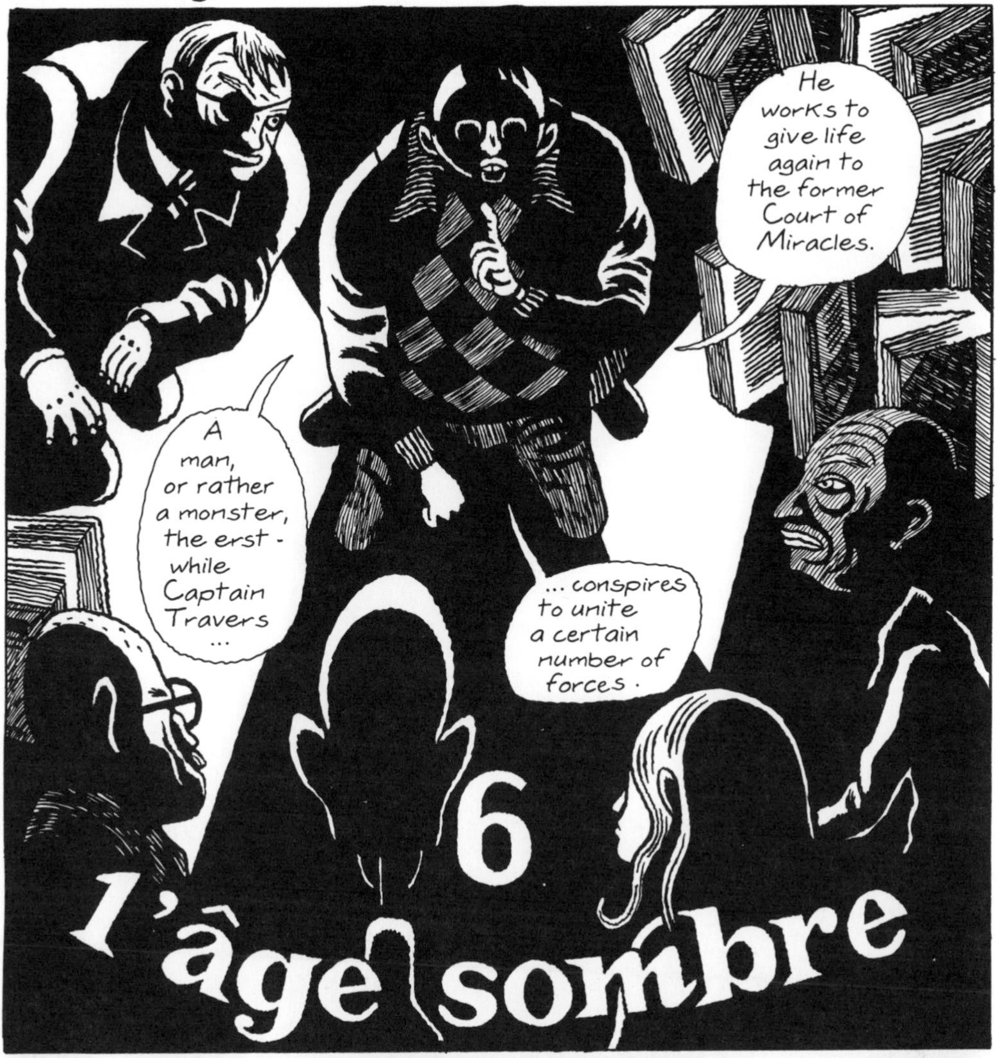
He works to give life again to the former Court of Miracles.
A man, or rather a monster, the erst - while Captain Travers ...
... conspires to unite a certain number of forces.
6
l'âge sombre

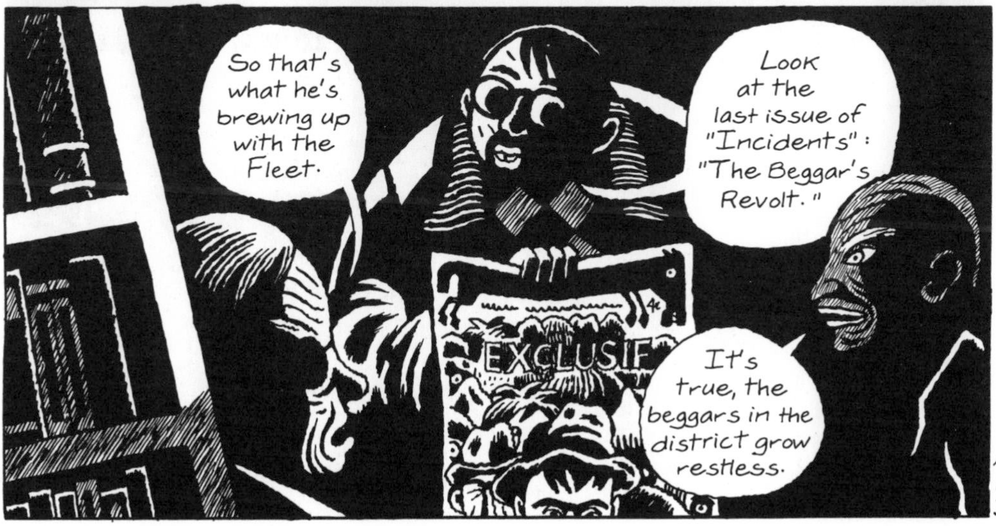
So that's what he's brewing up with the Fleet.
Look at the last issue of "Incidents" : "The Beggar's Revolt."
EXCLUSIF
It's true, the beggars in the district grow restless.

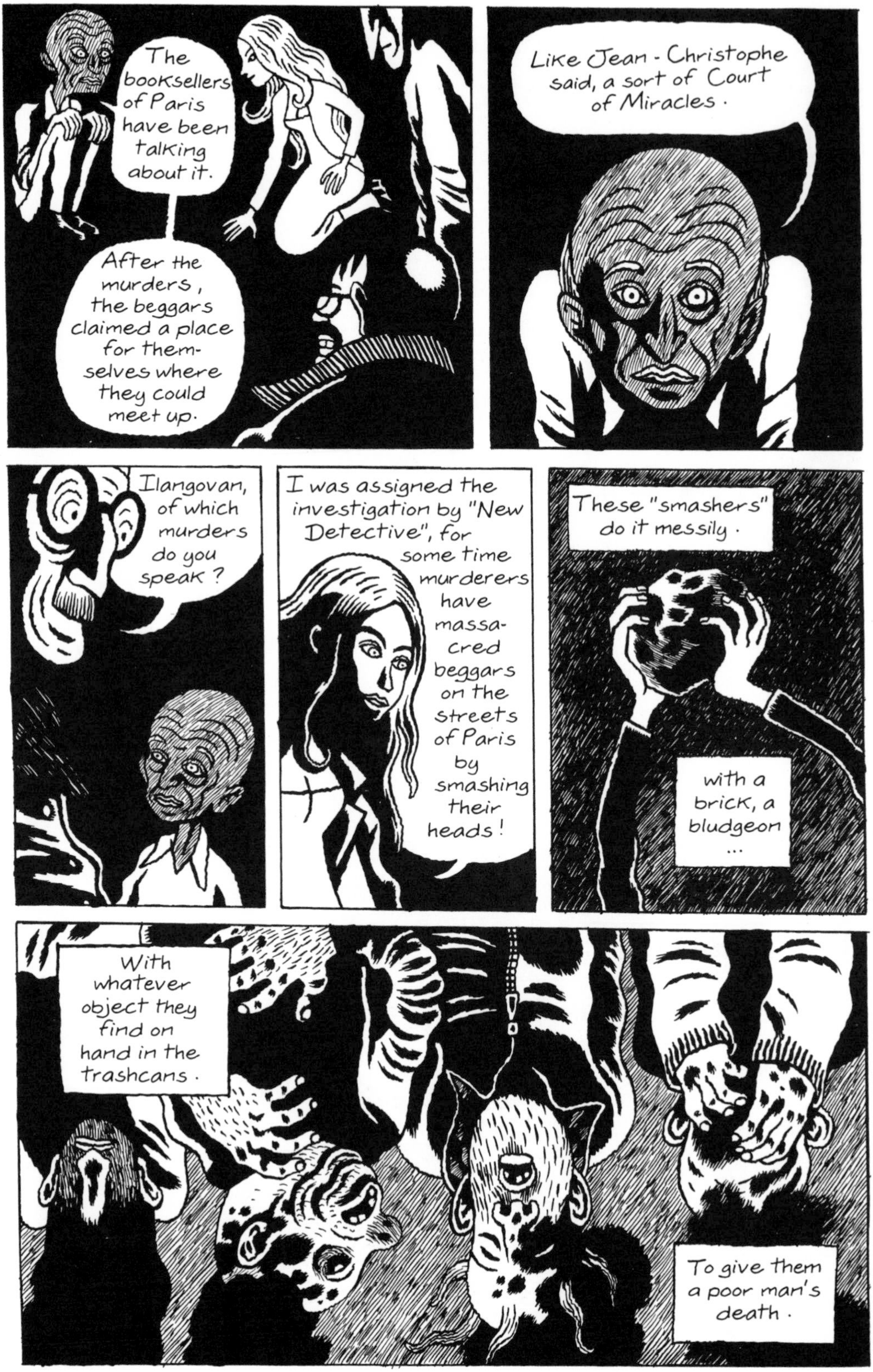
The booksellers of Paris have been talking about it.
After the murders, the beggars claimed a place for themselves where they could meet up.
Like Jean - Christophe said, a sort of Court of Miracles.
Ilangovan, of which murders do you speak?
I was assigned the investigation by "New Detective", for some time murderers have massacred beggars on the streets of Paris by smashing their heads!
These "smashers" do it messily.
with a brick, a bludgeon ...
With whatever object they find on hand in the trashcans.
To give them a poor man's death.

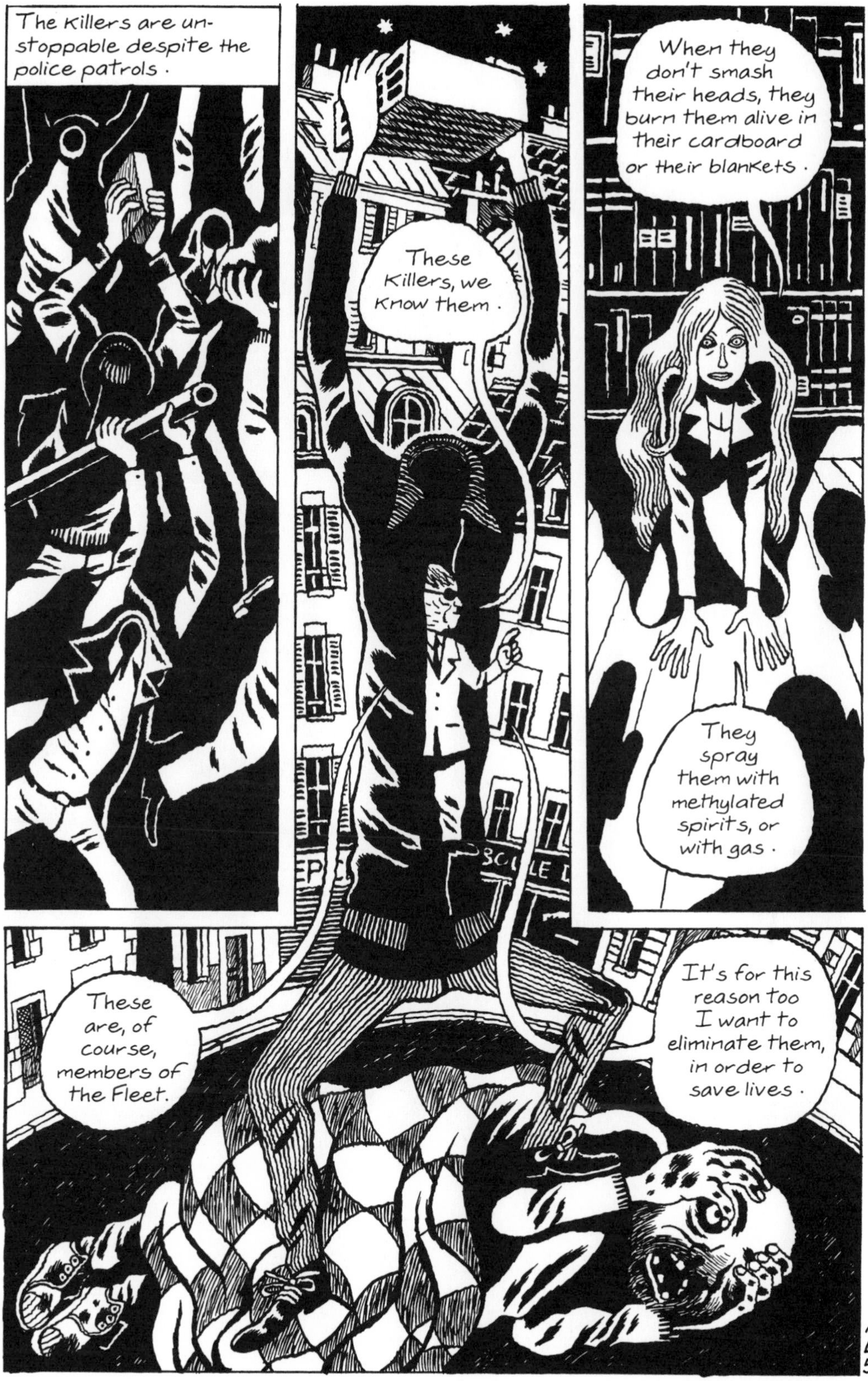
The Killers are unstoppable despite the police patrols.
These Killers, we Know them.
When they don't smash their heads, they burn them alive in their cardboard or their blankets.
They spray them with methylated spirits, or with gas.
These are, of course, members of the Fleet.
It's for this reason too I want to eliminate them, in order to save lives.

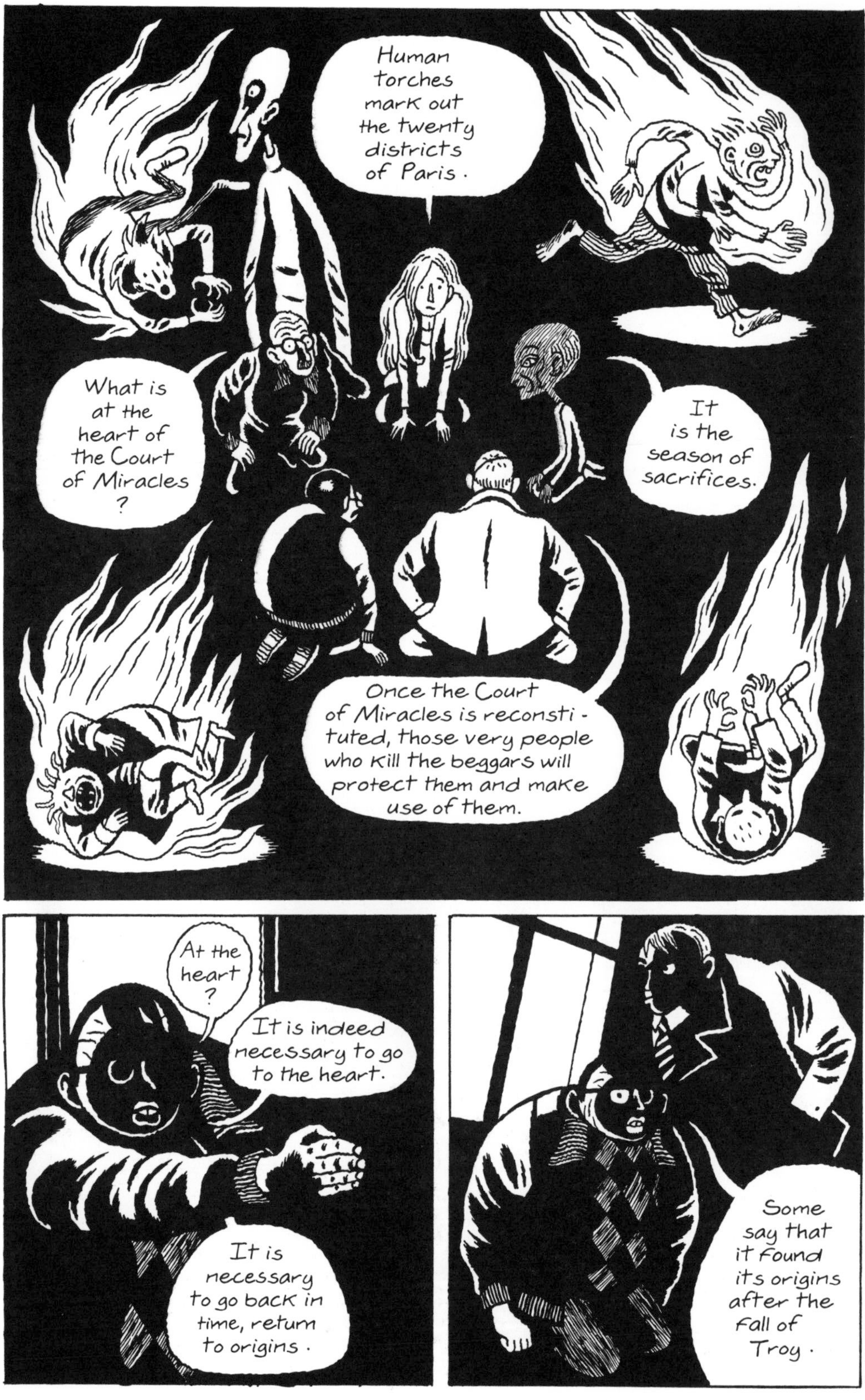
Human torches mark out the twenty districts of Paris.
What is at the heart of the Court of Miracles ?
It is the season of sacrifices.
Once the Court of Miracles is reconstituted, those very people who kill the beggars will protect them and make use of them.
At the heart ?
It is indeed necessary to go to the heart.
It is necessary to go back in time, return to origins.
Some say that it found its origins after the fall of Troy.

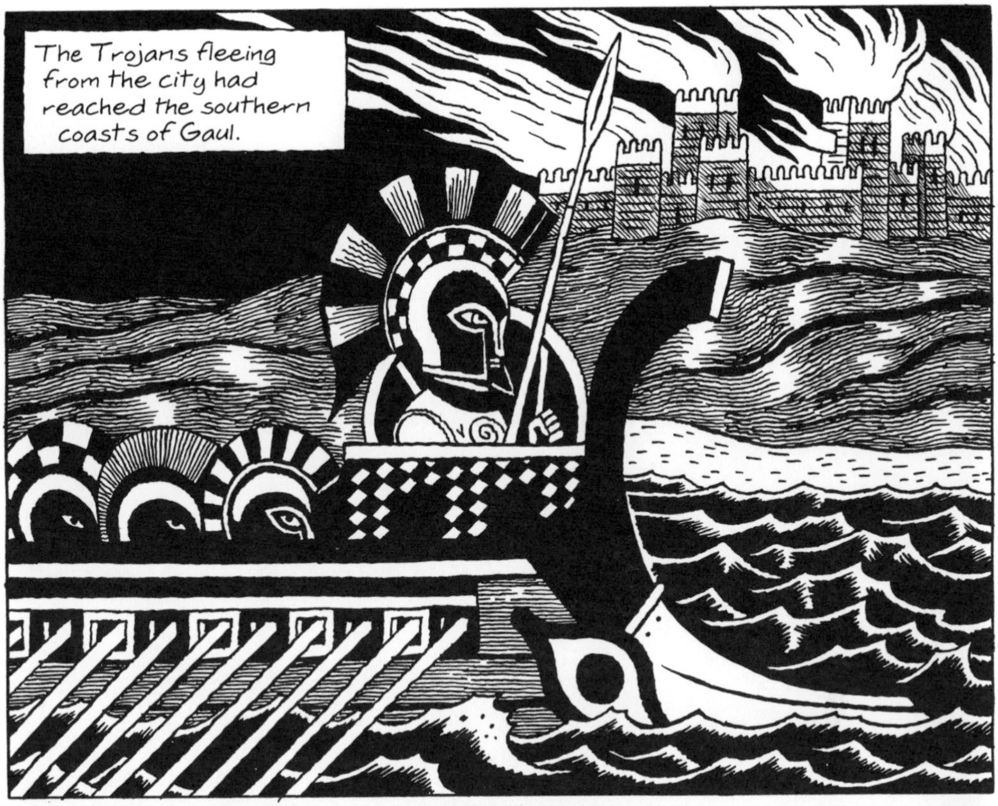
The Trojans fleeing from the city had reached the southern coasts of Gaul.

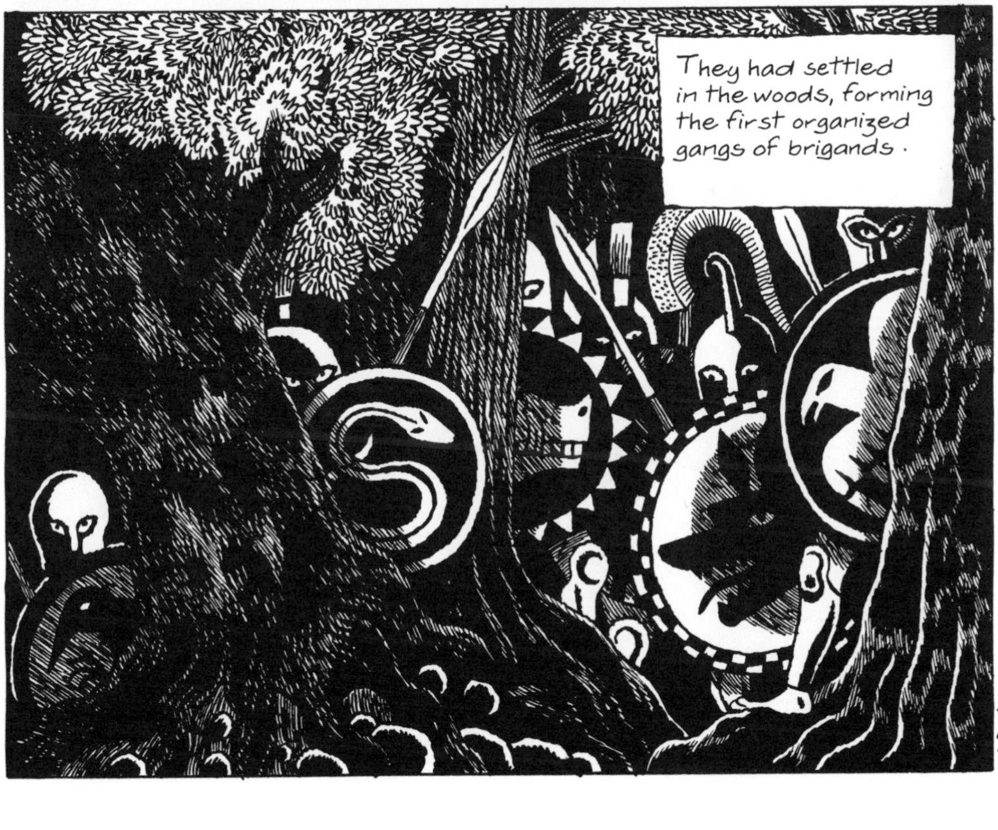
They had settled in the woods, forming the first organized gangs of brigands.

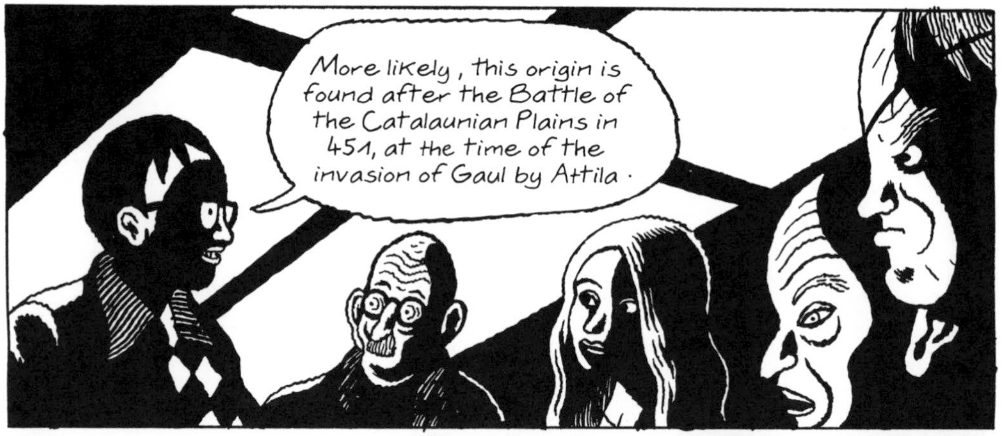
More likely, this origin is found after the Battle of the Catalaunian Plains in 451, at the time of the invasion of Gaul by Attila.

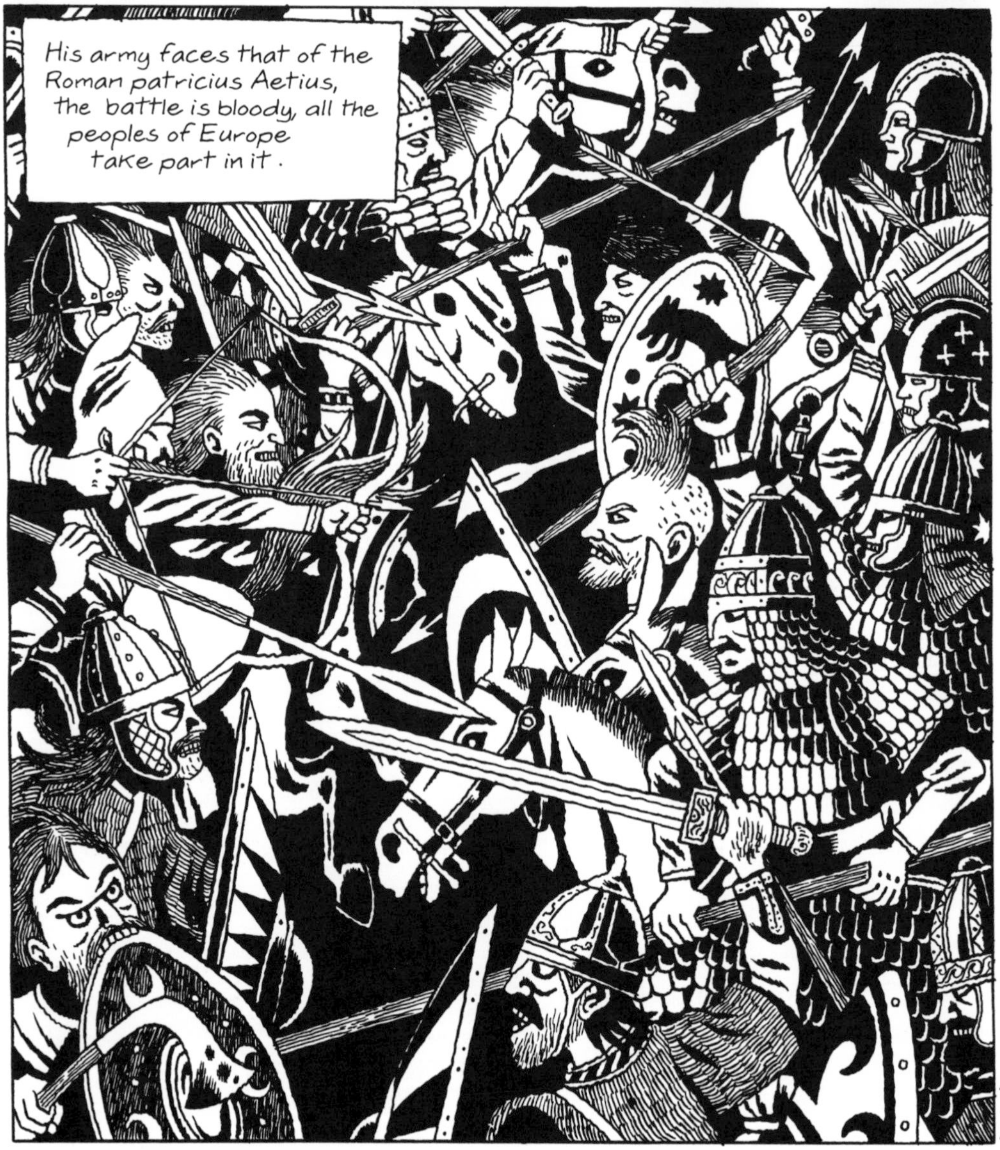
His army faces that of the Roman patricius Aetius, the battle is bloody, all the peoples of Europe take part in it.

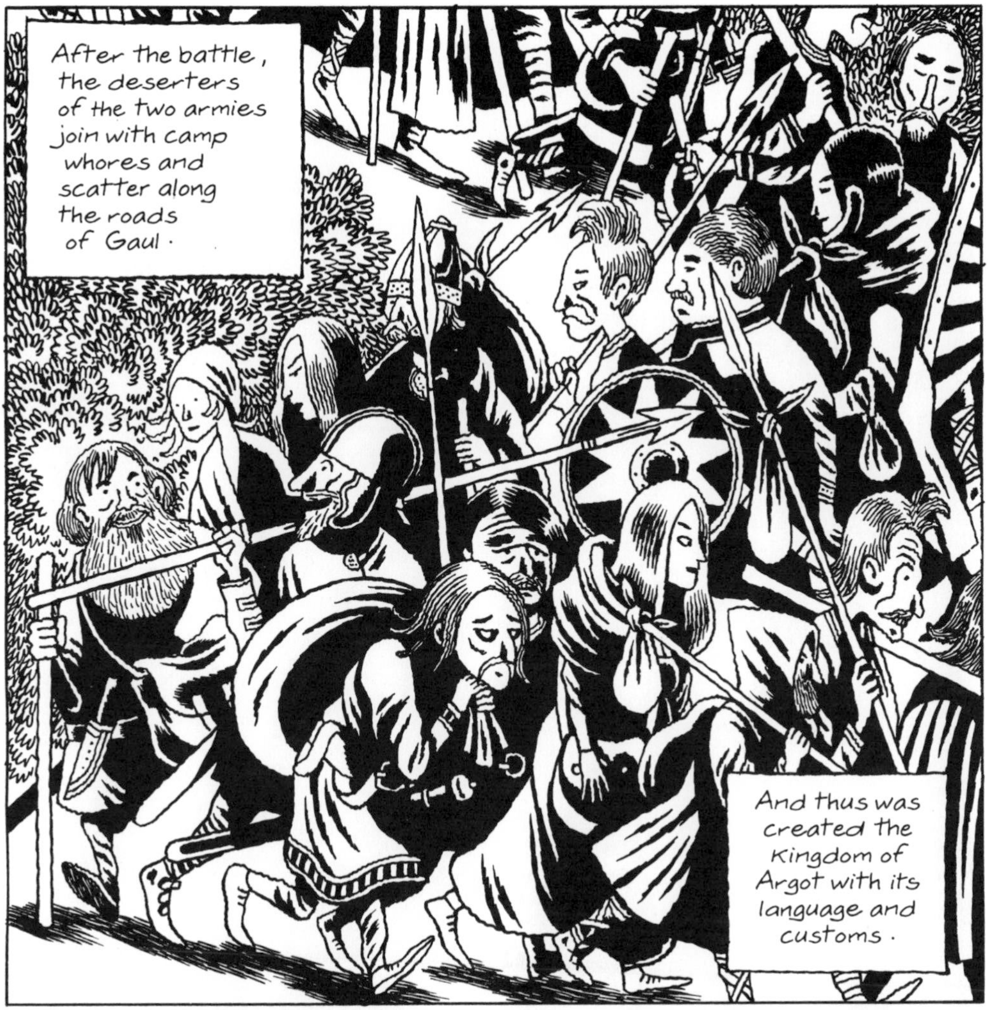
After the battle, the deserters of the two armies join with camp whores and scatter along the roads of Gaul.
And thus was created the Kingdom of Argot with its language and customs.

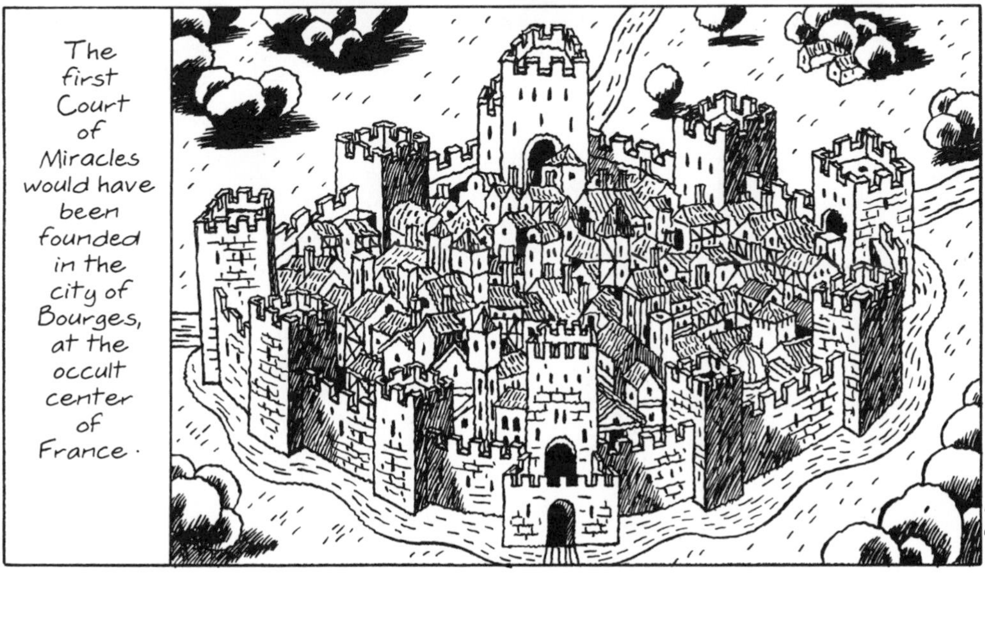
The first Court of Miracles would have been founded in the city of Bourges, at the occult center of France.

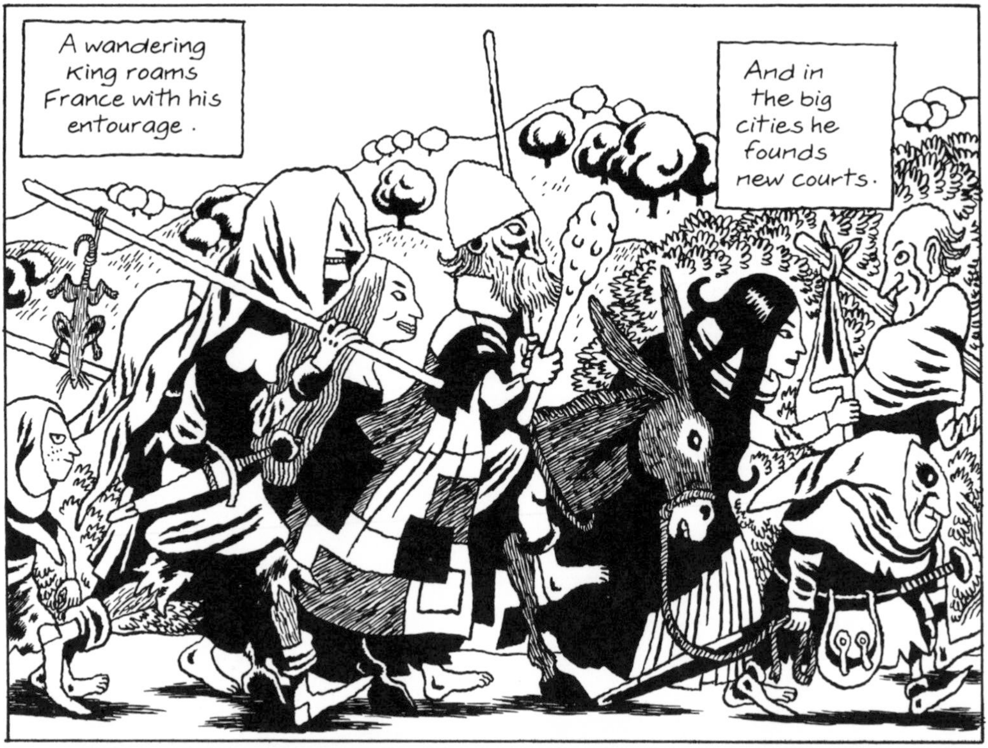
A wandering King roams France with his entourage.
And in the big cities he founds new courts.

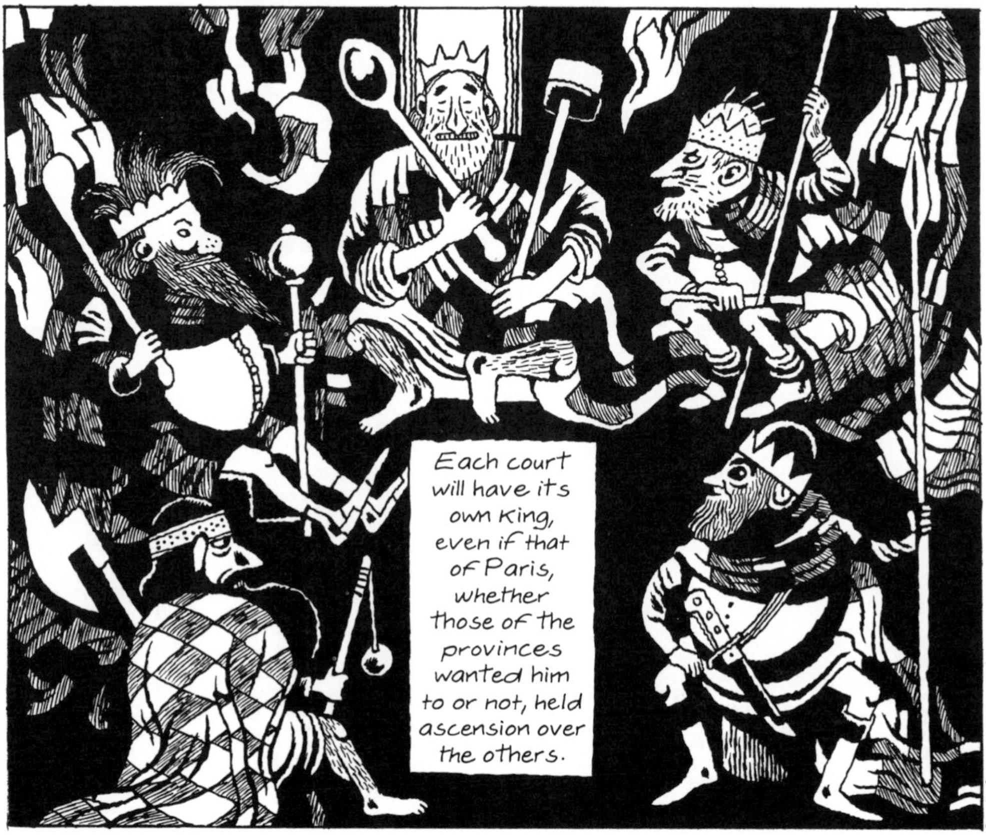
Each court will have its own King, even if that of Paris, whether those of the provinces wanted him to or not, held ascension over the others.

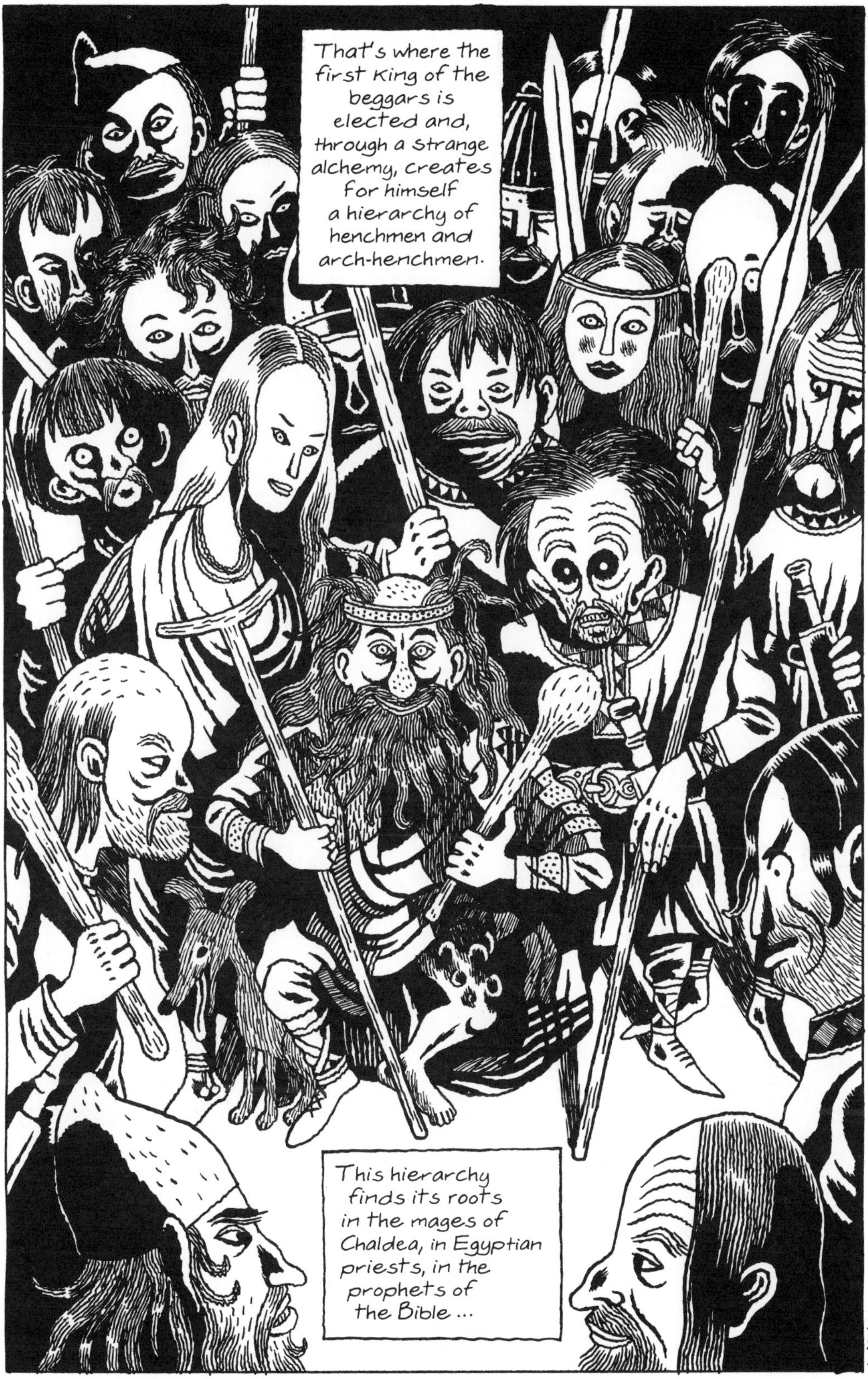
That's where the first King of the beggars is elected and, through a strange alchemy, creates for himself a hierarchy of henchmen and arch-henchmen.
This hierarchy finds its roots in the mages of Chaldea, in Egyptian priests, in the prophets of the Bible ...

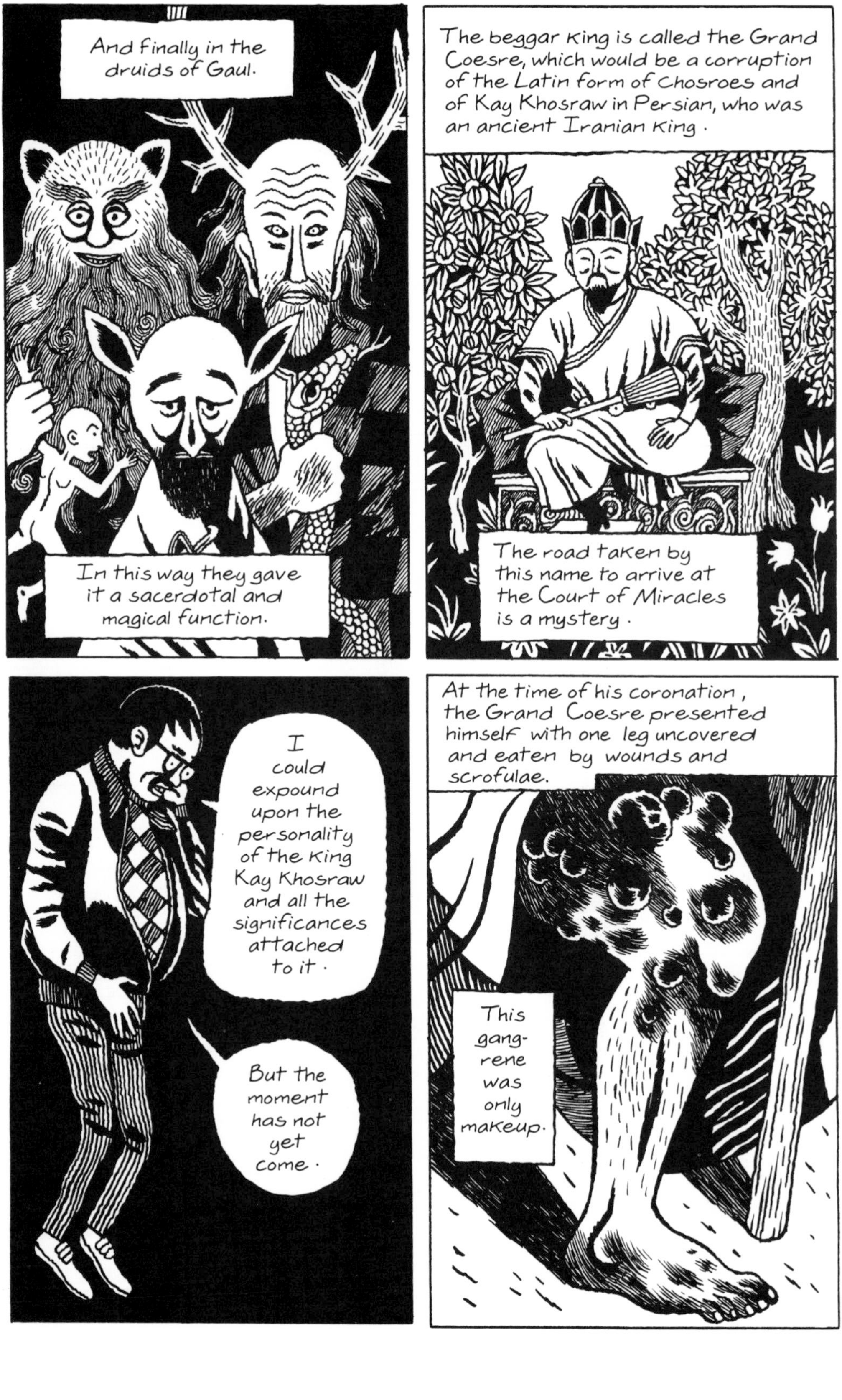
And finally in the druids of Gaul.
In this way they gave it a sacerdotal and magical function.
The beggar king is called the Grand Coesre, which would be a corruption of the Latin form of Chosroes and of Kay Khosraw in Persian, who was an ancient Iranian king.
The road taken by this name to arrive at the Court of Miracles is a mystery.
I could expound upon the personality of the King Kay Khosraw and all the significances attached to it.
But the moment has not yet come.
At the time of his coronation, the Grand Coesre presented himself with one leg uncovered and eaten by wounds and scrofulae.
This gang-rene was only makeup.

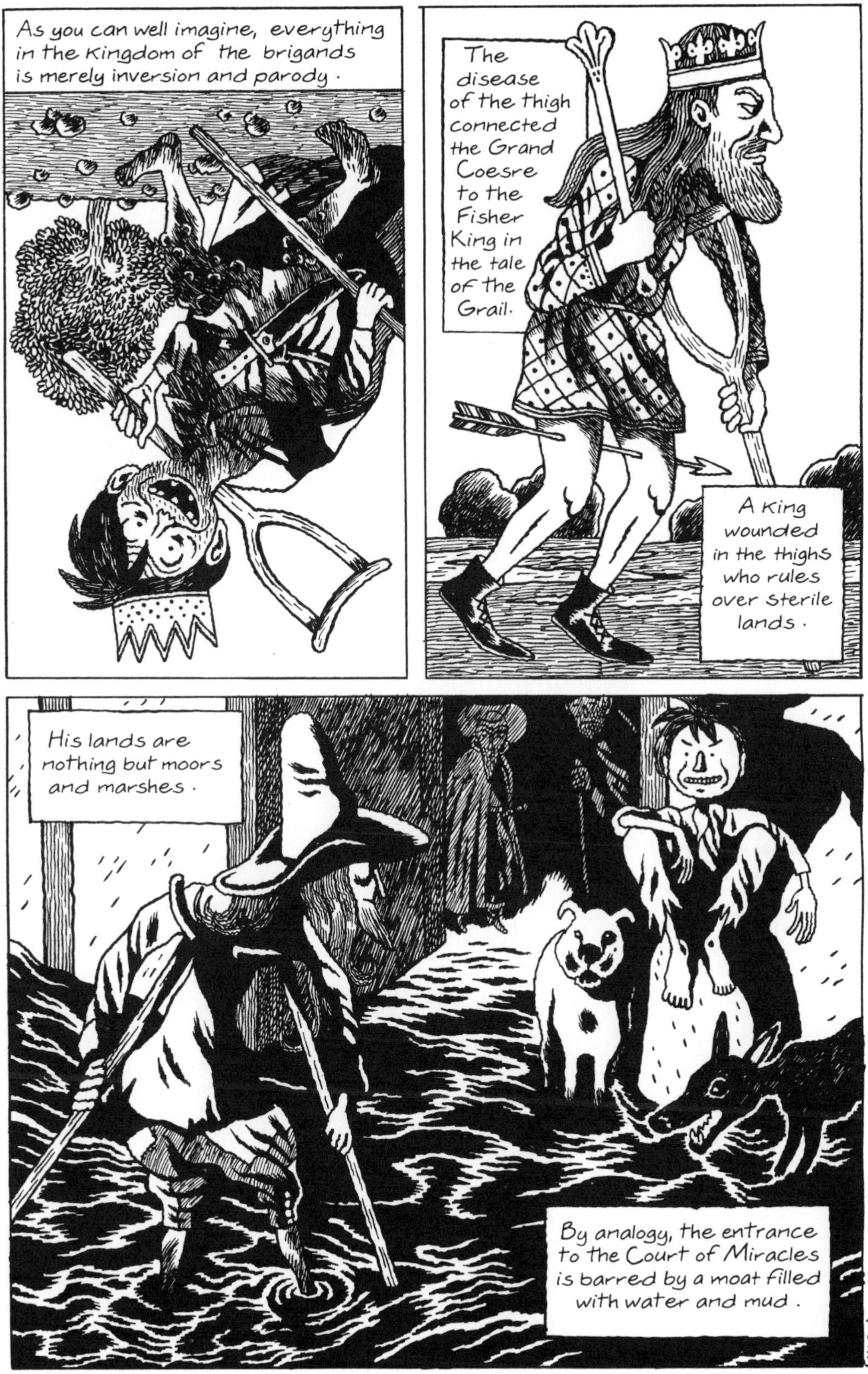
As you can well imagine, everything in the Kingdom of the brigands is merely inversion and parody.
The disease of the thigh connected the Grand Coesre to the Fisher King in the tale of the Grail.
A King wounded in the thighs who rules over sterile lands.
His lands are nothing but moors and marshes.
By analogy, the entrance to the Court of Miracles is barred by a moat filled with water and mud.

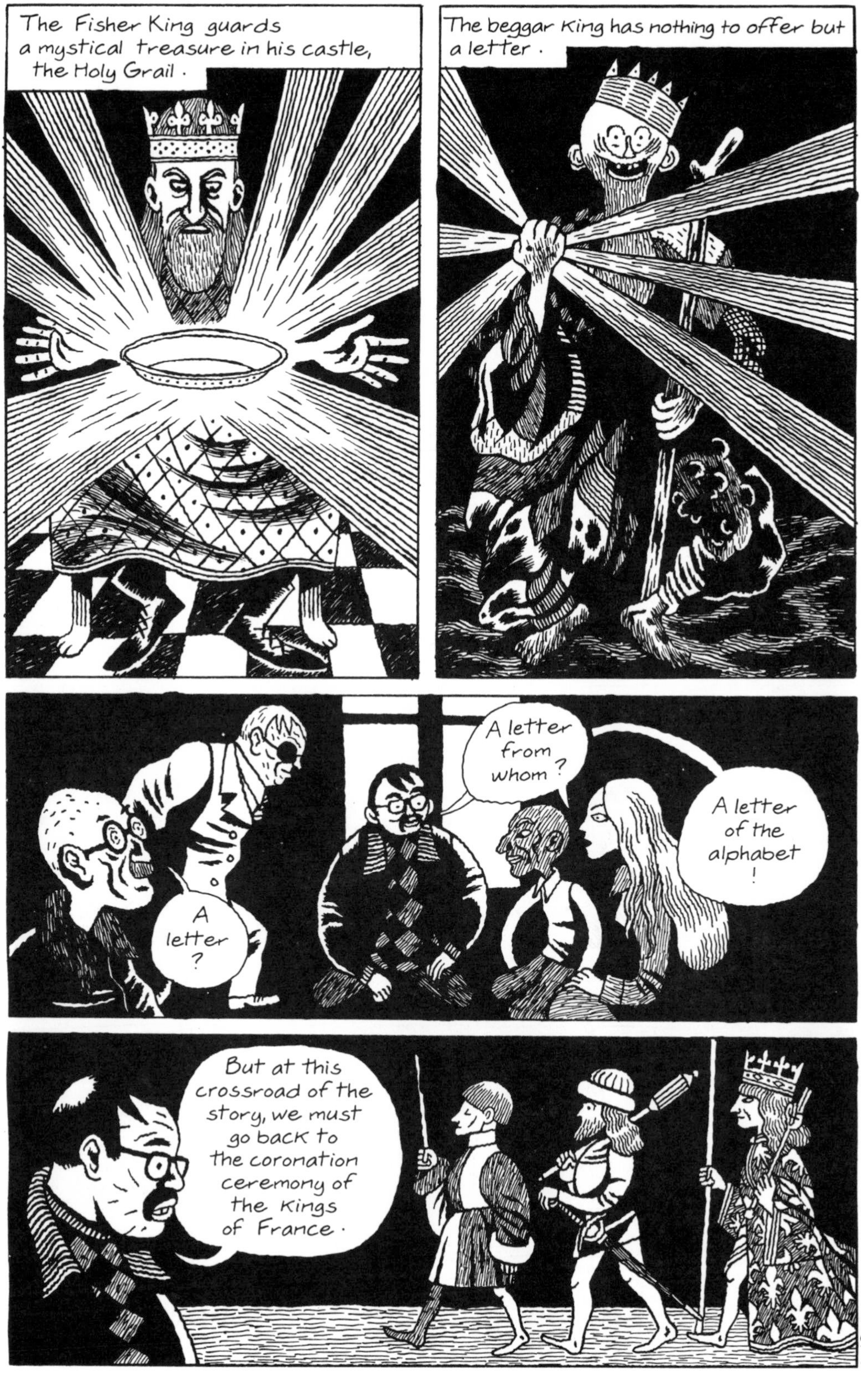
The Fisher King guards a mystical treasure in his castle, the Holy Grail.
The beggar King has nothing to offer but a letter.
A letter?
A letter from whom?
A letter of the alphabet!
But at this crossroad of the story, we must go back to the coronation ceremony of the Kings of France.

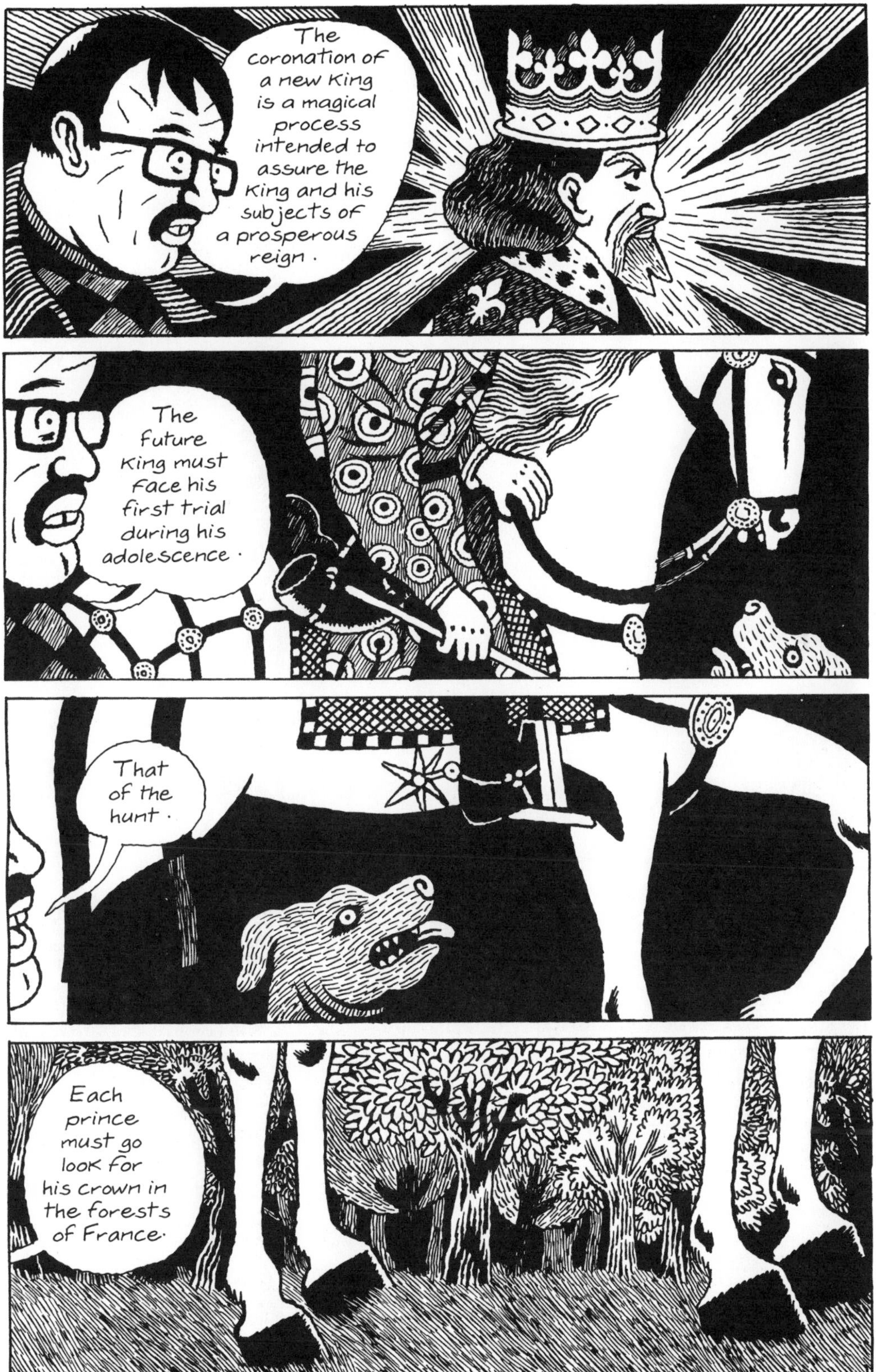
The coronation of a new King is a magical process intended to assure the King and his subjects of a prosperous reign.
The future King must face his first trial during his adolescence.
That of the hunt.
Each prince must go look for his crown in the forests of France.

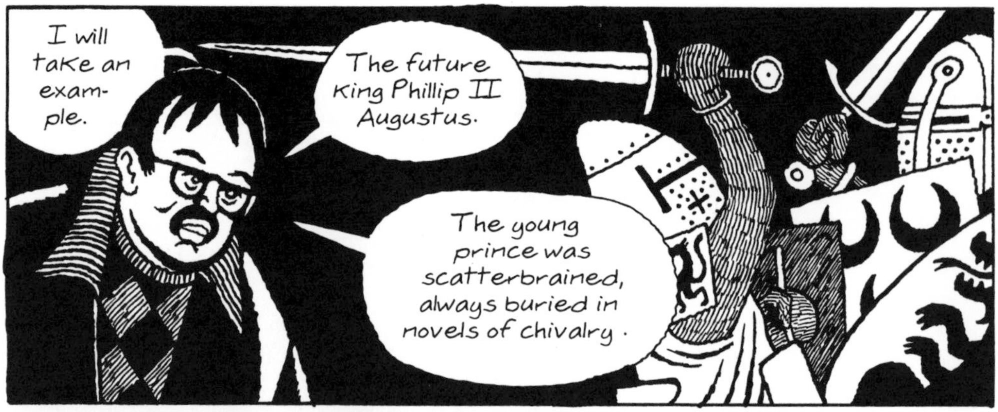
I will take an exam-ple.
The future King Phillip II Augustus.
The young prince was scatterbrained, always buried in novels of chivalry.

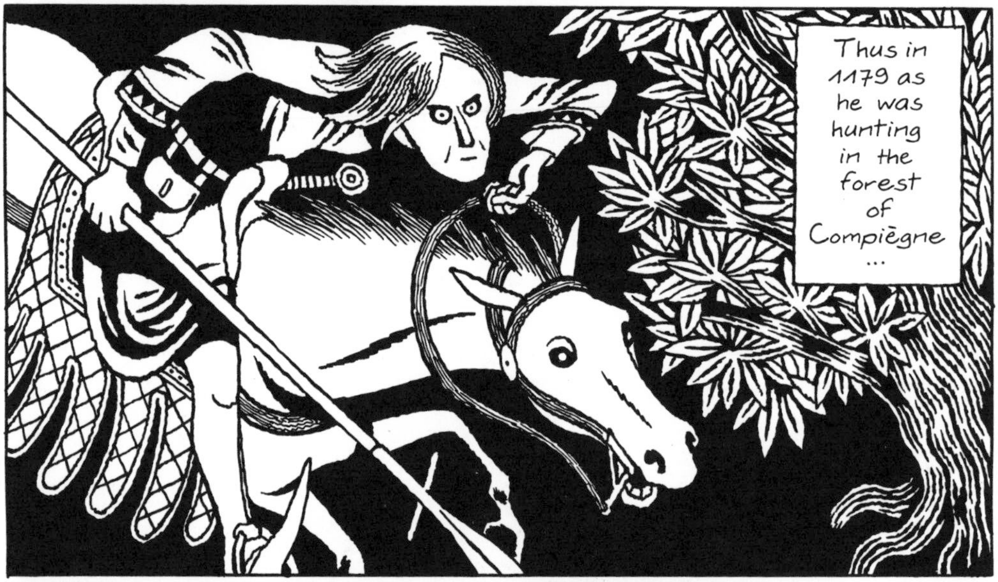
Thus in 1179 as he was hunting in the forest of Compiègne ...

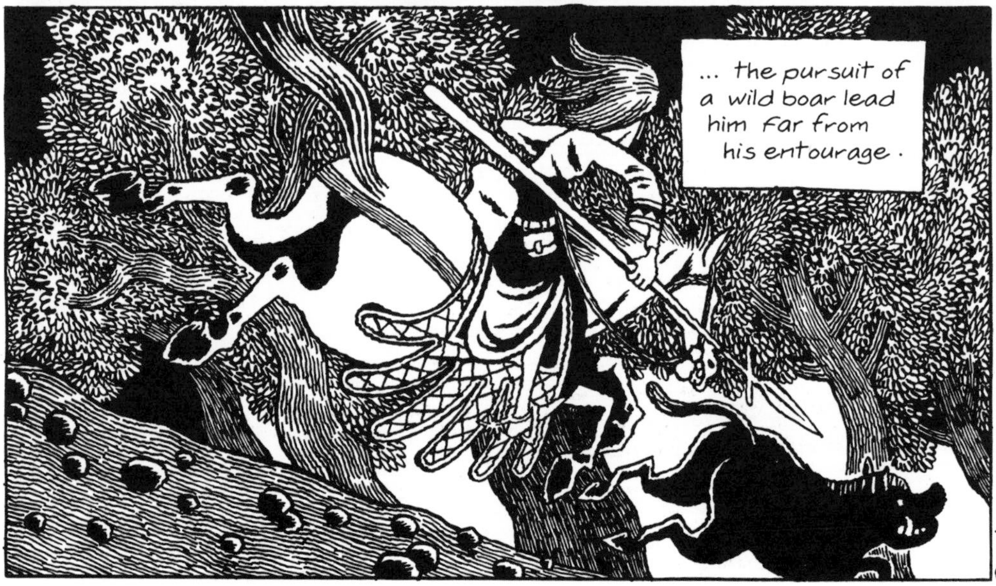
... the pursuit of a wild boar lead him far from his entourage.

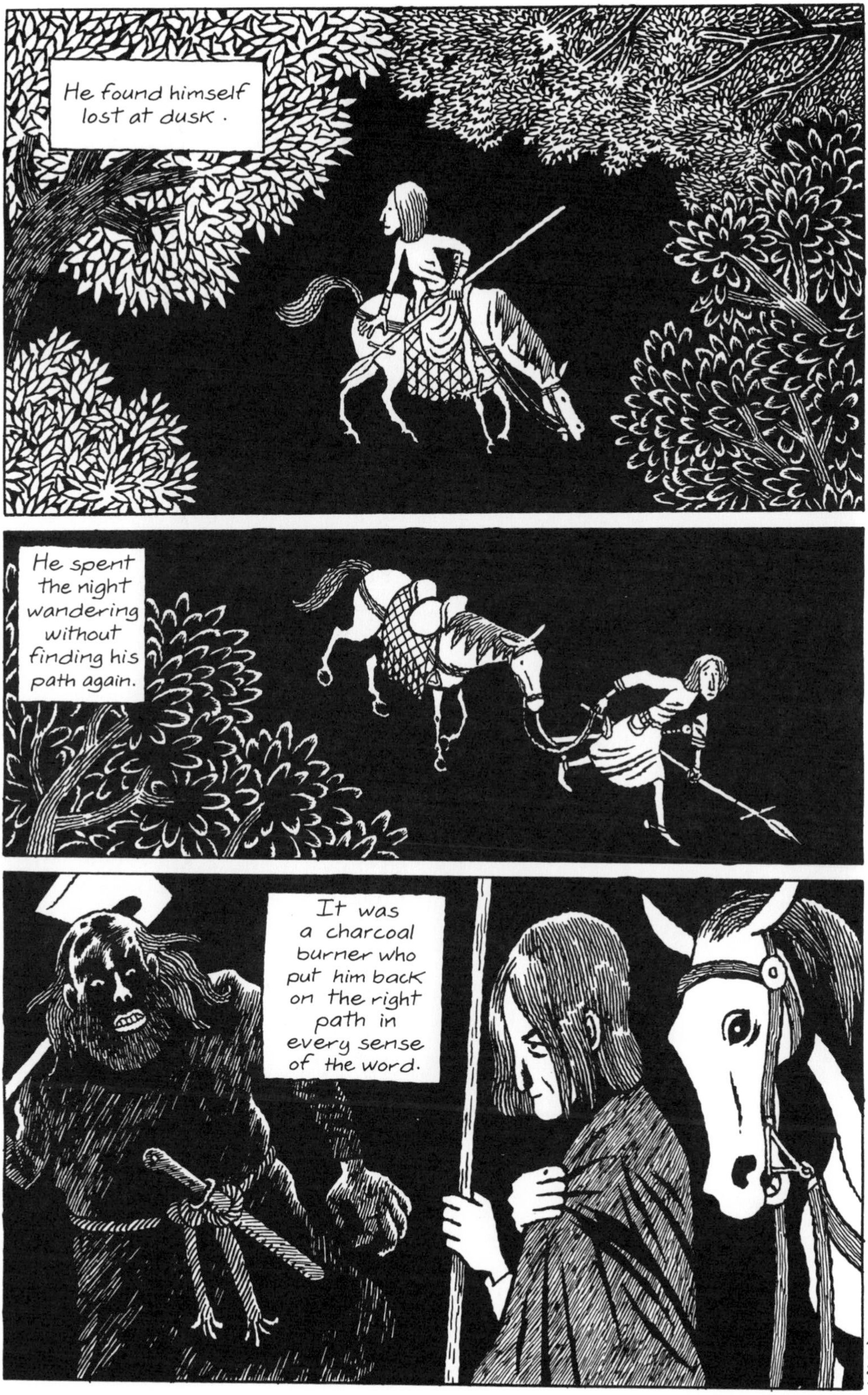
He found himself lost at dusk .
He spent the night wandering without finding his path again.
It was a charcoal burner who put him back on the right path in every sense of the word.

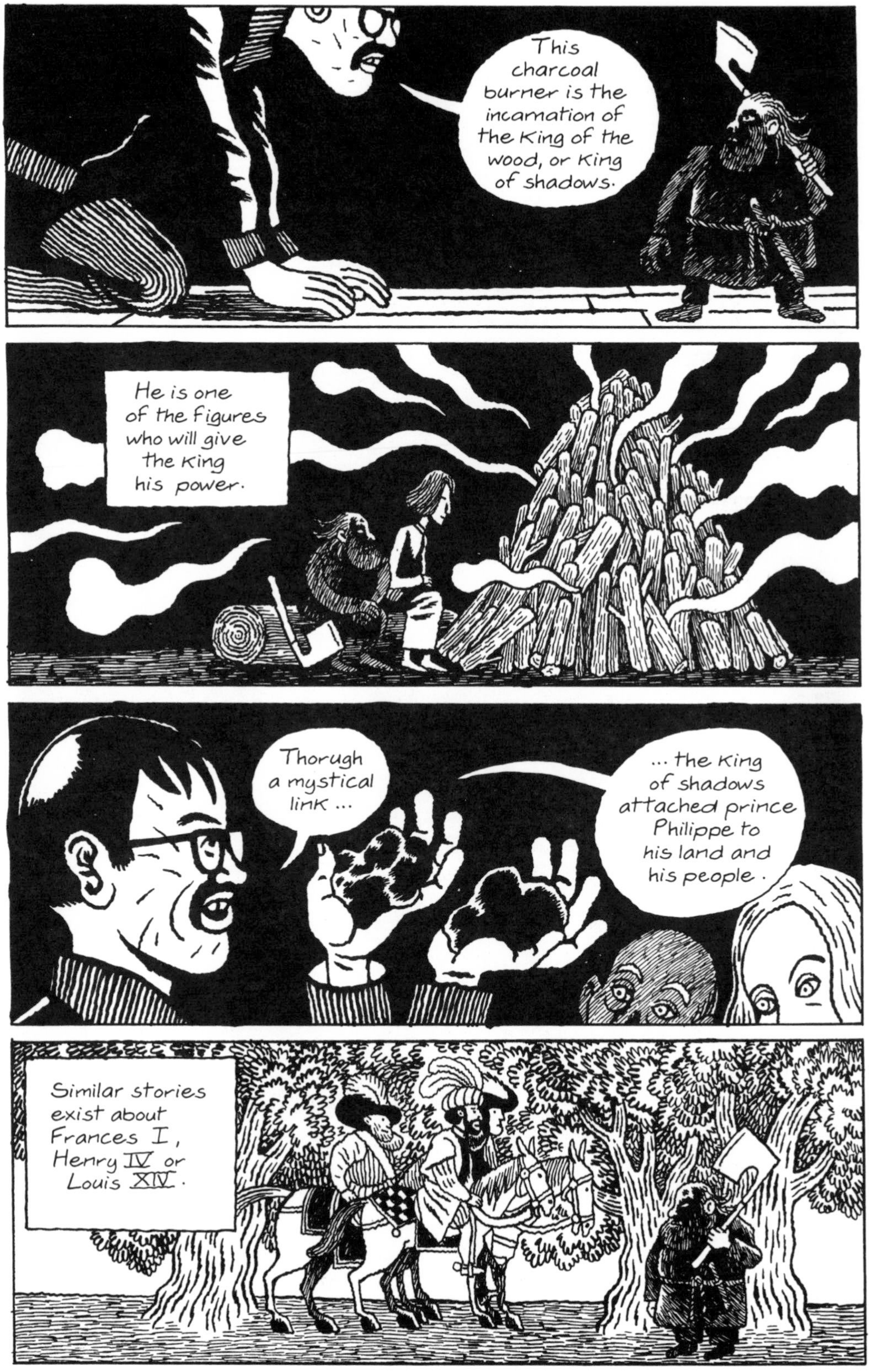
This charcoal burner is the incarnation of the King of the wood, or King of shadows.
He is one of the figures who will give the King his power.
Thorugh a mystical link ...
... the King of shadows attached prince Philippe to his land and his people.
Similar stories exist about Frances I, Henry IV or Louis XIV.

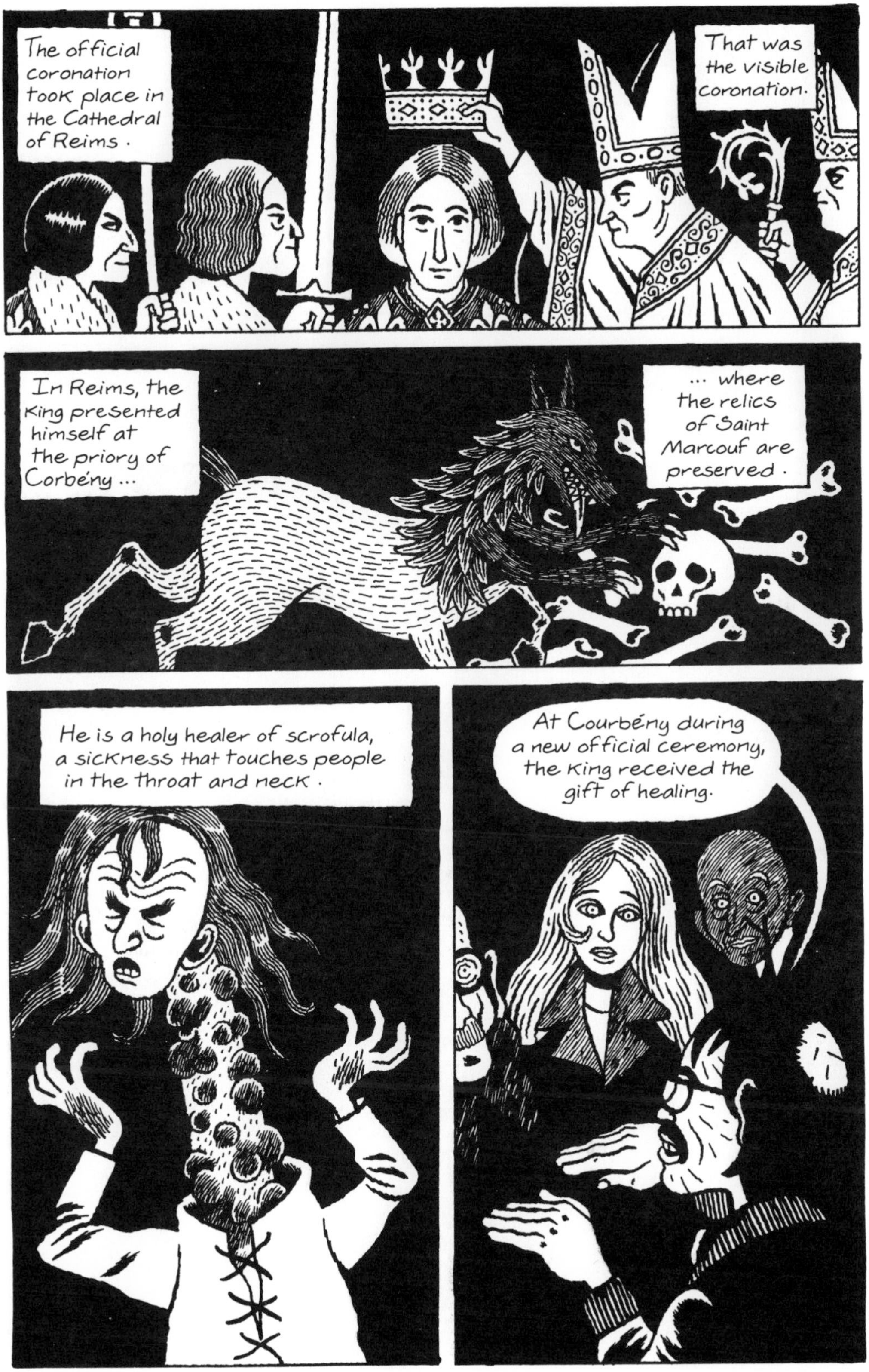
The official coronation took place in the Cathedral of Reims.
That was the visible coronation.
In Reims, the King presented himself at the priory of Corbény...
... where the relics of Saint Marcouf are preserved.
He is a holy healer of scrofula, a sickness that touches people in the throat and neck.
At Courbény during a new official ceremony, the King received the gift of healing.

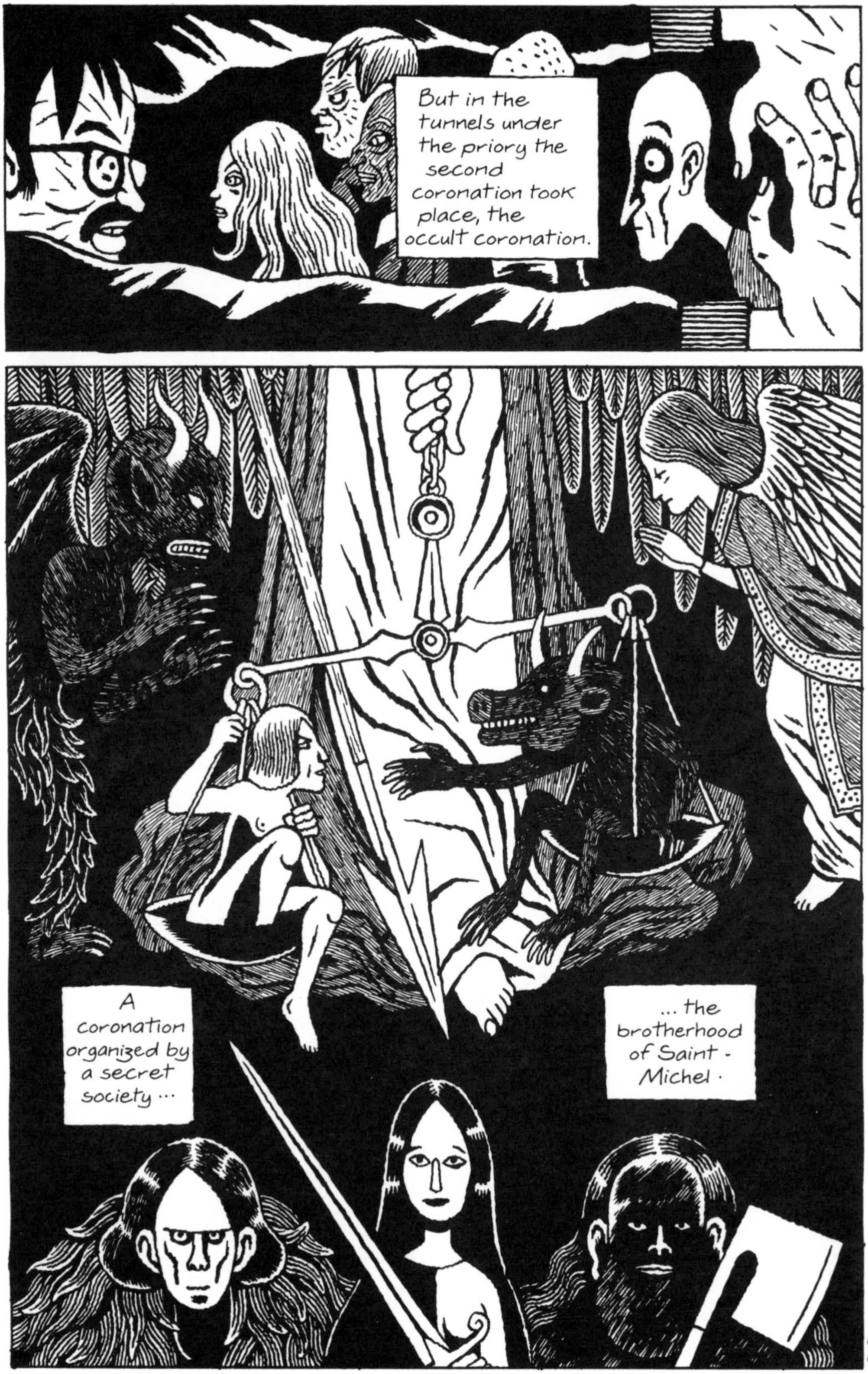
But in the tunnels under the priory the second coronation took place, the occult coronation.
A coronation organized by a secret society ...
... the brotherhood of Saint - Michel ·

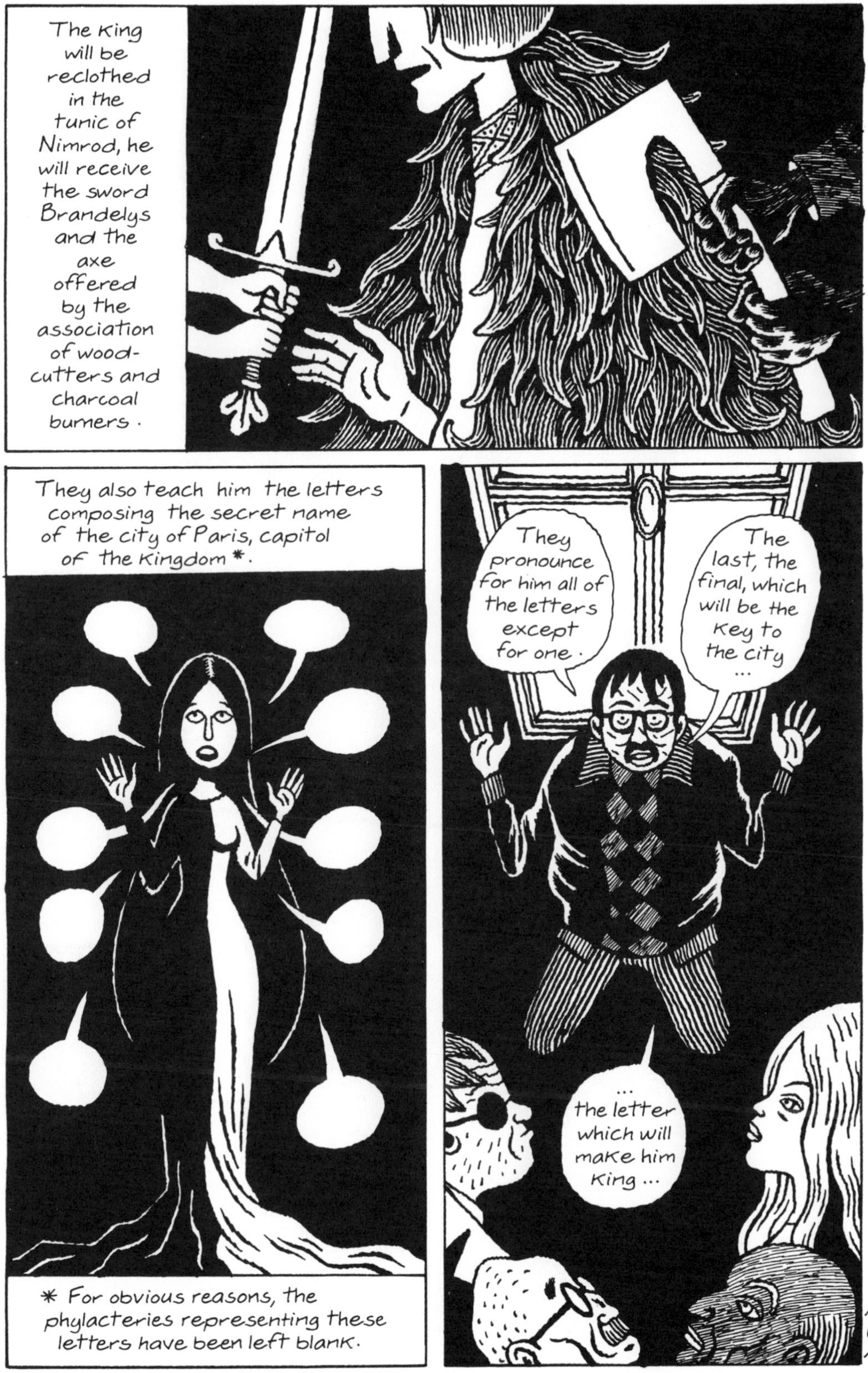
The King will be reclothed in the tunic of Nimrod, he will receive the sword Brandelys and the axe offered by the association of wood-cutters and charcoal burners .
They also teach him the letters composing the secret name of the city of Paris, capitol of the Kingdom *.
They pronounce for him all of the letters except for one .
The last, the final, which will be the Key to the city ...
... the letter which will make him King ...
* For obvious reasons, the phylacteries representing these letters have been left blank.

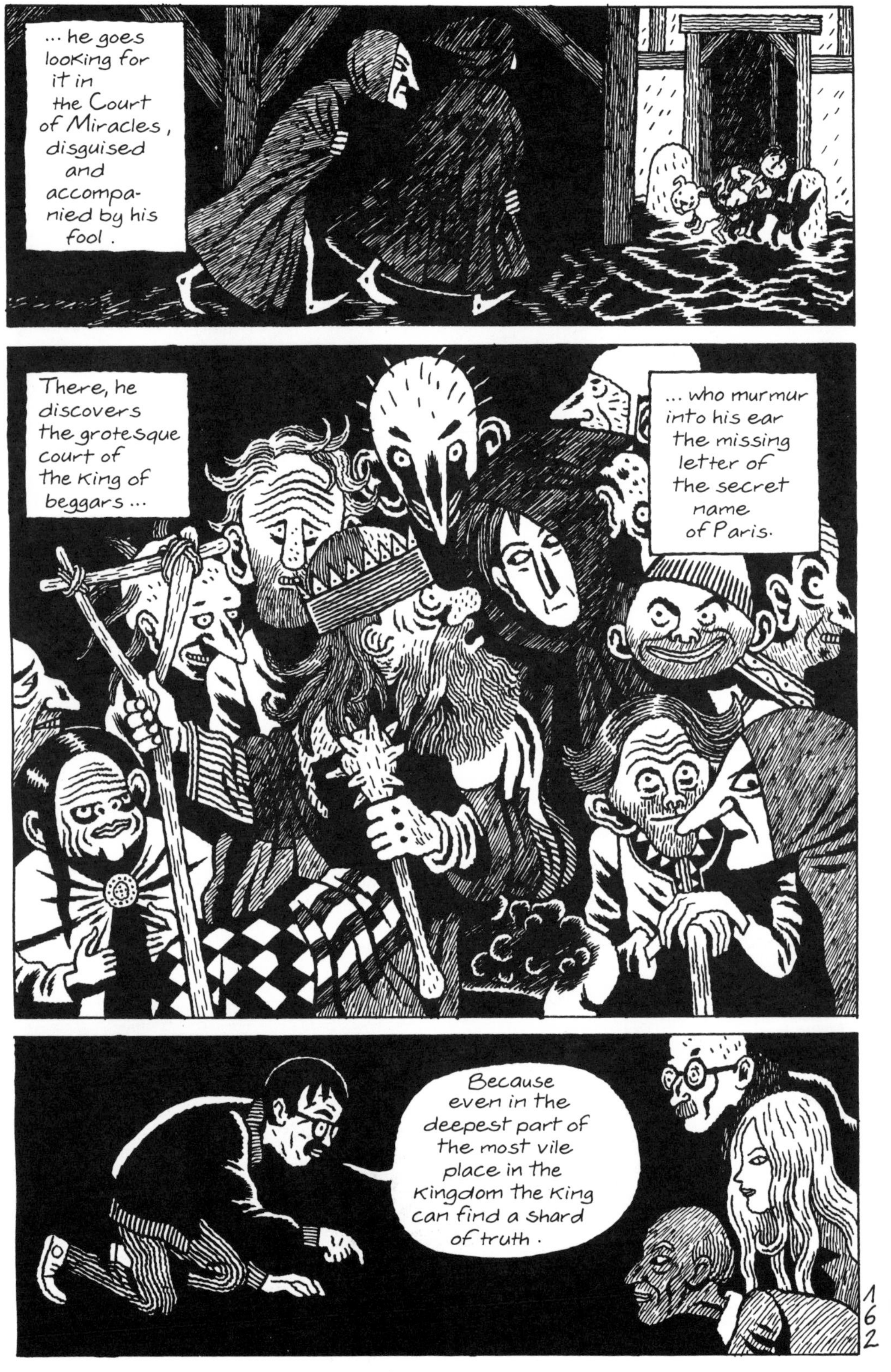
... he goes looking for it in the Court of Miracles, disguised and accompanied by his fool.
There, he discovers the grotesque court of the King of beggars ...
... who murmur into his ear the missing letter of the secret name of Paris.
Because even in the deepest part of the most vile place in the kingdom the king can find a shard of truth.

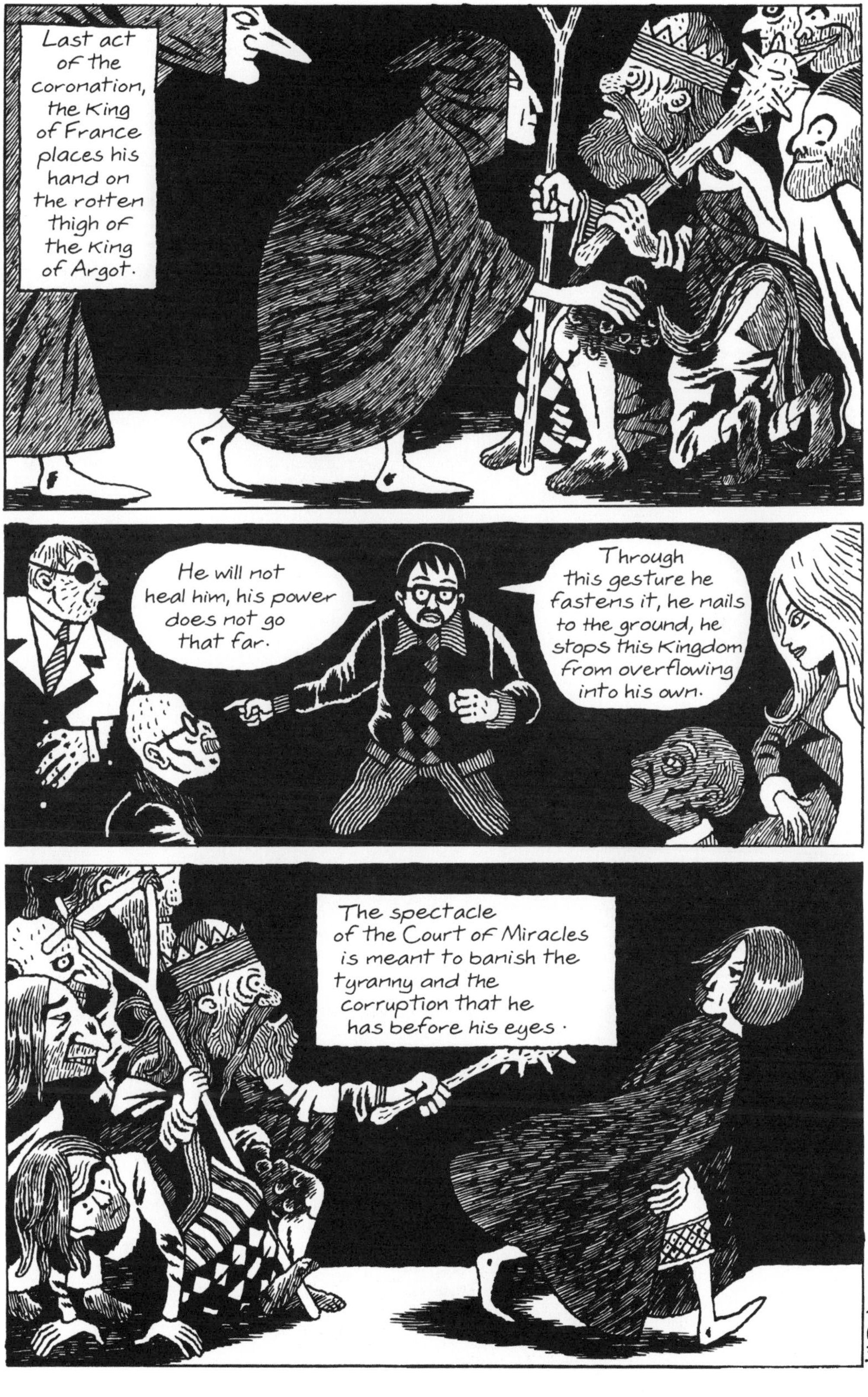

Last act of the coronation, the King of France places his hand on the rotten thigh of the King of Argot.
He will not heal him, his power does not go that far.
Through this gesture he fastens it, he nails to the ground, he stops this Kingdom from overflowing into his own.
The spectacle of the Court of Miracles is meant to banish the tyranny and the corruption that he has before his eyes.

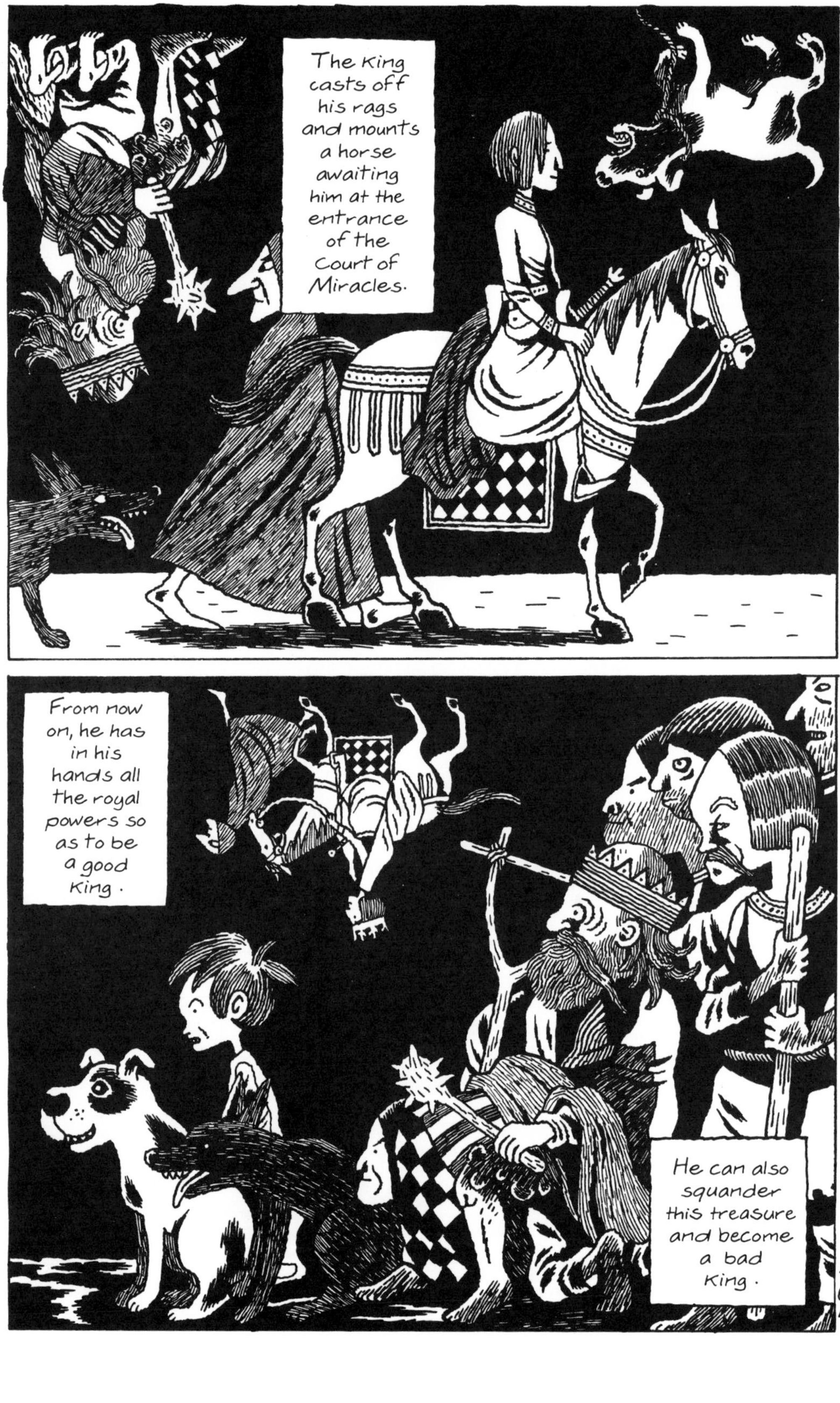
The King casts off his rags and mounts a horse awaiting him at the entrance of the Court of Miracles.
From now on, he has in his hands all the royal powers so as to be a good King.
He can also squander this treasure and become a bad King.

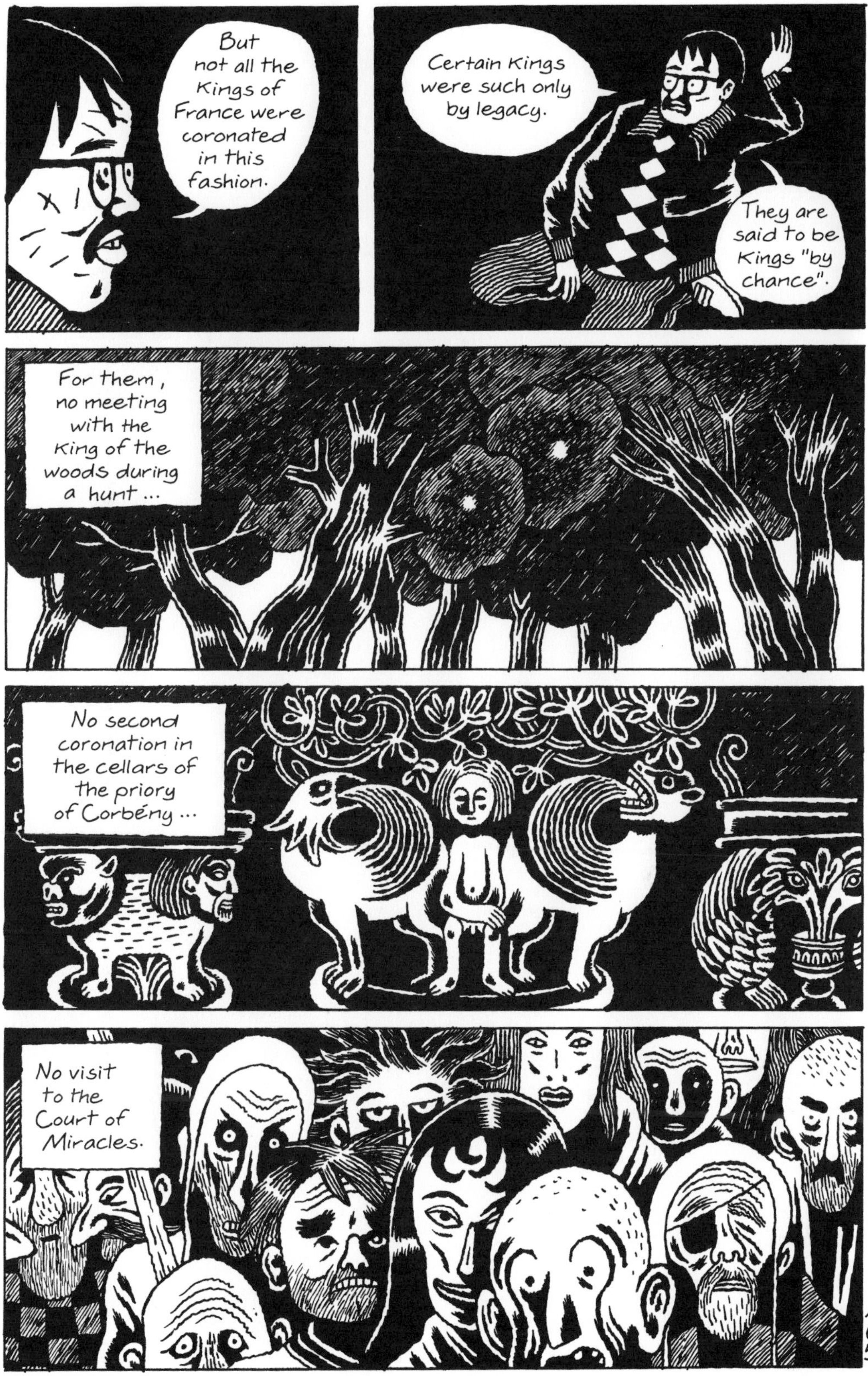
But not all the Kings of France were coronated in this fashion.
Certain Kings were such only by legacy.
They are said to be Kings "by chance".
For them, no meeting with the King of the woods during a hunt ...
No second coronation in the cellars of the priory of Corbény ...
No visit to the Court of Miracles.

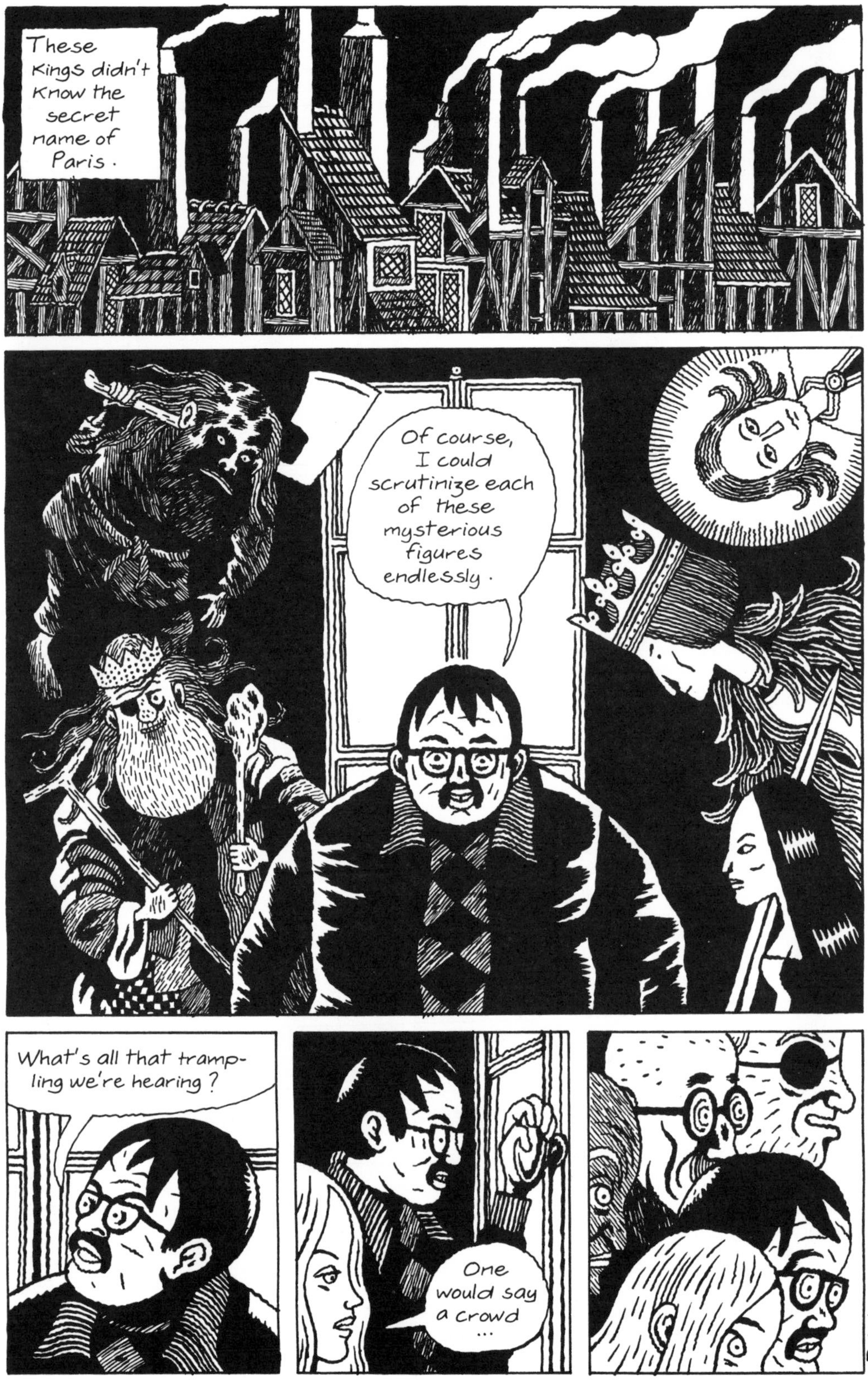
These Kings didn't Know the secret name of Paris.
Of course, I could scrutinize each of these mysterious figures endlessly.
What's all that trampling we're hearing?
One would say a crowd ...

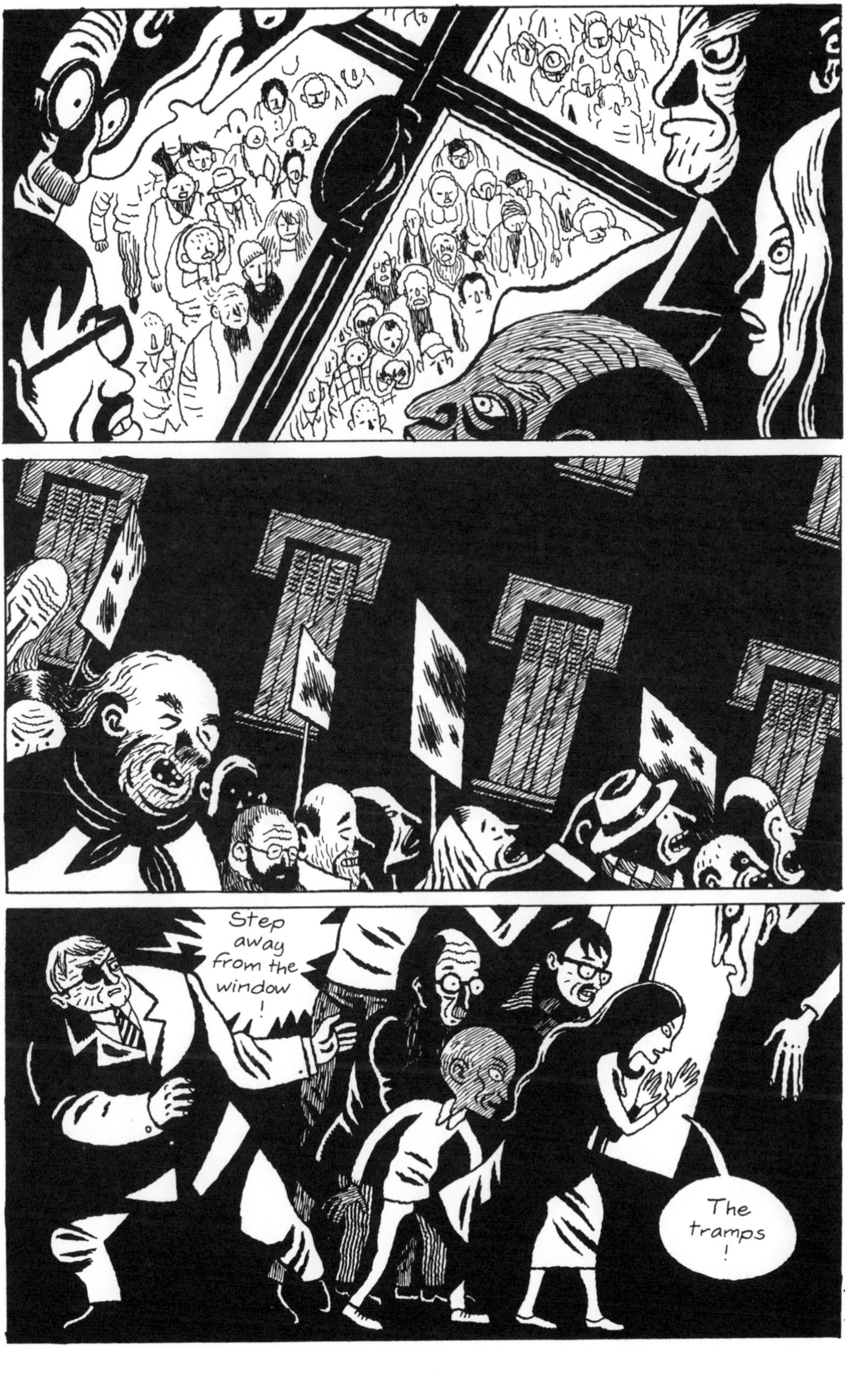
Step away from the window !
The tramps !

The dirty placards carried no slogan.

What made this demonstration terrible was that it unfolded in an absolute silence.

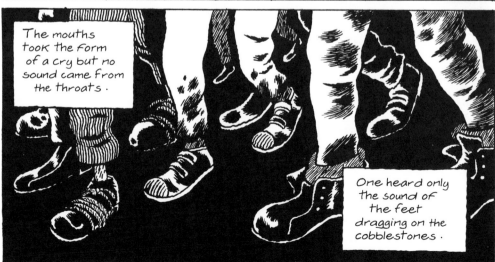

The mouths took the form of a cry but no sound came from the throats.

One heard only the sound of the feet dragging on the cobblestones.

168

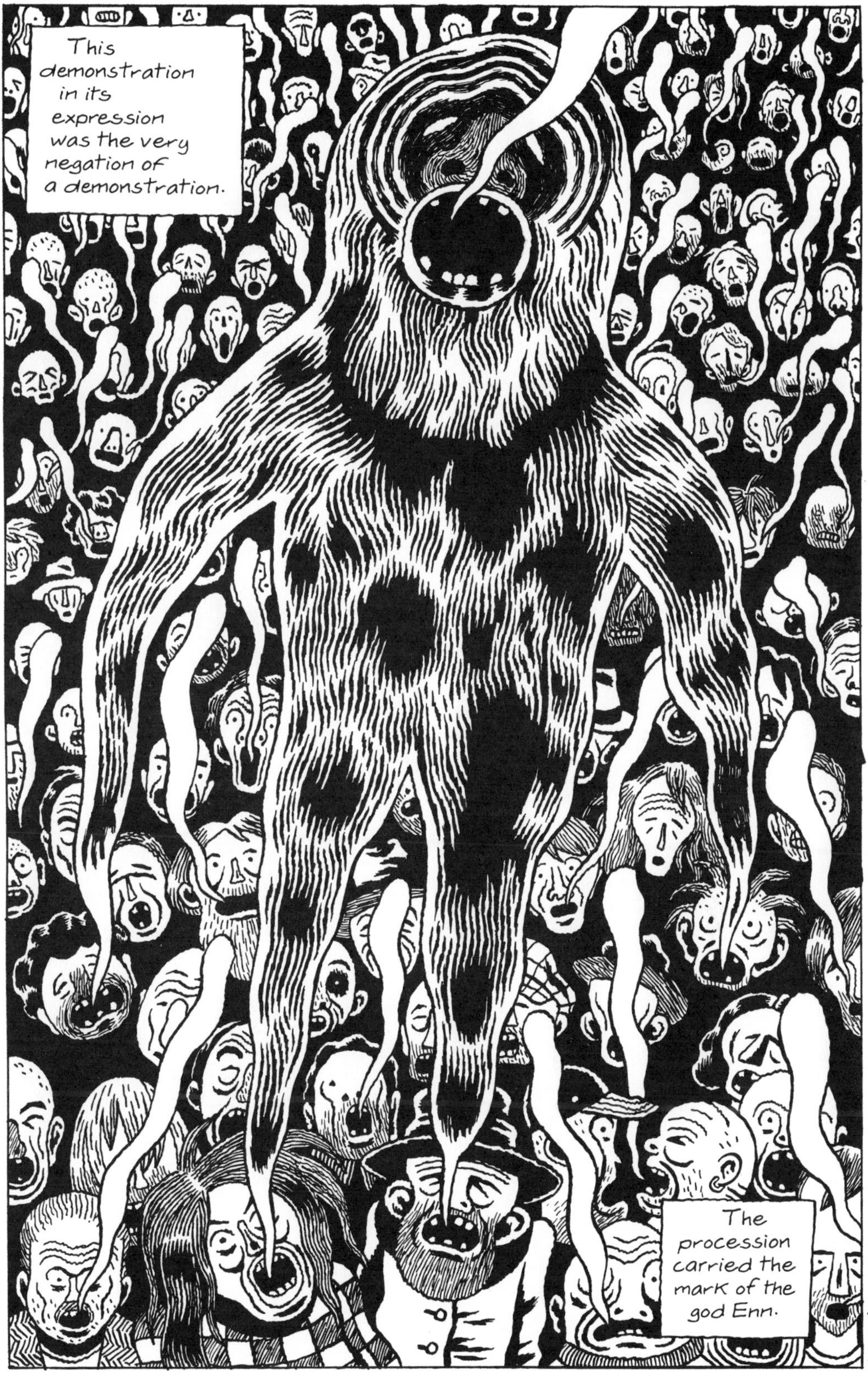
This demonstration in its expression was the very negation of a demonstration.
The procession carried the mark of the god Enn.

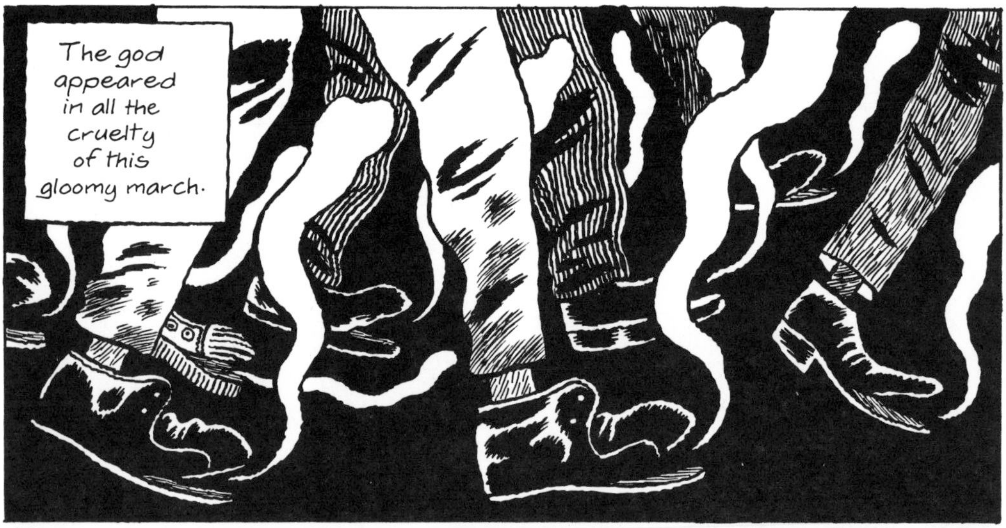
The god appeared in all the cruelty of this gloomy march.

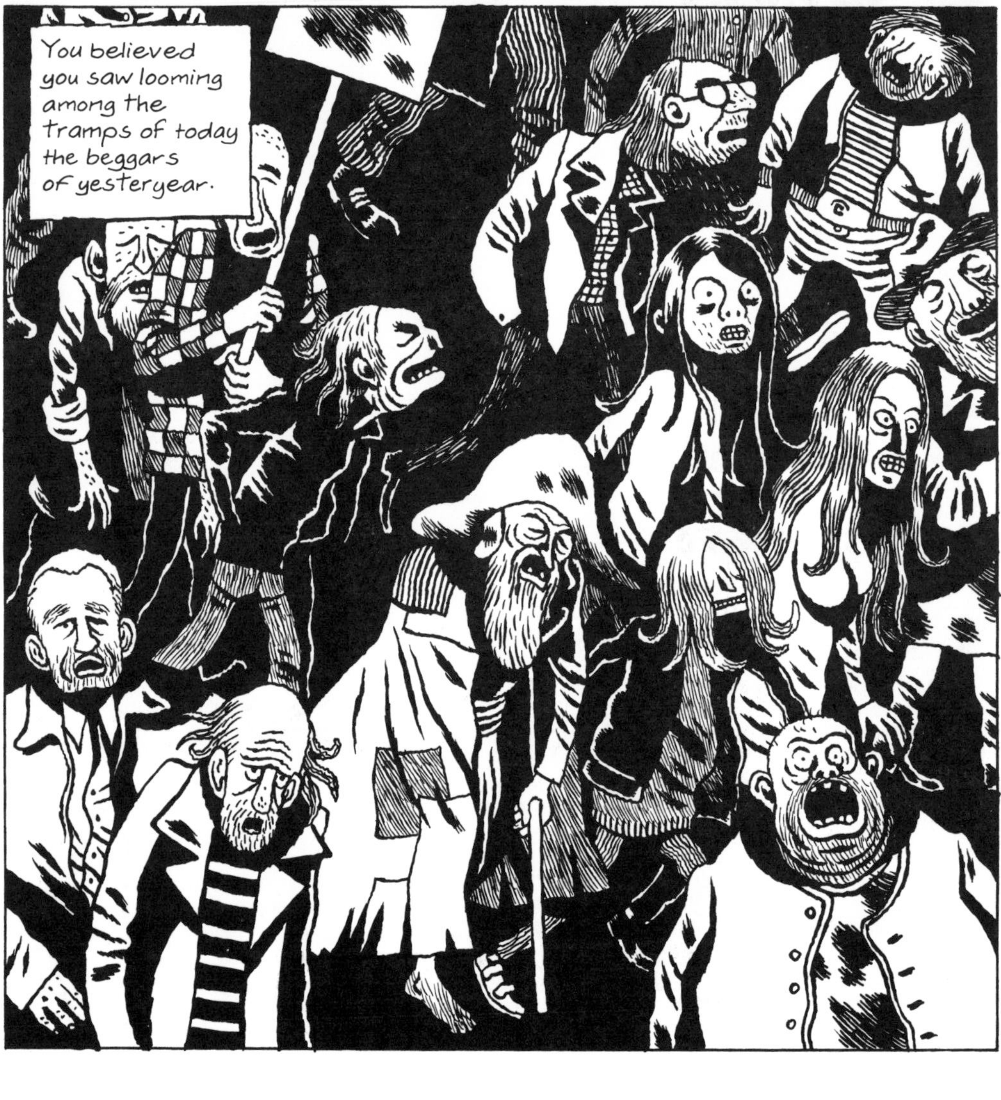
You believed you saw looming among the tramps of today the beggars of yesteryear.

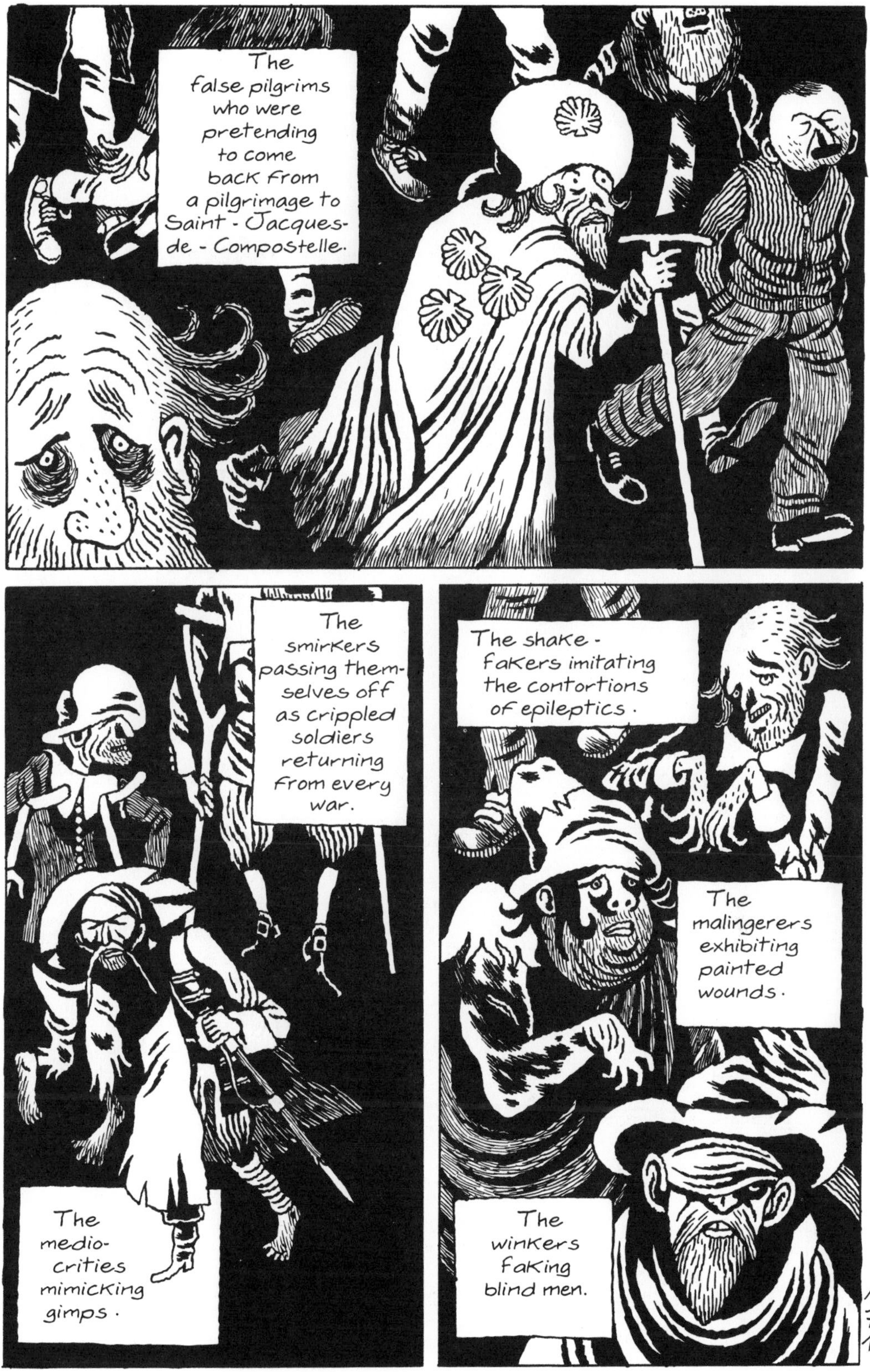
The false pilgrims who were pretending to come back from a pilgrimage to Saint - Jacques-de - Compostelle.
The smirkers passing them-selves off as crippled soldiers returning from every war.
The medio-crities mimicking gimps.
The shake-fakers imitating the contortions of epileptics.
The malingerers exhibiting painted wounds.
The winkers faking blind men.

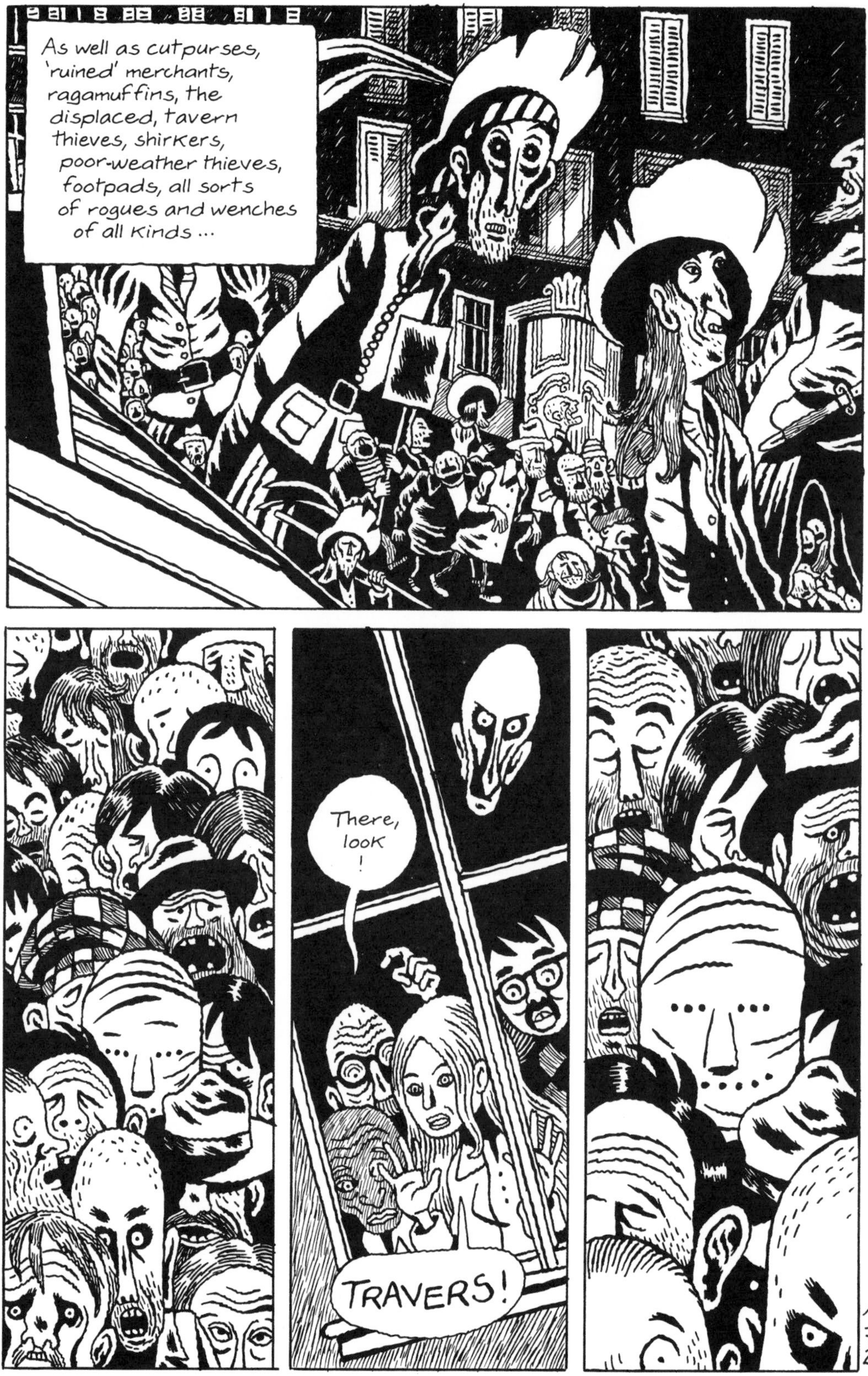
As well as cutpurses, 'ruined' merchants, ragamuffins, the displaced, tavern thieves, shirkers, poor-weather thieves, footpads, all sorts of rogues and wenches of all kinds ...
There, look !
TRAVERS!

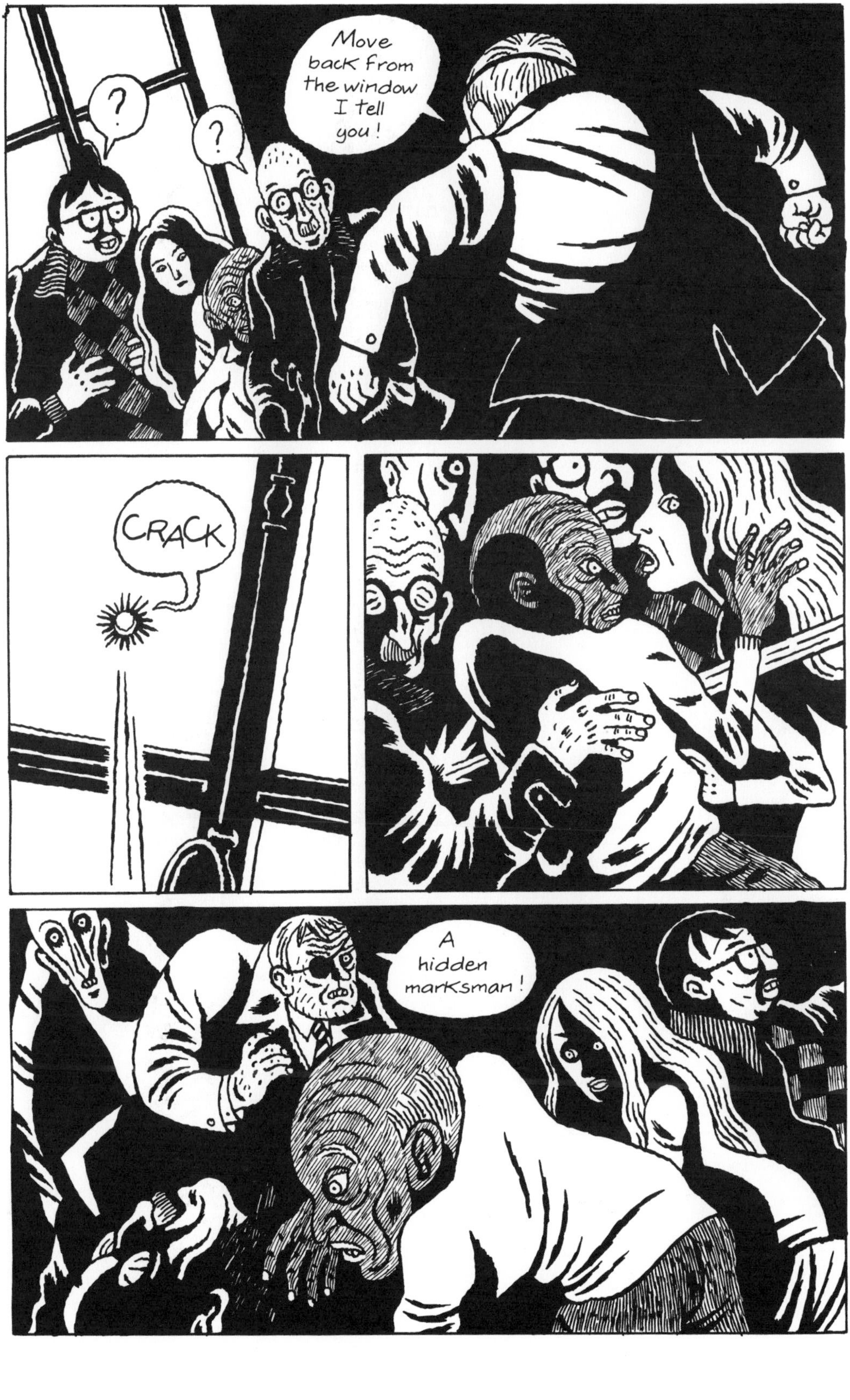
?
?
Move back from the window I tell you!
CRACK
A hidden marksman!

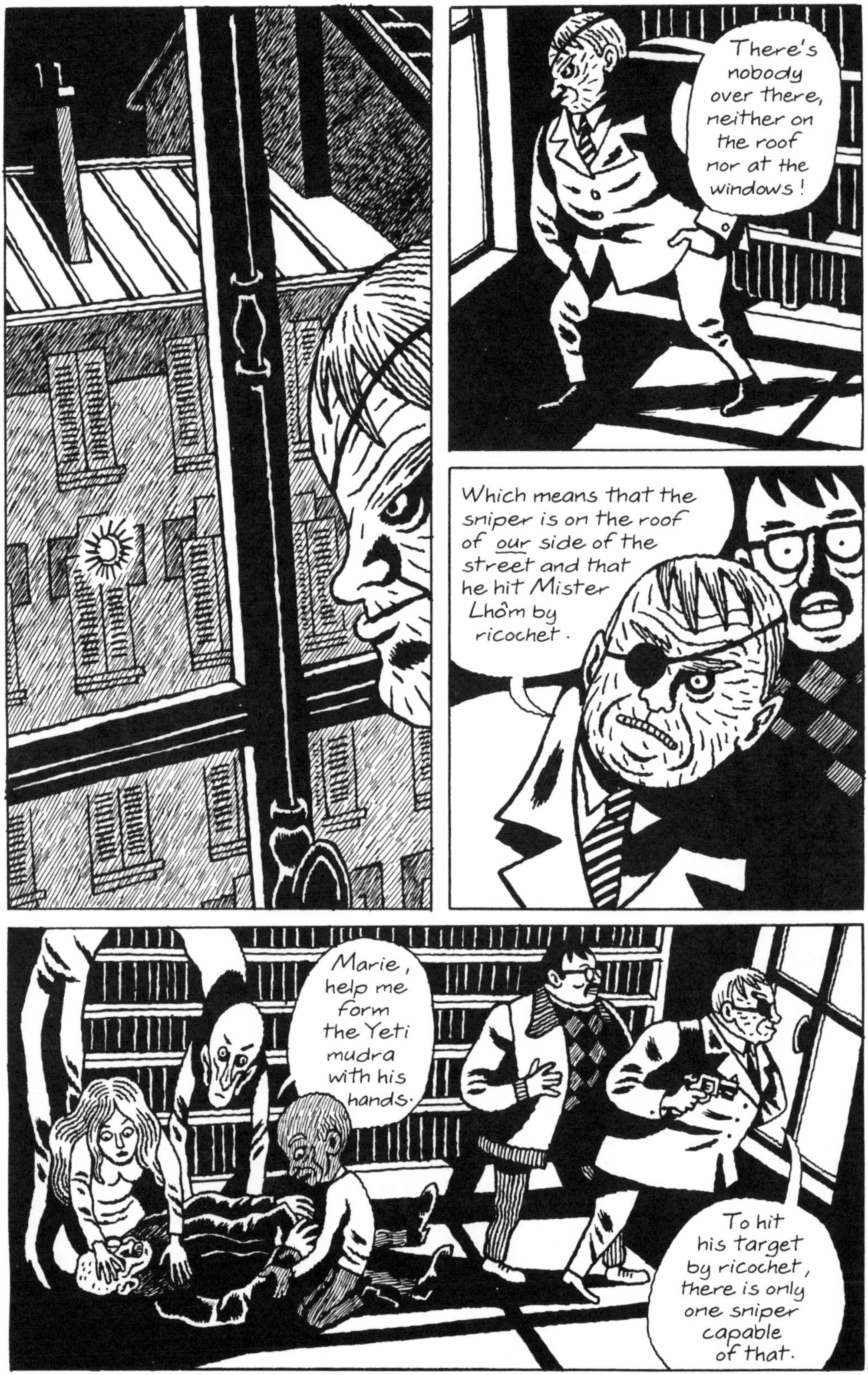
There's nobody over there, neither on the roof nor at the windows!
Which means that the sniper is on the roof of our side of the street and that he hit Mister Lhôm by ricochet.
Marie, help me form the Yeti mudra with his hands.
To hit his target by ricochet, there is only one sniper capable of that.

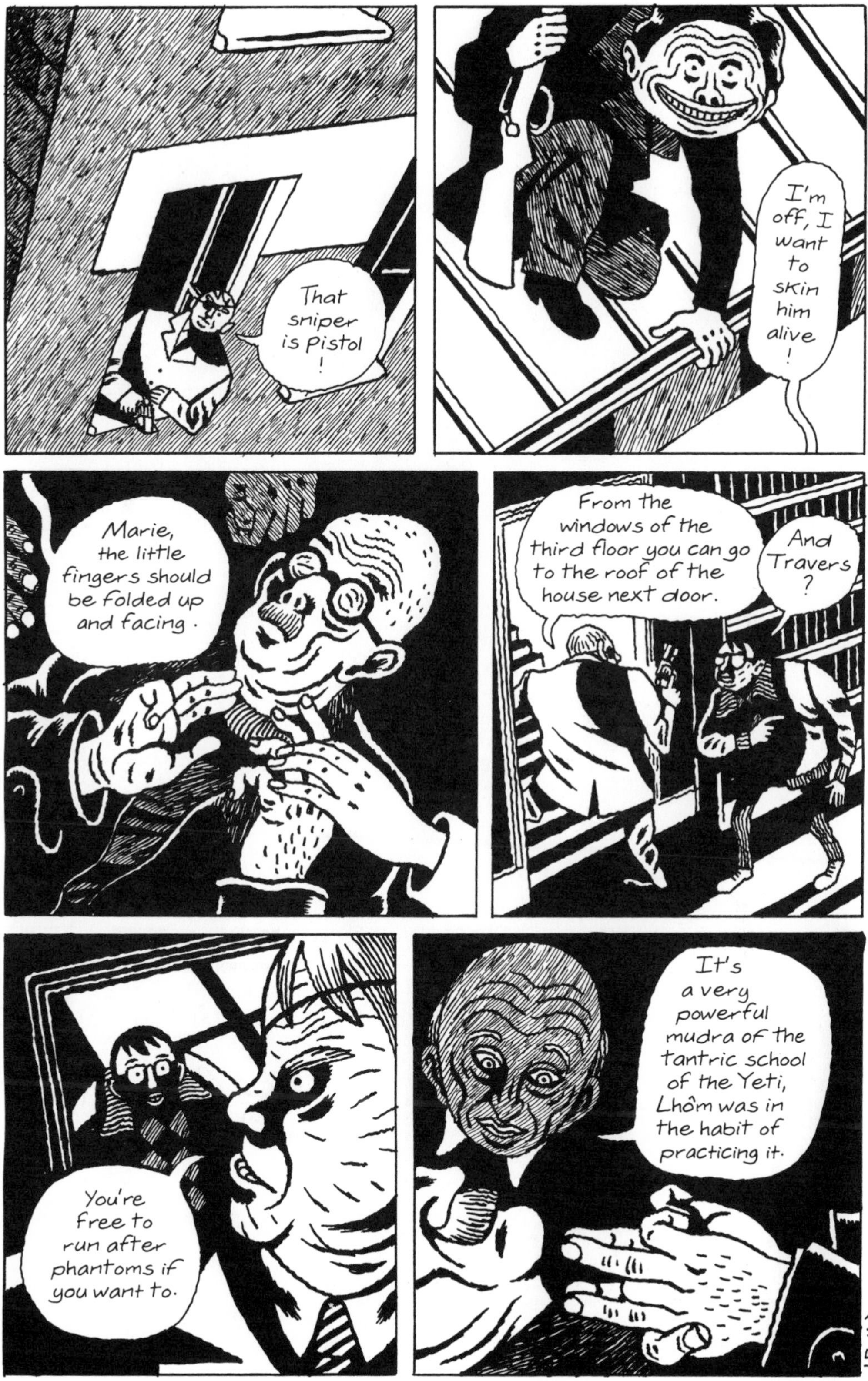
That sniper is Pistol !
I'm off, I want to skin him alive !
Marie, the little fingers should be folded up and facing .
From the windows of the third floor you can go to the roof of the house next door.
And Travers ?
You're free to run after phantoms if you want to.
It's a very powerful mudra of the tantric school of the Yeti, Lhôm was in the habit of practicing it.

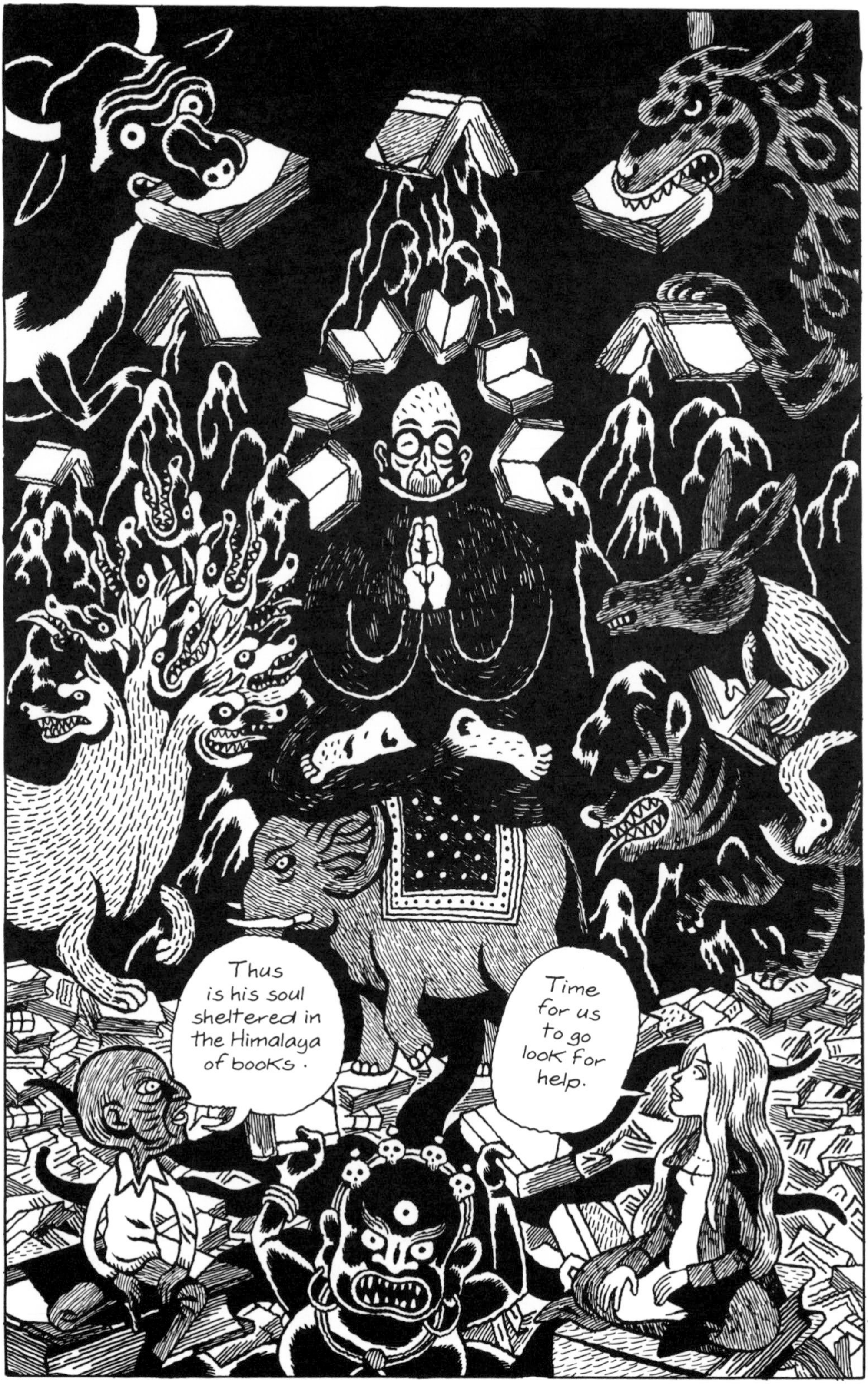
Thus is his soul sheltered in the Himalaya of books.
Time for us to go look for help.

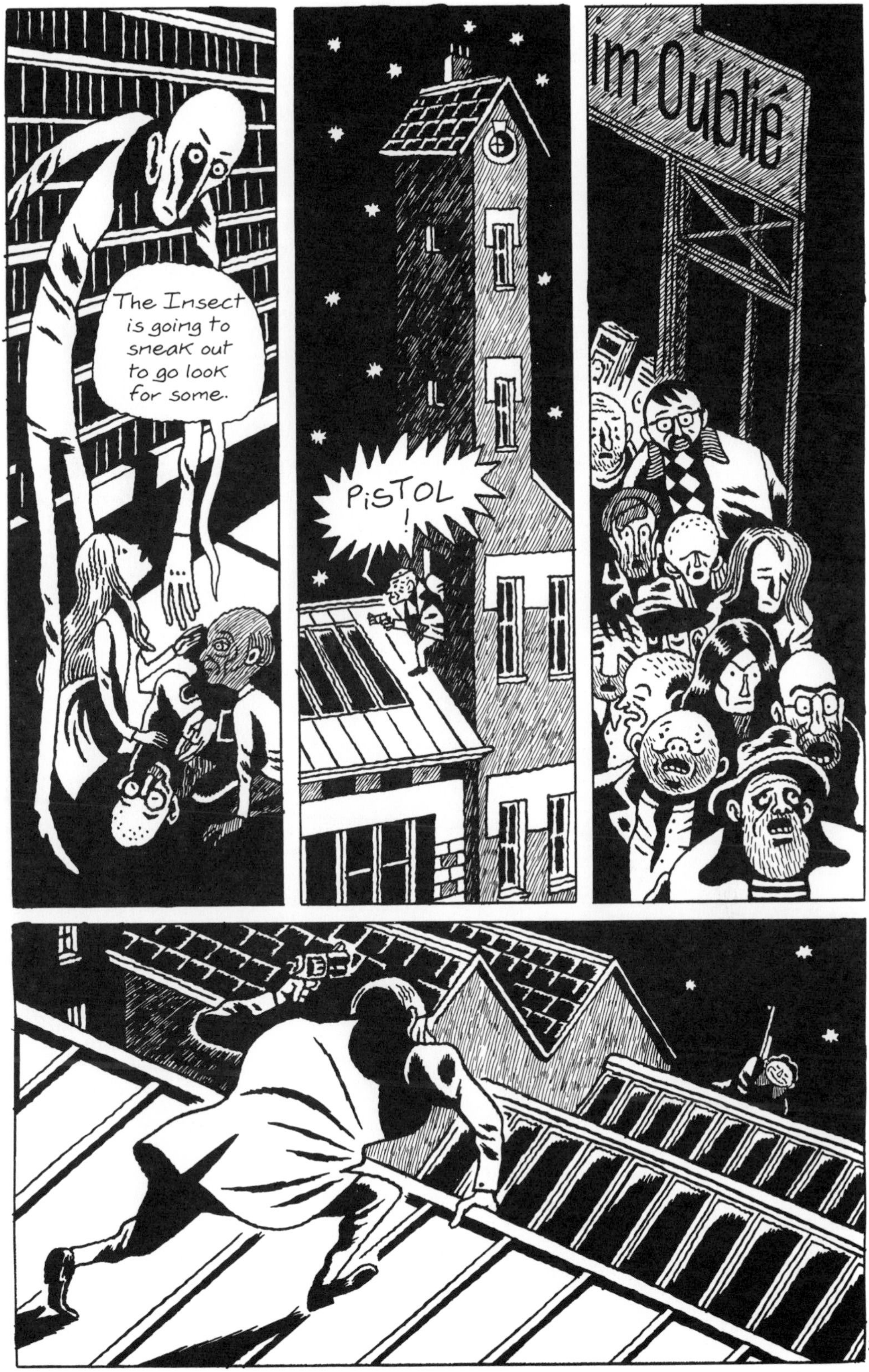
The Insect is going to sneak out to go look for some.
PiSTOL!
im Oublié

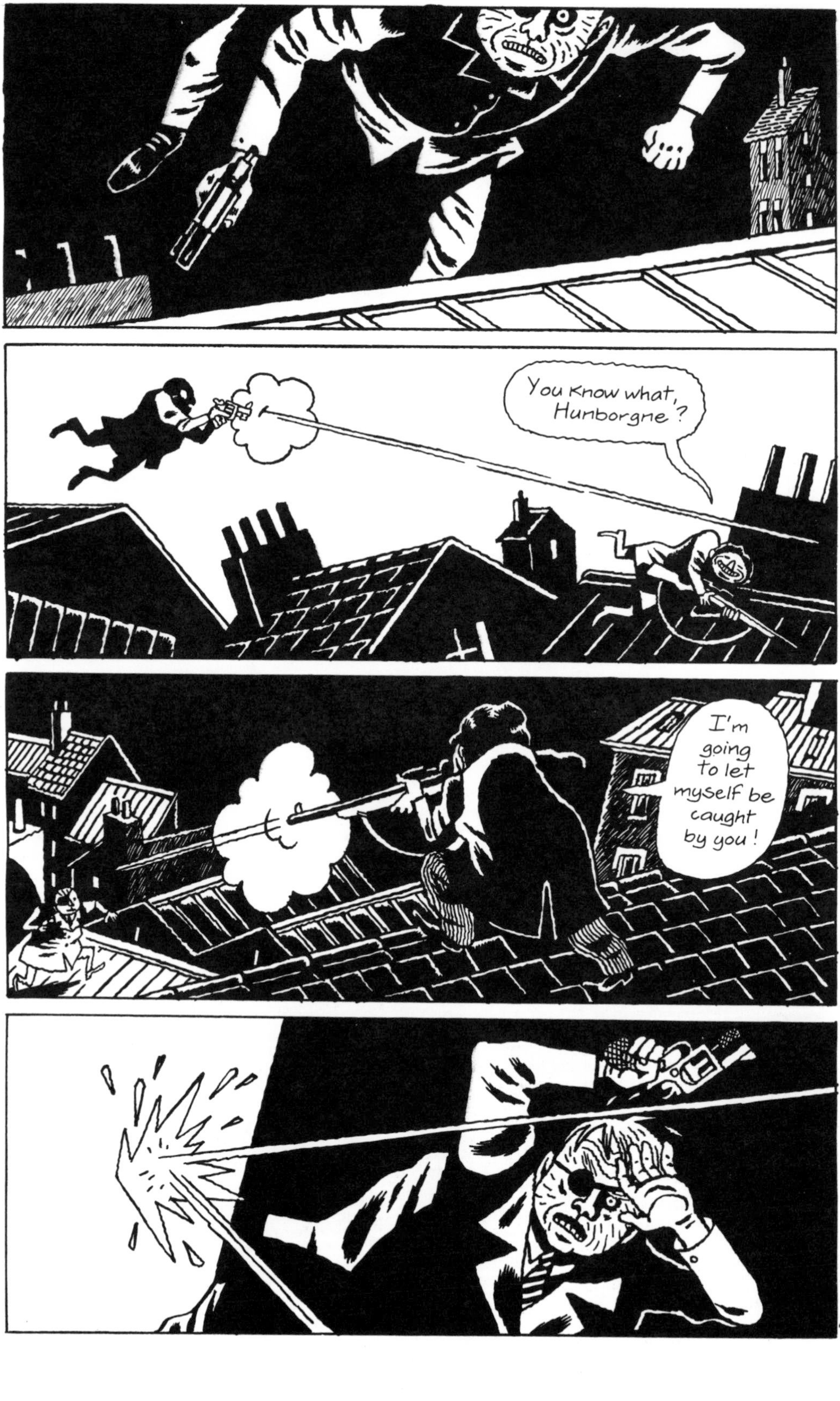
You know what, Humborgne ?
I'm going to let myself be caught by you !

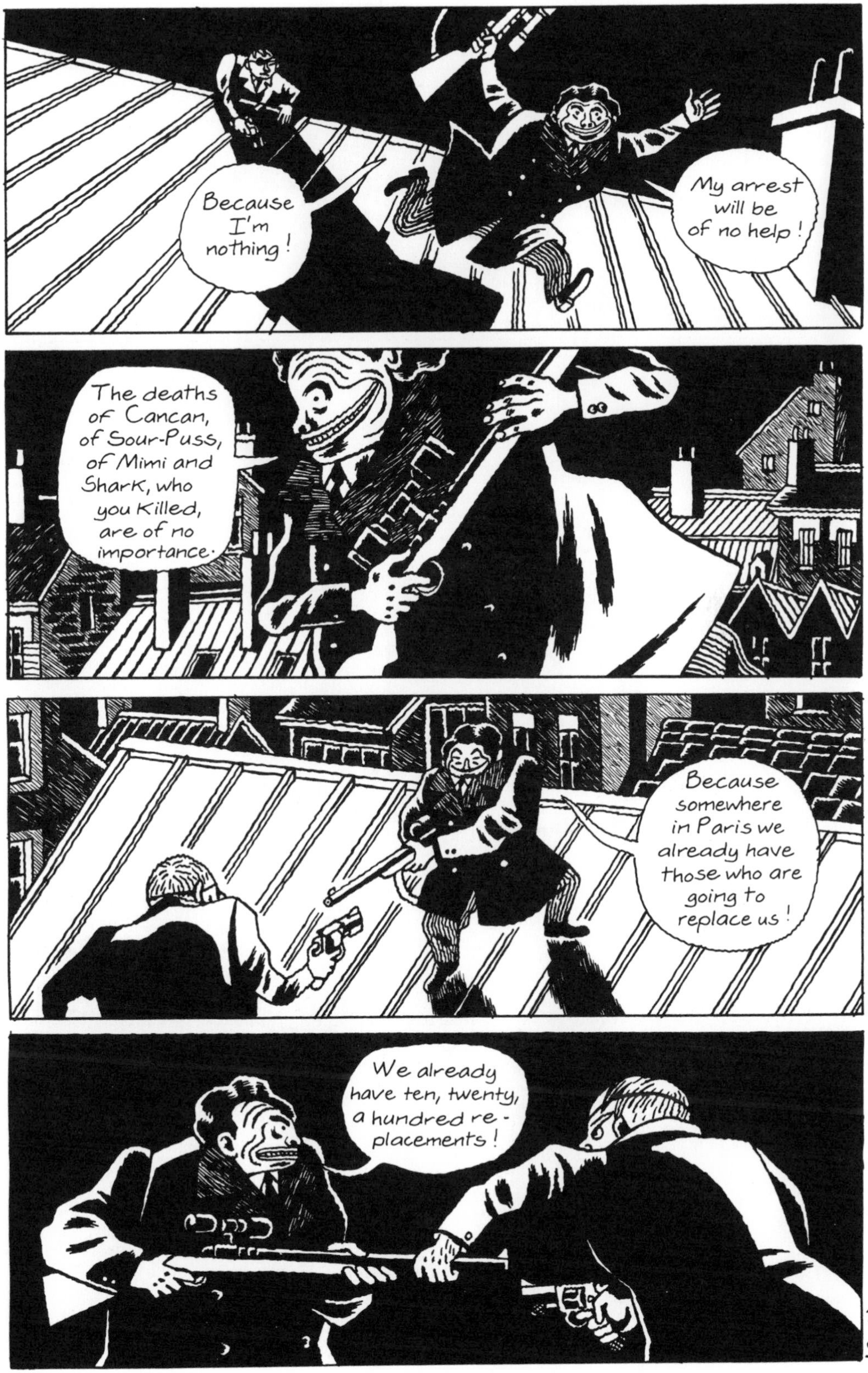
Because I'm nothing !
My arrest will be of no help !
The deaths of Cancan, of Sour-Puss, of Mimi and Shark, who you Killed, are of no importance.
Because somewhere in Paris we already have those who are going to replace us !
We already have ten, twenty, a hundred re-placements !

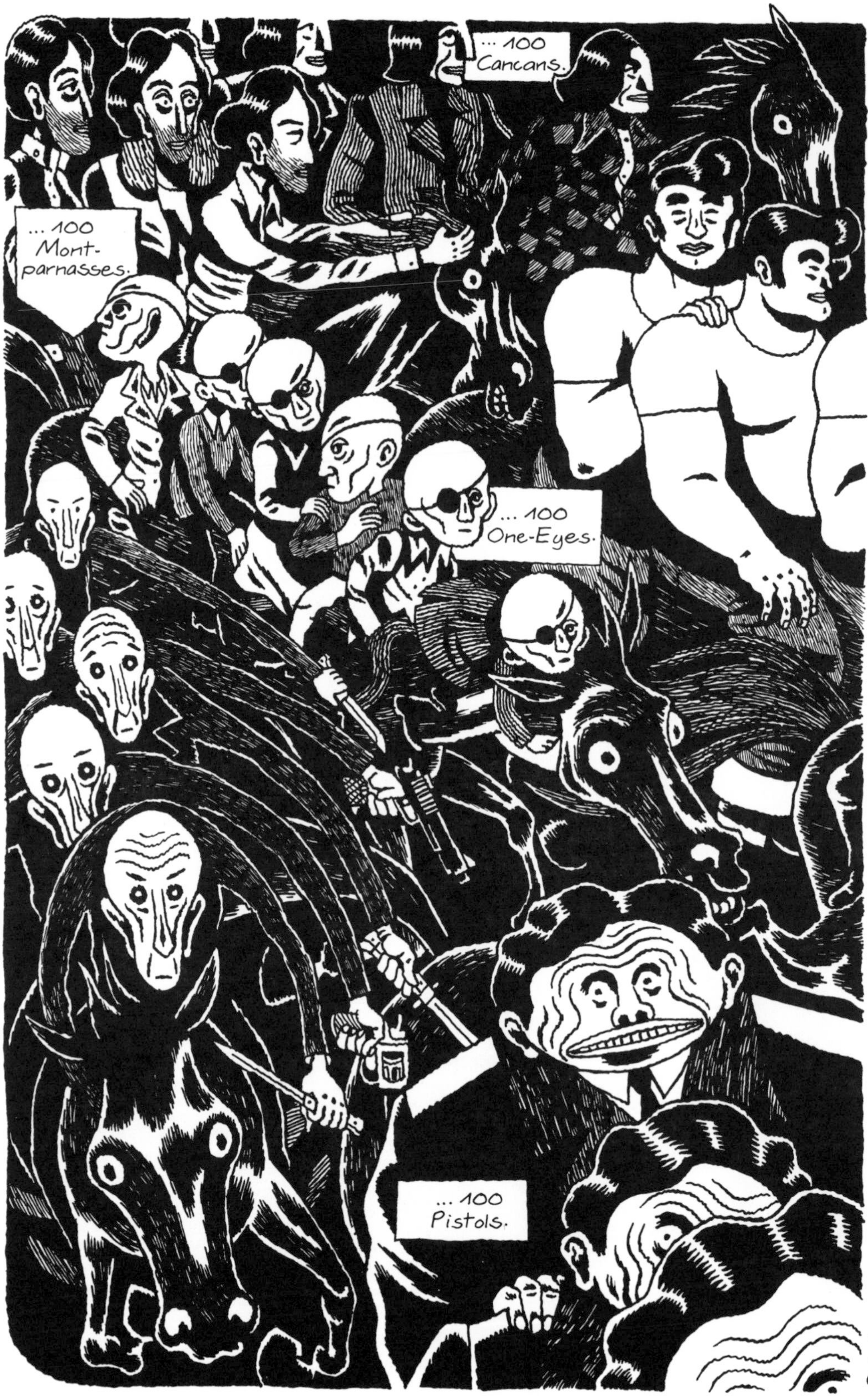

... 100
Cancans.
... 100
Mont-
parnasses.
... 100
One-Eyes.
... 100
Pistols.

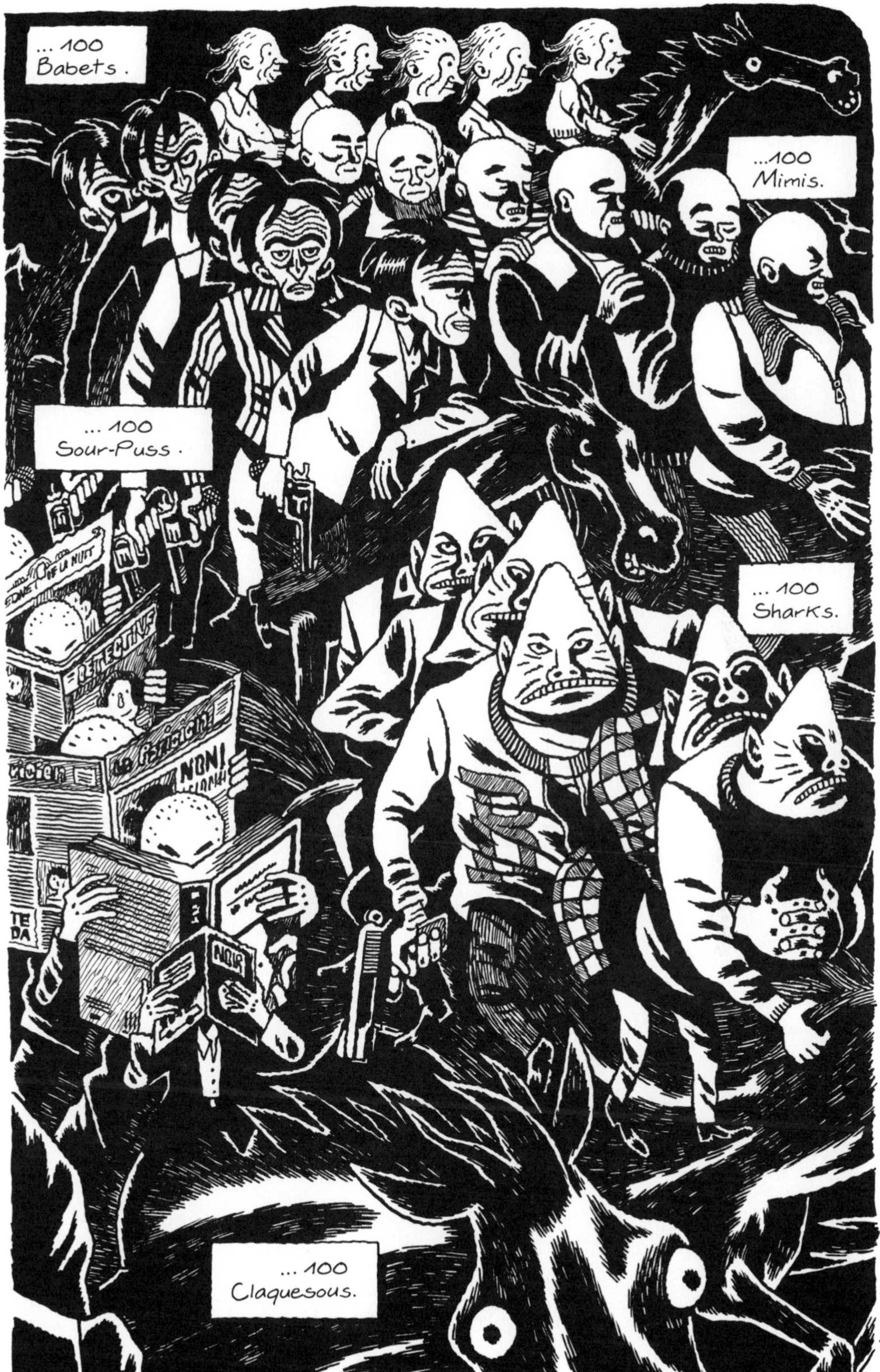

... 100 Babets.
...100 Mimis.
... 100 Sour-Puss.
... 100 Sharks.
... 100 Claquesous.

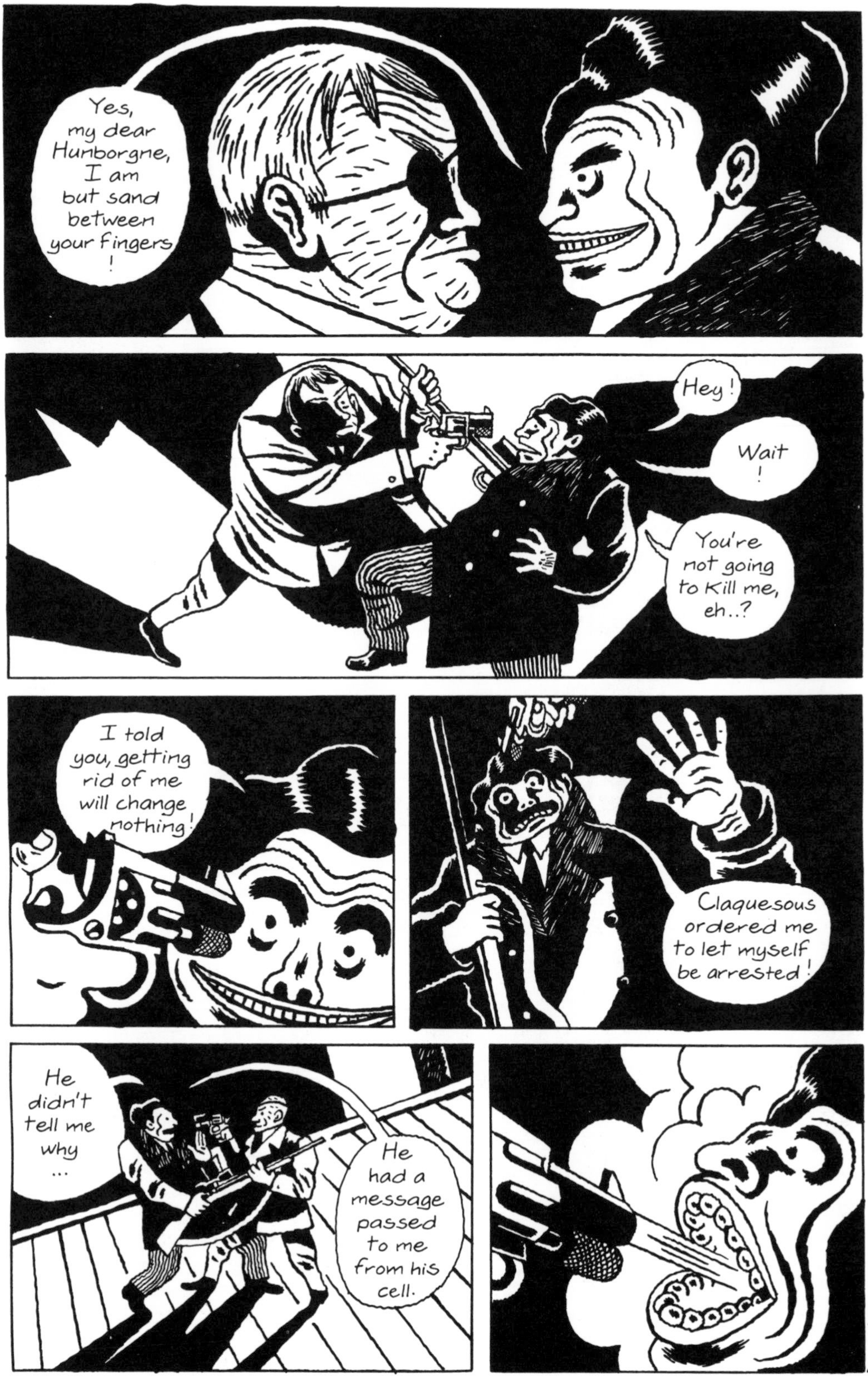
Yes, my dear Humborgne, I am but sand between your fingers !
Hey !
Wait !
You're not going to kill me, eh..?
I told you, getting rid of me will change nothing !
Claquesous ordered me to let myself be arrested !
He didn't tell me why ...
He had a message passed to me from his cell.

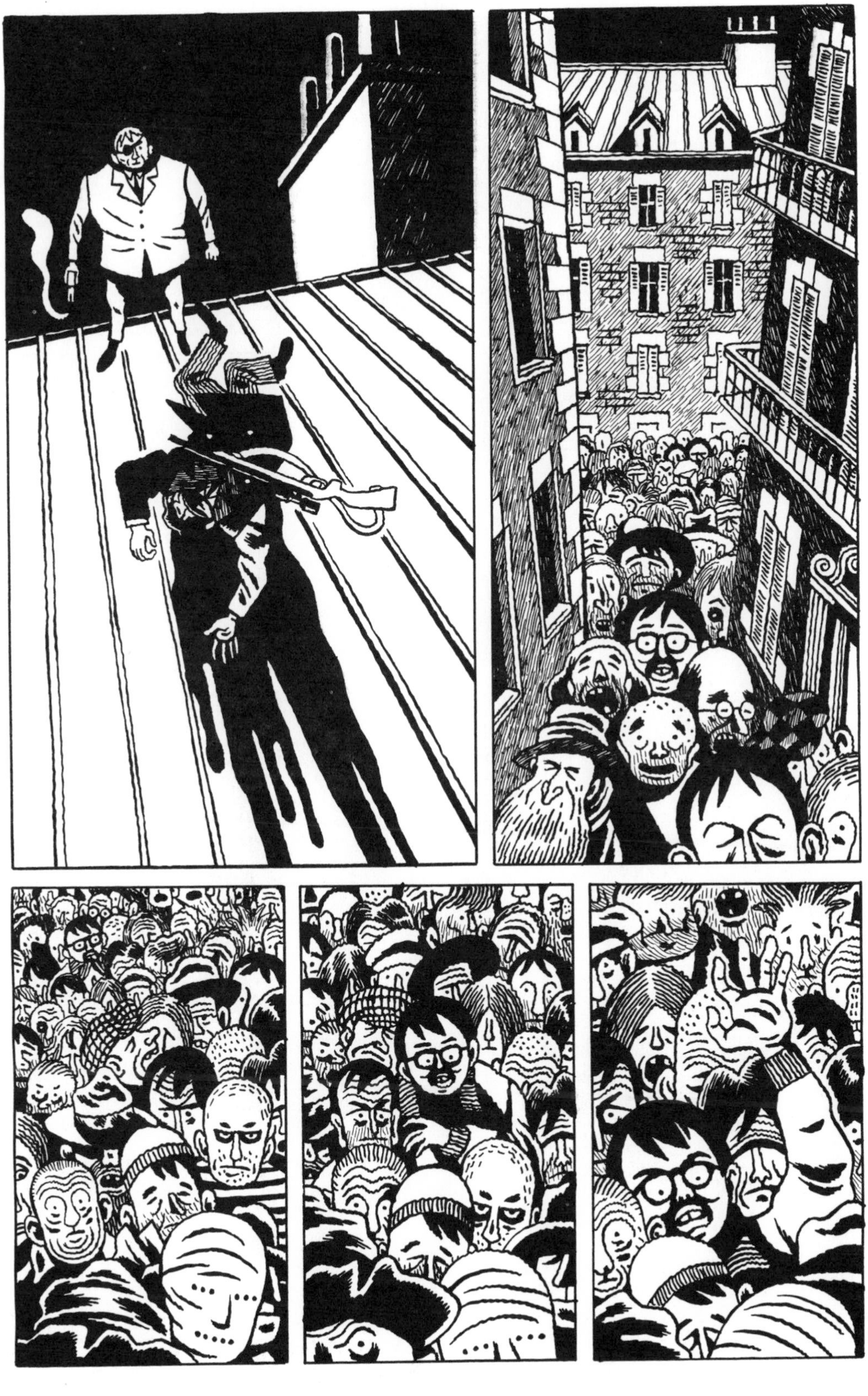

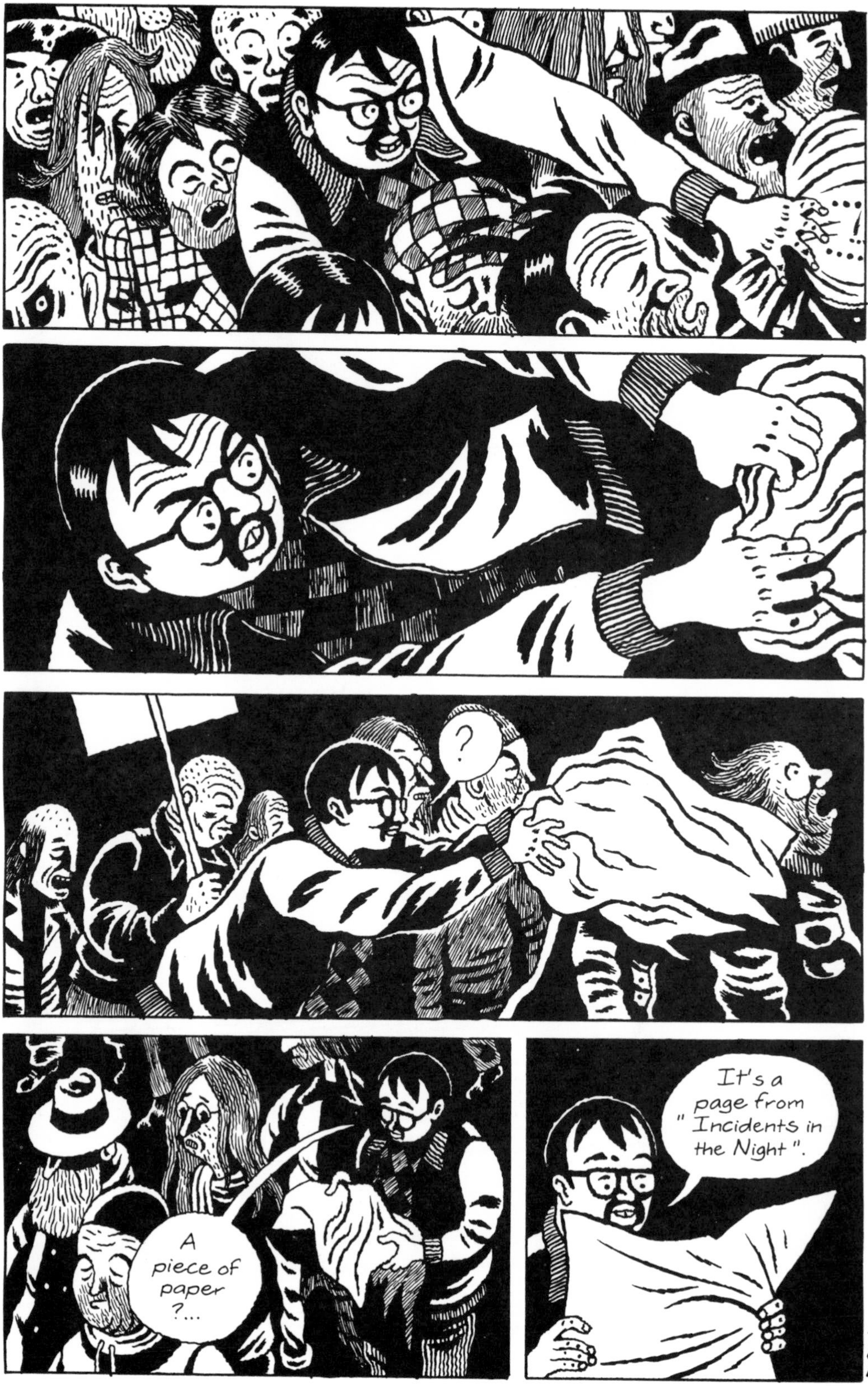
?
A piece of paper ?...
It's a page from "Incidents in the Night".

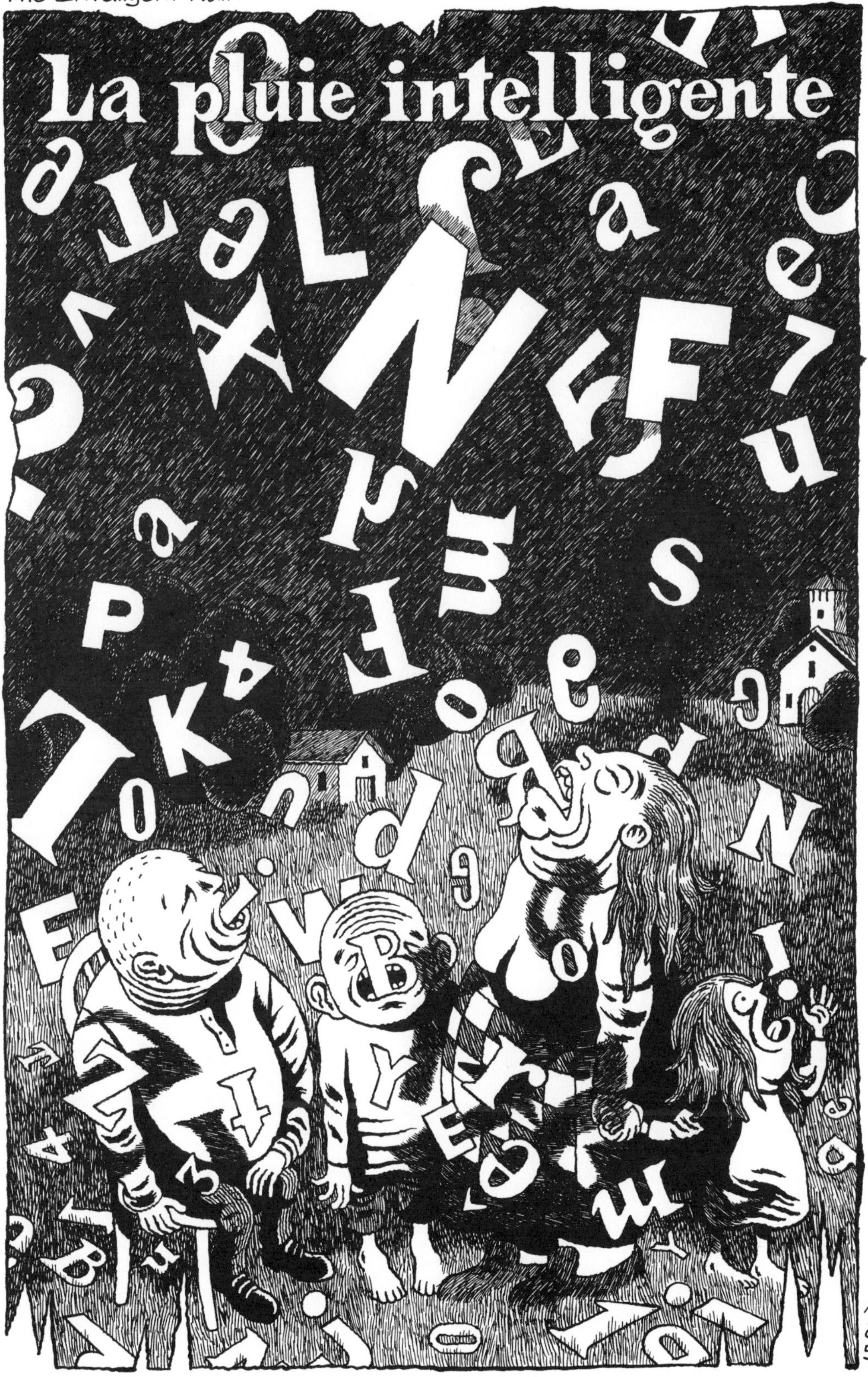
La pluie intelligente

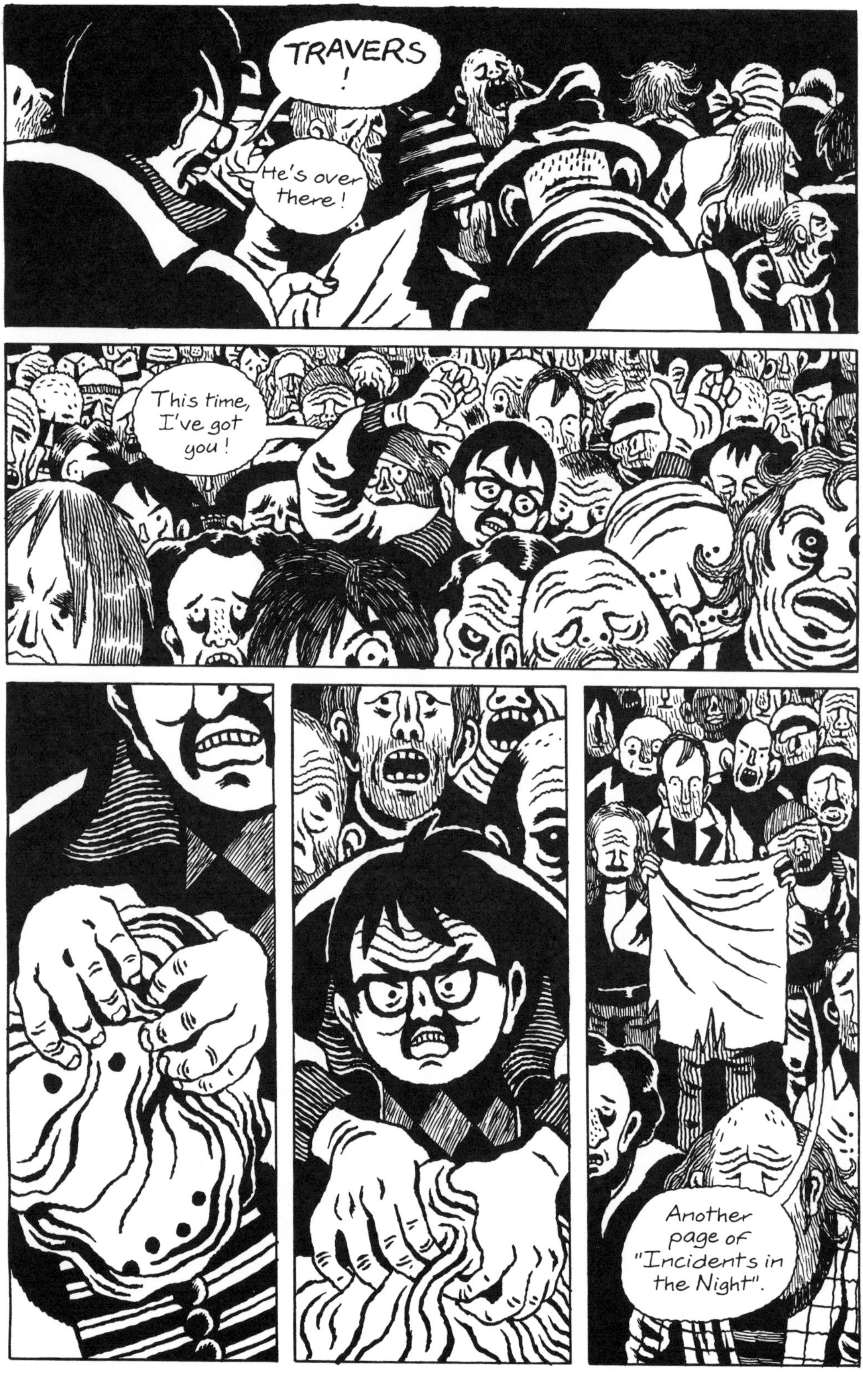
TRAVERS !
He's over there !
This time, I've got you !
Another page of "Incidents in the Night".

The Spectator Eater

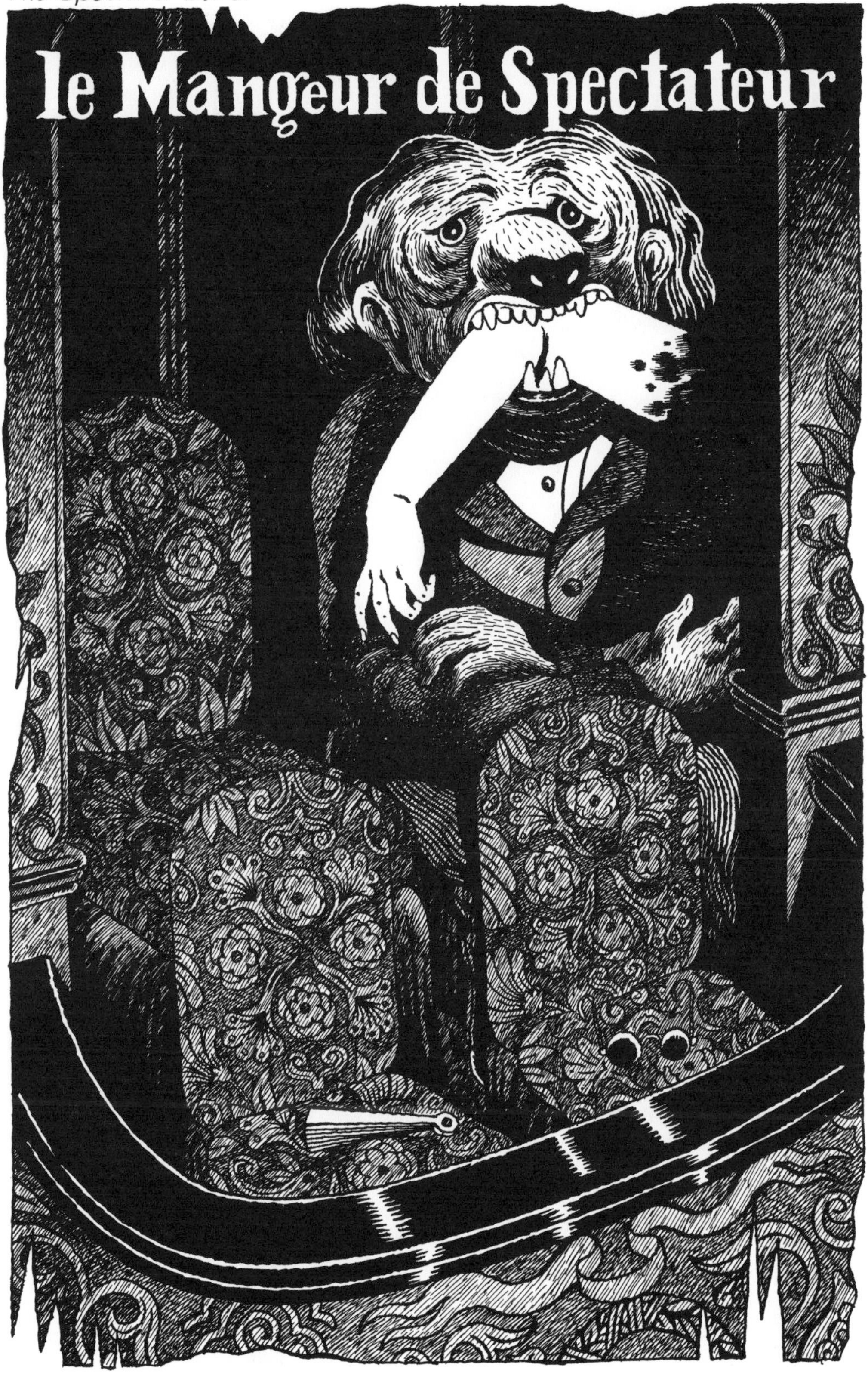
le Mangeur de Spectateur

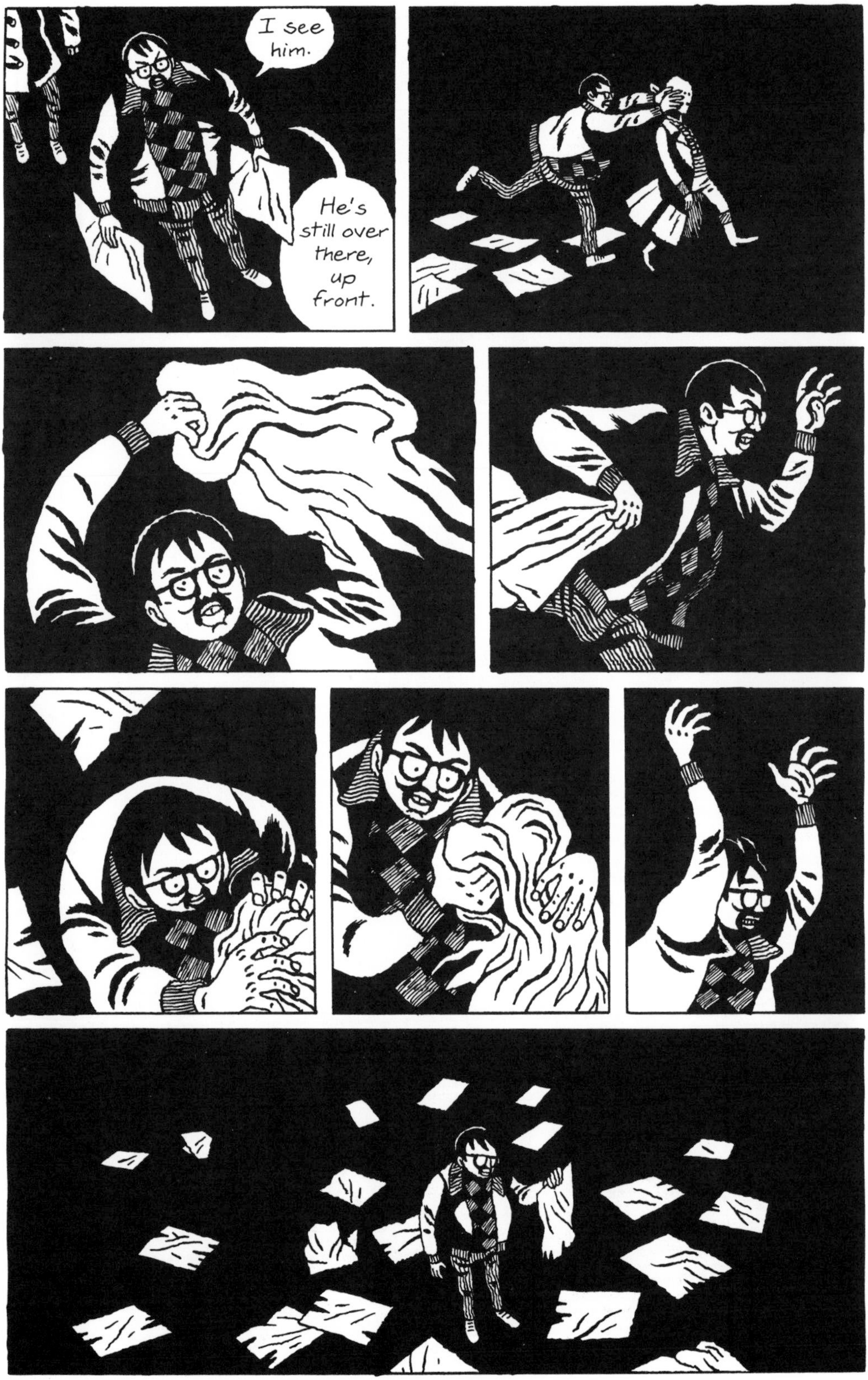
I see him.
He's still over there, up front.

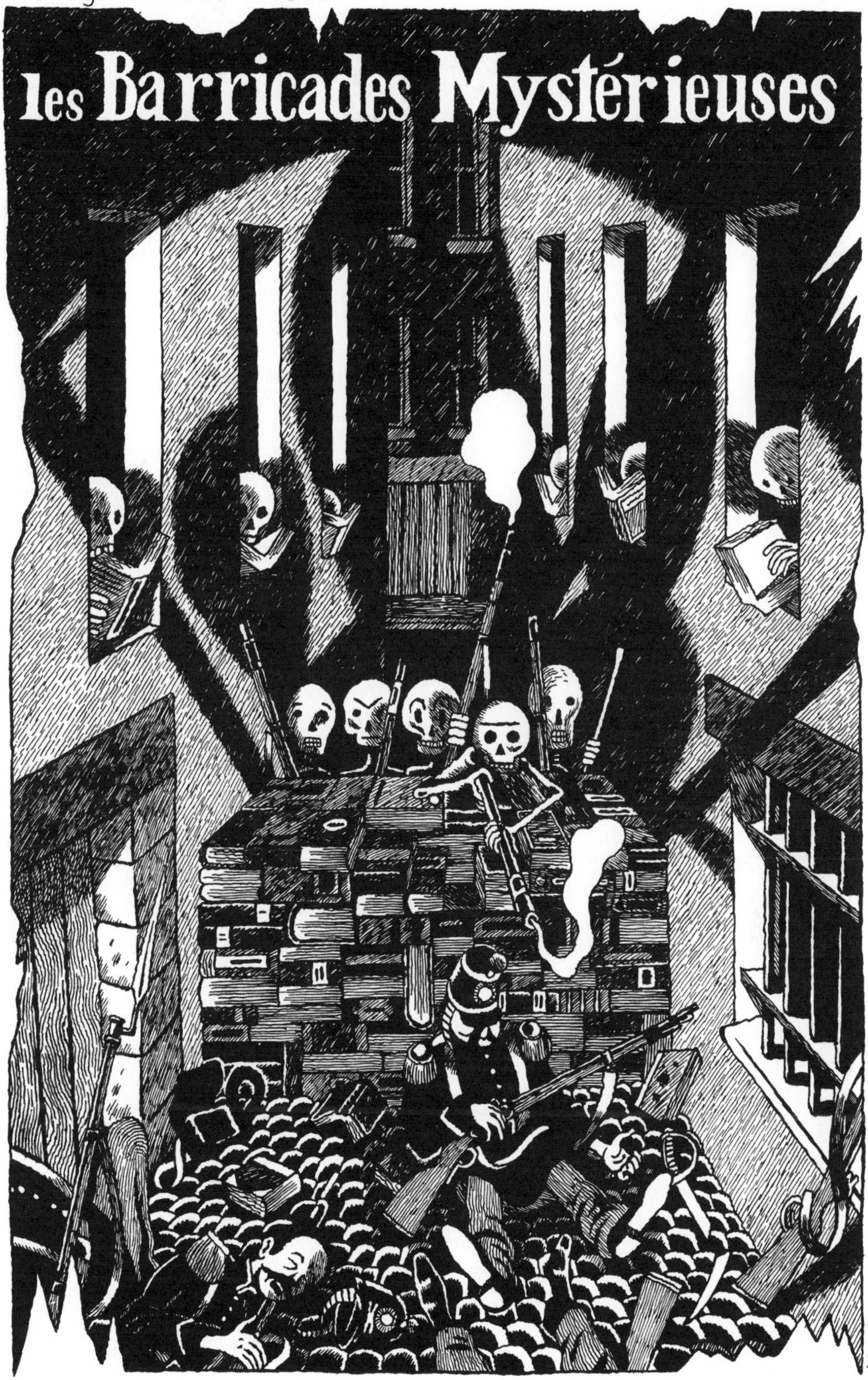
les Barricades Mystérieuses

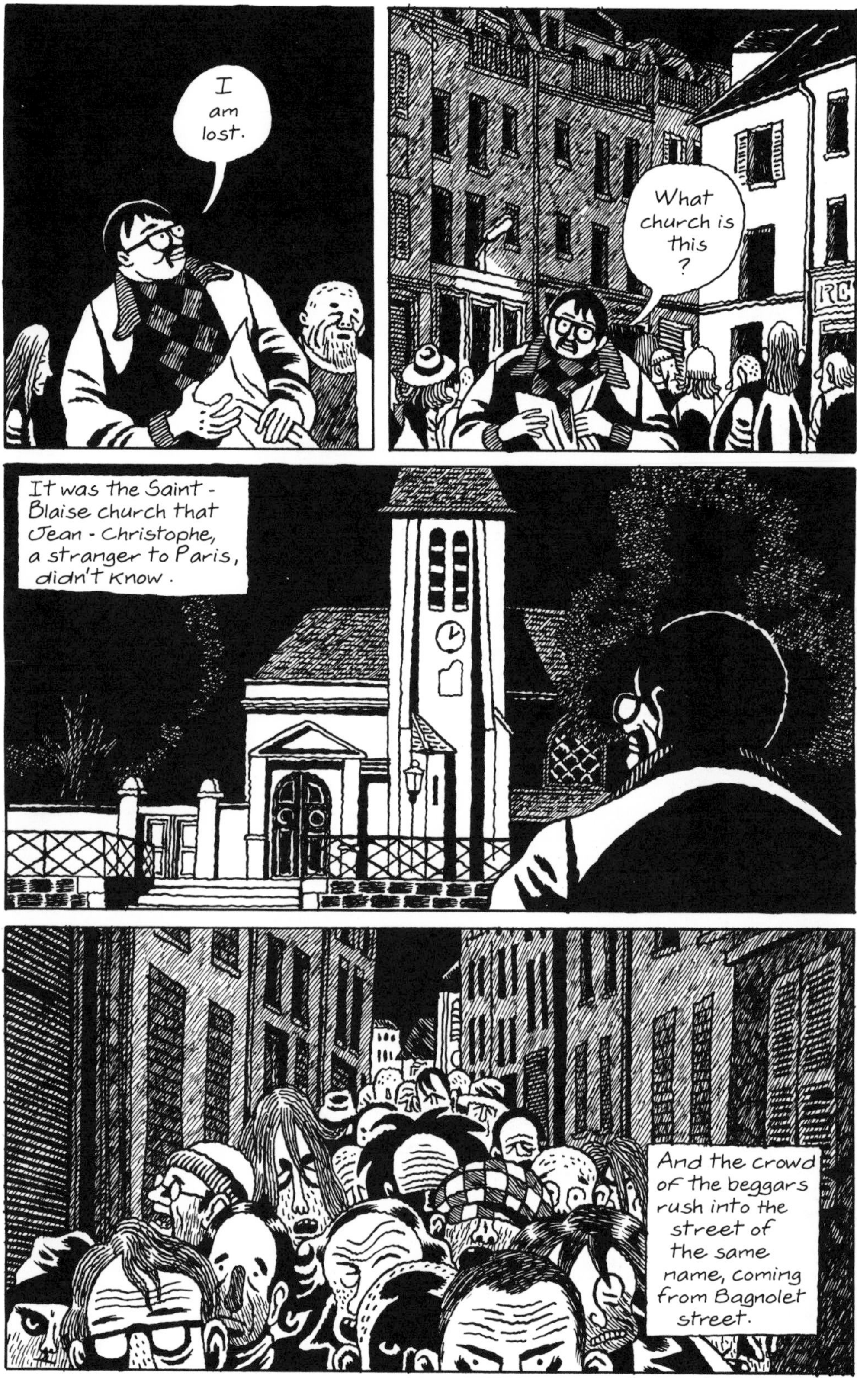
I am lost.
What church is this ?
It was the Saint - Blaise church that Jean - Christophe, a stranger to Paris, didn't know .
And the crowd of the beggars rush into the street of the same name, coming from Bagnolet street.

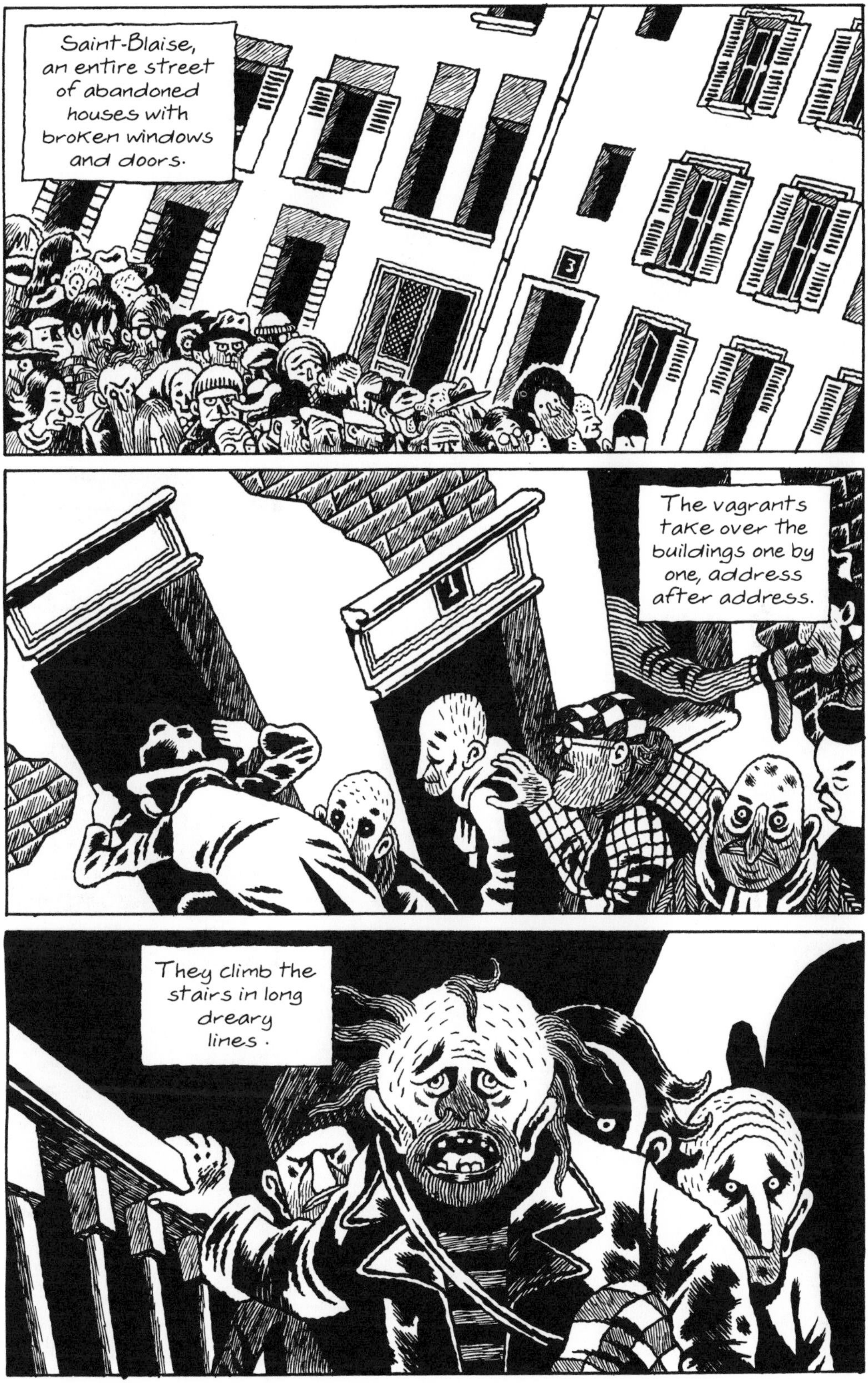
Saint-Blaise, an entire street of abandoned houses with broken windows and doors.
The vagrants take over the buildings one by one, address after address.
They climb the stairs in long dreary lines.

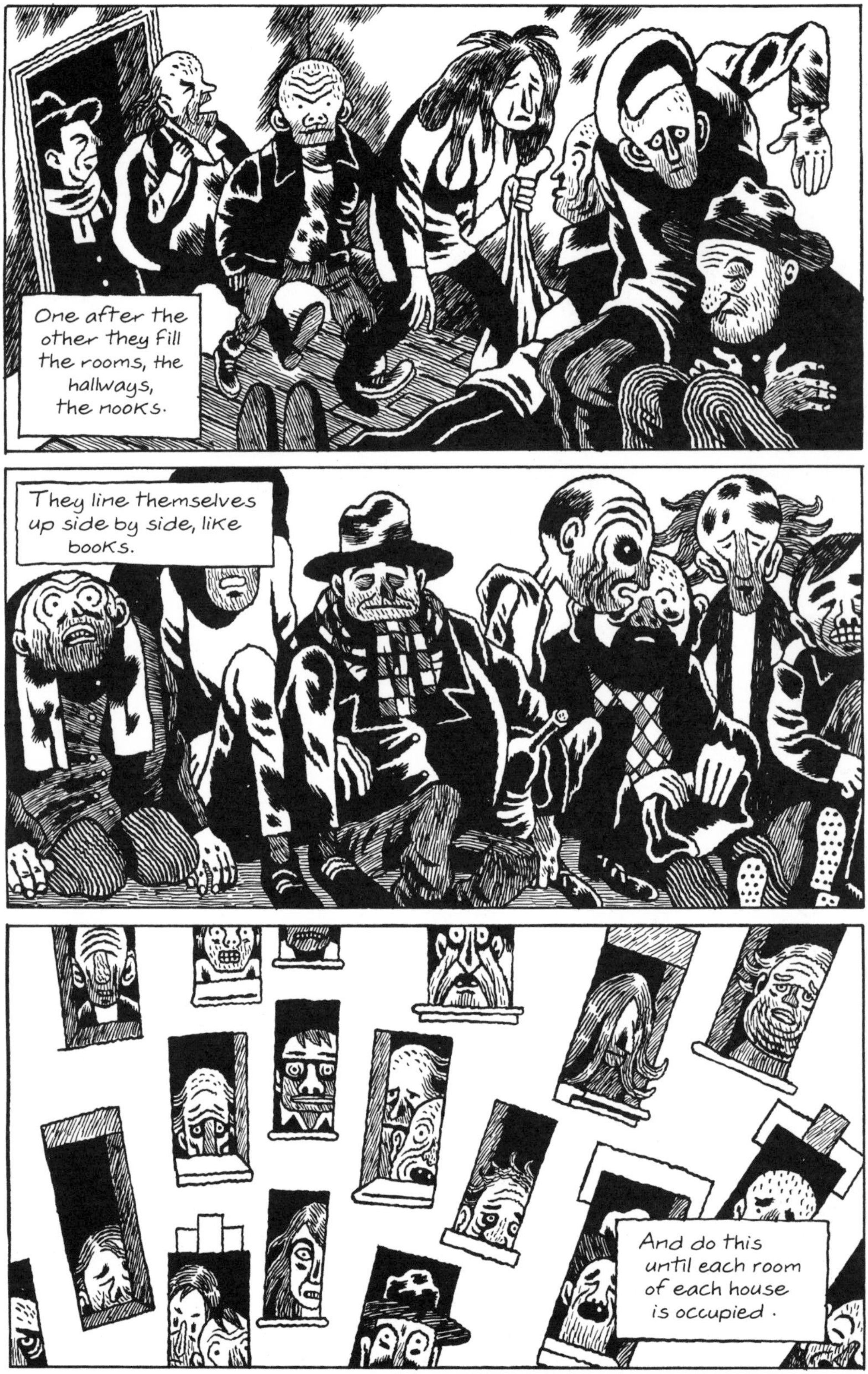
One after the other they fill the rooms, the hallways, the nooks.
They line themselves up side by side, like books.
And do this until each room of each house is occupied .

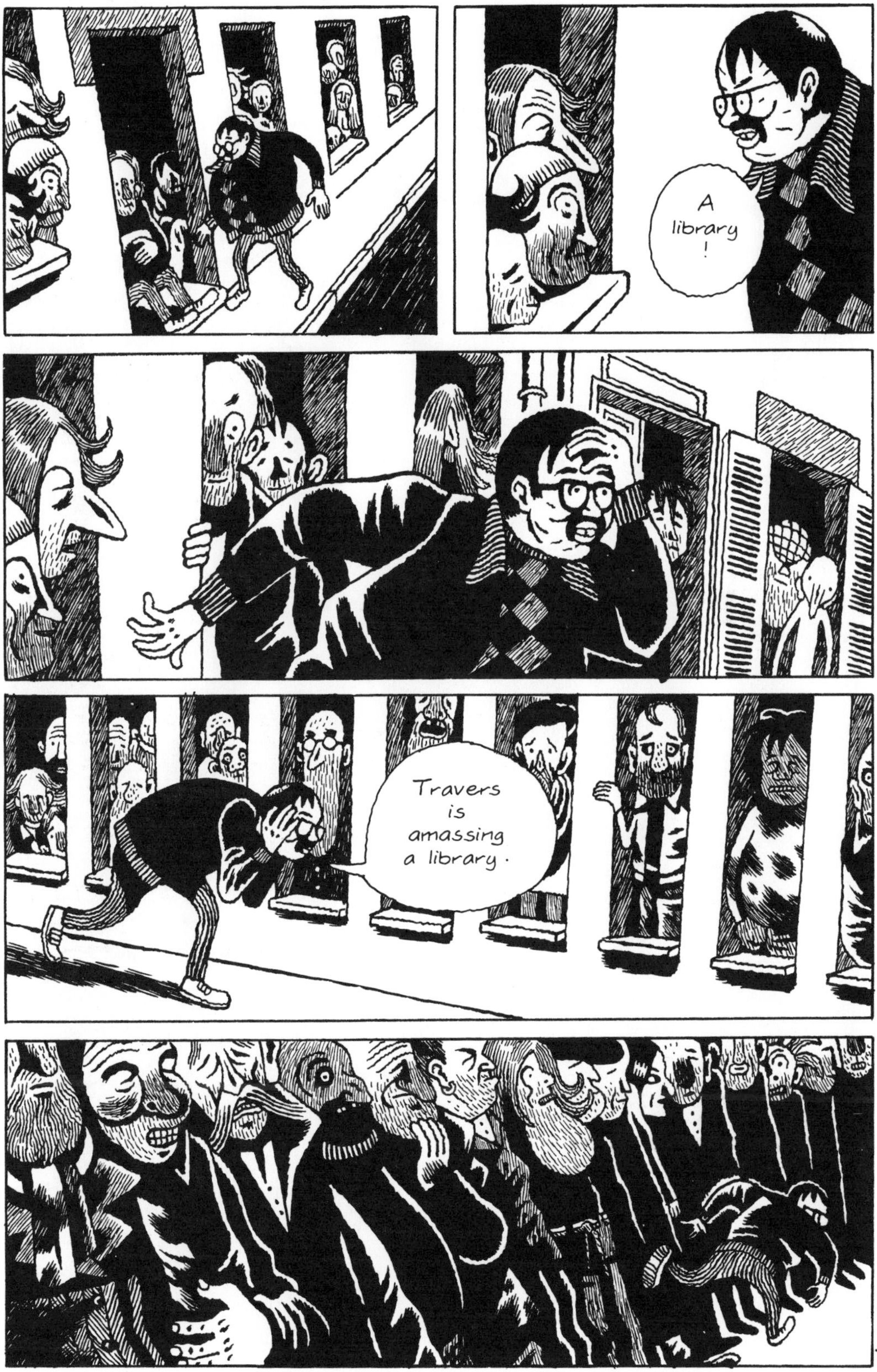
A library !
Travers is amassing a library.

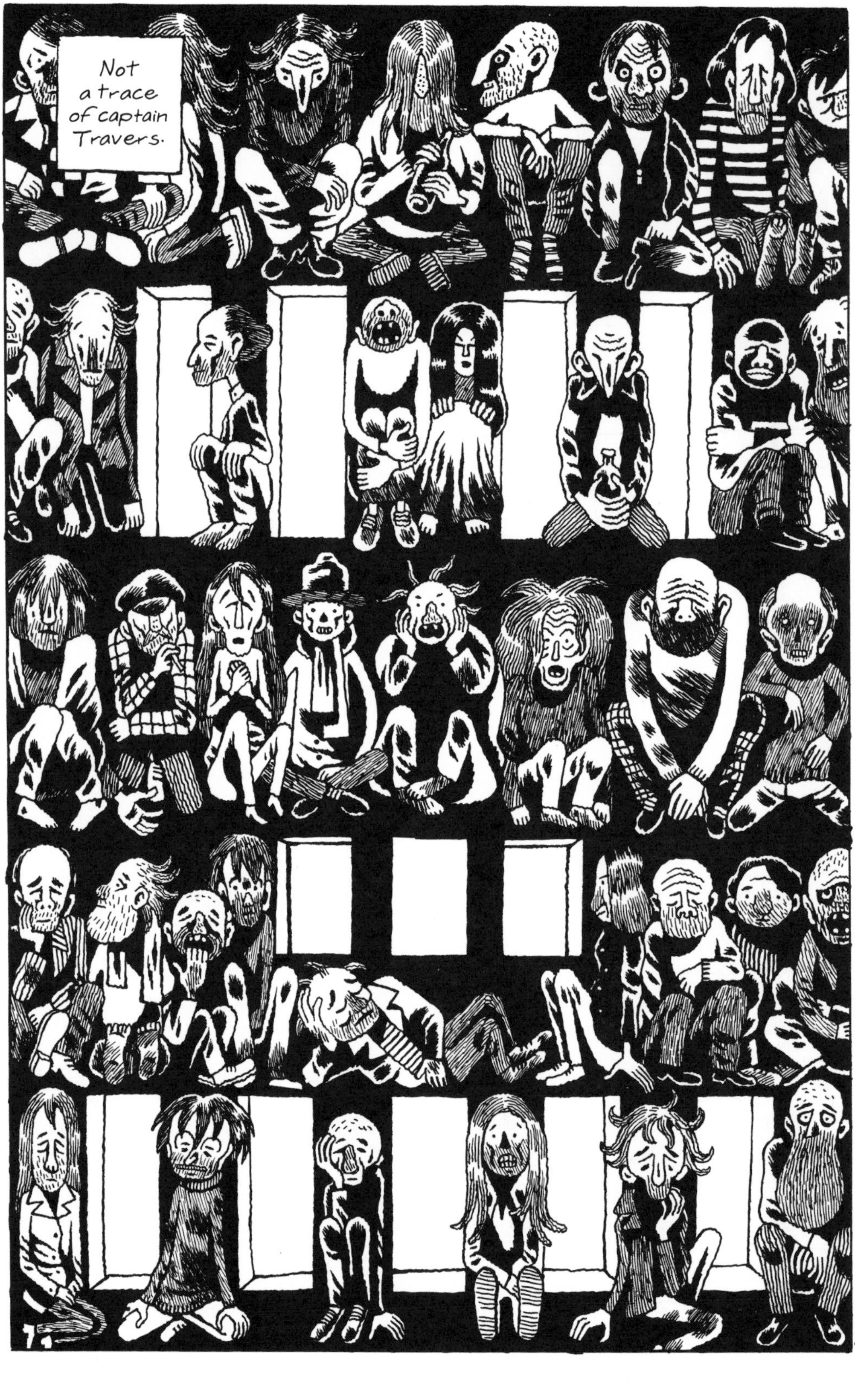
Not a trace of captain Travers.

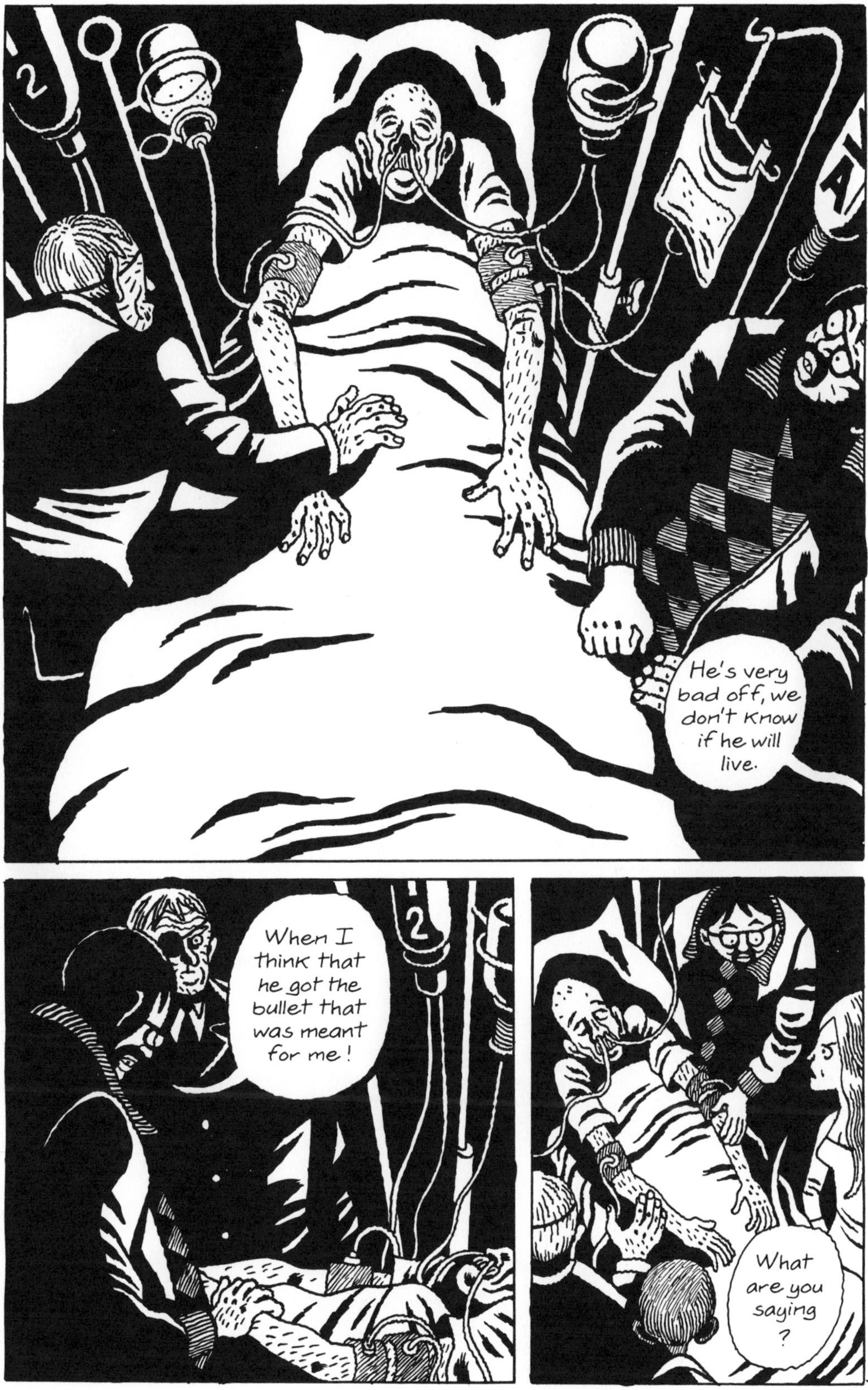
He's very bad off, we don't know if he will live.
When I think that he got the bullet that was meant for me!
What are you saying ?

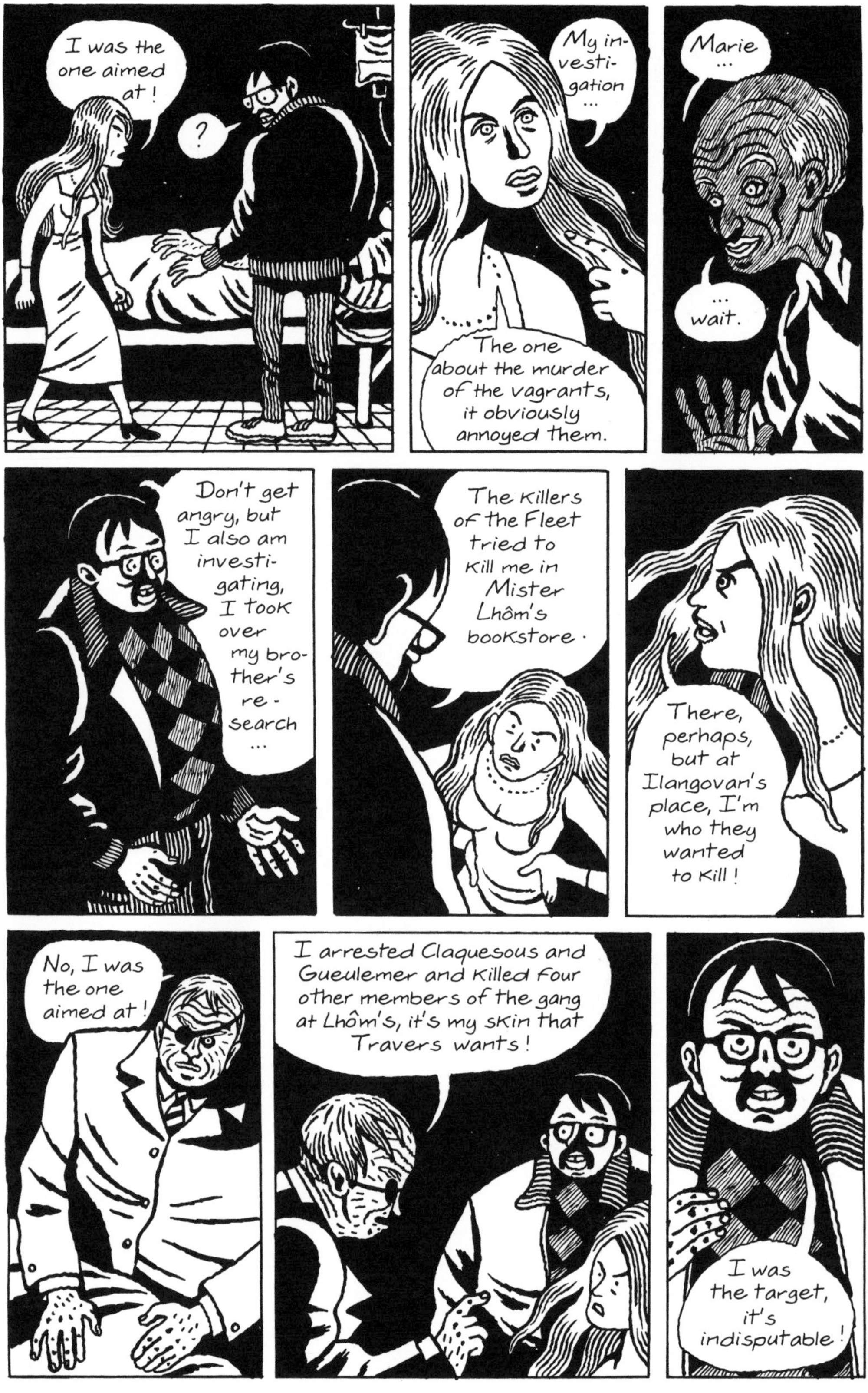
I was the one aimed at !
?
My investigation ...
The one about the murder of the vagrants, it obviously annoyed them.
Marie ...
... wait.
Don't get angry, but I also am investigating, I took over my brother's research ...
The Killers of the Fleet tried to Kill me in Mister Lhôm's bookstore.
There, perhaps, but at Ilangovan's place, I'm who they wanted to Kill !
No, I was the one aimed at !
I arrested Claquesous and Gueulemer and Killed four other members of the gang at Lhôm's, it's my skin that Travers wants !
I was the target, it's indisputable !

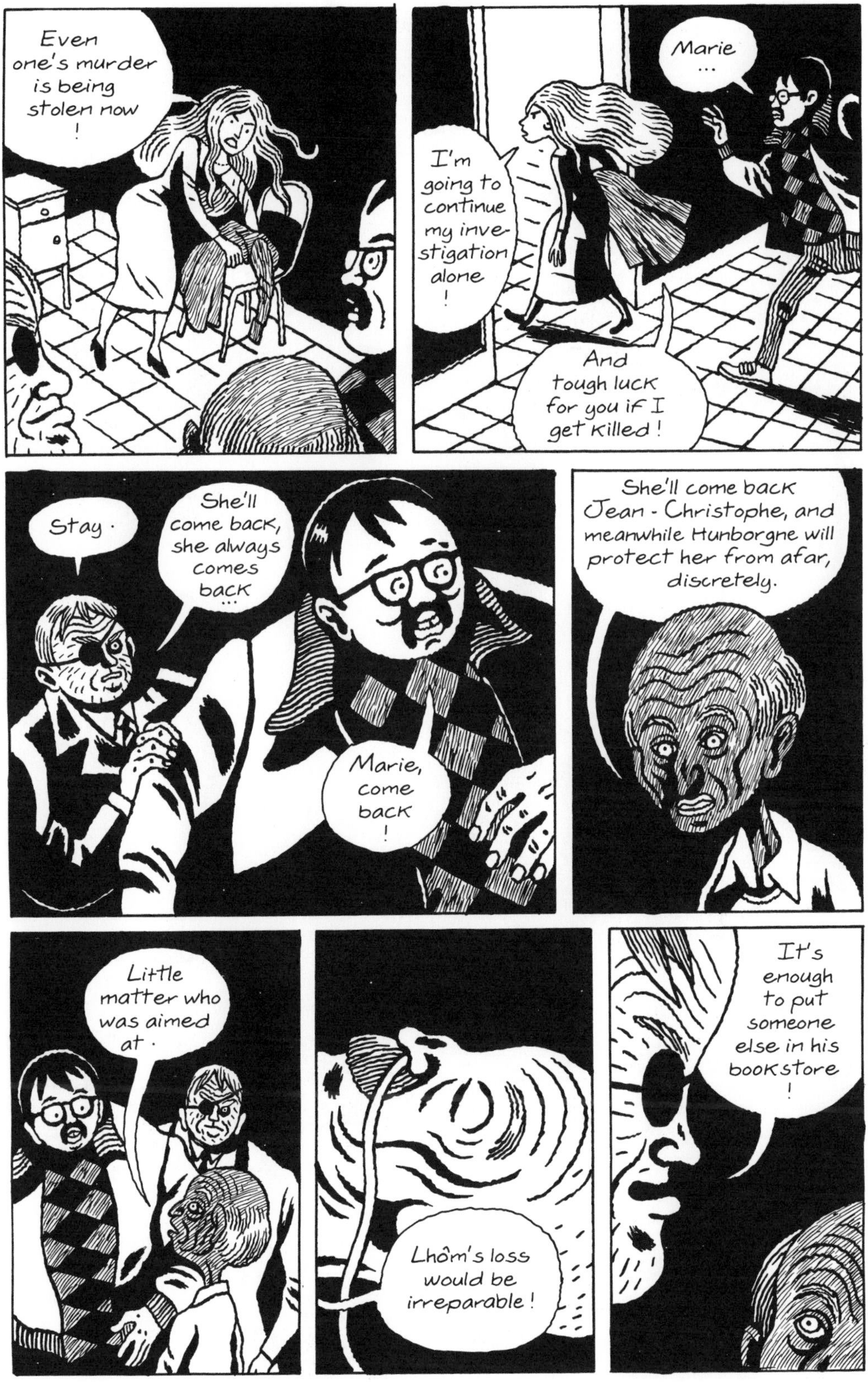
Even one's murder is being stolen now !
Marie ...
I'm going to continue my investigation alone !
And tough luck for you if I get killed !
Stay.
She'll come back, she always comes back ...
Marie, come back !
She'll come back Jean - Christophe, and meanwhile Hunborgne will protect her from afar, discretely.
Little matter who was aimed at.
Lhôm's loss would be irreparable !
It's enough to put someone else in his bookstore !

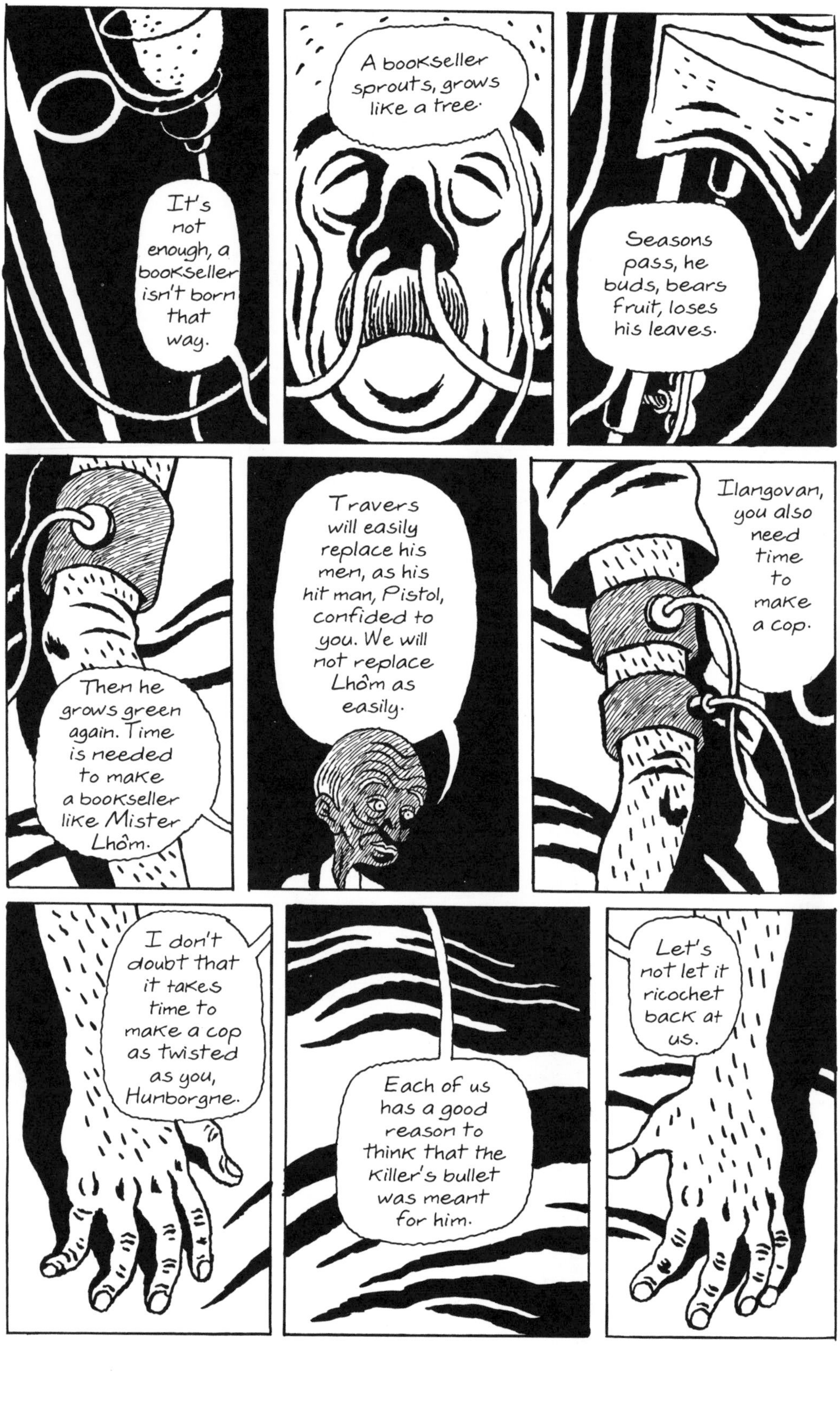
It's not enough, a bookseller isn't born that way.
A bookseller sprouts, grows like a tree.
Seasons pass, he buds, bears fruit, loses his leaves.
Then he grows green again. Time is needed to make a bookseller like Mister Lhôm.
Travers will easily replace his men, as his hit man, Pistol, confided to you. We will not replace Lhôm as easily.
Ilangovan, you also need time to make a cop.
I don't doubt that it takes time to make a cop as twisted as you, Hunborgne.
Each of us has a good reason to think that the killer's bullet was meant for him.
Let's not let it ricochet back at us.

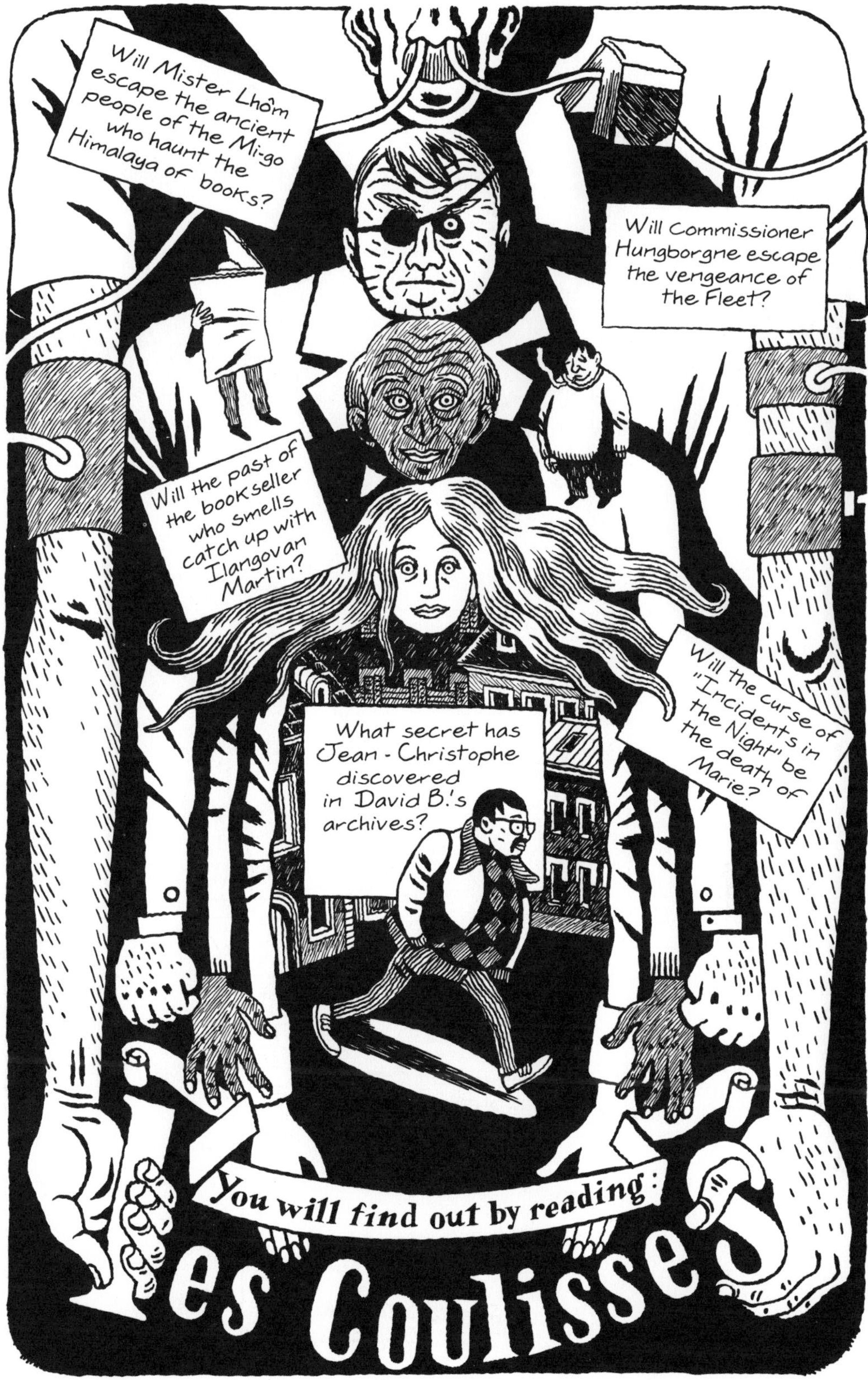
Will Mister Lhôm escape the ancient people of the Mi-go who haunt the Himalaya of books?
Will Commissioner Hungborgne escape the vengeance of the Fleet?
Will the past of the bookseller who smells catch up with Ilangovan Martin?
Will the curse of "Incidents in the Night" be the death of Marie?
What secret has Jean - Christophe discovered in David B.'s archives?
You will find out by reading:
Les Coulisses

Backstage

David B.

David B. is one of France's finest cartoonists and a co-founder of the legendary L'Association collective. He is the author of many books of comics including *The Armed Garden*, *Noctural Conspiracies*, and *Epileptic* which was awarded Angoulême International Comics Festival Prize for Scenario and the Ignatz Award for Outstanding Artist. *Incidents in the Night Book One* was nominated for the L.A. Times Book Prize and the Eisner Awards. He lives and works in Paris, France.

Brian Evenson

Brian Evenson is the author of eleven prize-winning books of fiction, including *The Open Curtain*, *Last Days*, *Windeye*, and *Immobility*. His work has been translated into over a dozen languages. He lives and works in Providence, Rhode Island, where he teaches at Brown University.

Sarah Evenson

Sarah Evenson is also the co-translator of Manuela Draeger's *Belle-Medusa*. She lives and works in Minneapolis as a freelance illustrator. Visit her on the web at sarahevenson.tumblr.com.

UNCIVILIZED BOOKS CATALOGUE

The Voyeurs by Gabrielle Bell

Truth is Fragmentary by Gabrielle Bell

An Iranian Metamorphosis by Mana Neyestani

Incidents in the Night Book One by David B.; Translated by Brian Evenson

Amazing Facts & Beyond by Kevin Huizenga & Dan Zettwoch

War of Streets and Houses by Sophie Yanow

Post York by James Romberger & Crosby

It Never Happened Again by Sam Alden

Eel Mansions by Derek Van Gieson

Over the Wall by Peter Wartman

Sammy The Mouse by Zak Sally

True Swamp by Jon Lewis

Pascin by Joann Sfar

Borb by Jason Little

CRITICAL CARTOONS SERIES:

Ed vs. Yummy Fur by Brian Evenson

Carl Bark' Duck by Peter Schilling Jr.

and more...

uncivilizedbooks.com